Exploring the Superstitions

Also by John Annerino

Photography & Essay Books
Indian Country: Sacred Ground, Native Peoples
Apache: The Sacred Path to Womanhood
People of Legend: Native Americans of the Southwest
Vanishing Borderlands: The Fragile Landscape of the U.S.-Mexico Border
Colorado Plateau Wild and Beautiful
New Mexico: A Photographic Tribute
Arizona: A Photographic Tribute
Desert Light: A Photographer's Journey Through America's Desert Southwest
Canyon Country: A Photographic Journey
Grand Canyon Wild: A Photographic Journey
The Wild Country of Mexico: La tierra salvaje de México
*Canyons of the Southwest: A Tour of the Great Canyon Country
from Colorado to Northern Mexico*
High Risk Photography: The Adventure Behind the Image

Exploring the Superstitions

Trails and Tales of the Southwest's Mystery Mountains

BY JOHN ANNERINO

Skyhorse Publishing

Text, photographs, appendix, and glossary Copyright © 2018 by John Annerino

All rights reserved. No part of this book may be reproduced in any manner without the express written consent of the publisher, except in the case of brief excerpts in critical reviews or articles. All inquiries should be addressed to Skyhorse Publishing, 307 West 36th Street, 11th Floor, New York, NY 10018.

Skyhorse Publishing books may be purchased in bulk at special discounts for sales promotion, corporate gifts, fund-raising, or educational purposes. Special editions can also be created to specifications. For details, contact the Special Sales Department, Skyhorse Publishing, 307 West 36th Street, 11th Floor, New York, NY 10018 or info@skyhorsepublishing.com.

Skyhorse® and Skyhorse Publishing® are registered trademarks of Skyhorse Publishing, Inc.®, a Delaware corporation.

Visit our website at www.skyhorsepublishing.com.

Disclaimer: Hiking, exploring, and prospecting in the Superstition Moutains is dangerous and too often has proven deadly. The author and publisher accept no responsibility for any injury, loss, or inconvenience by any person using this book.

10 9 8 7 6 5 4 3 2 1

Library of Congress Cataloging-in-Publication Data is available on file.

Cover design by Tom Lau.
Cover photo Copyright © John Annerino

Historical and Contemporary Photo and Illustration Credits: Edward S. Curtis, Edward H. Davis, Maynard Dixon, Camilius Sidney Fly, William J. Lubken, Andrew Miller, Frank A. Russell, A. Frank Randall, John Annerino / LIFE, and DeGrazia Gallery in the Sun.

Print ISBN: 978-1-5107-2373-3
Ebook ISBN: 978-1-5107-2374-0

Printed in China

In memory of my father and mother, who nurtured my teens from our home in the long morning shadows of the Superstition Mountains; my white shepherd who accompanied me on my first solo explorations afoot in the Superstition's daunting canyons; for my wife and family who later joined me exploring its spectacular ramparts; the late artist Ettore "Ted" DeGrazia; and for its Native Peoples who more often than not have been unfairly portrayed with more fiction than fact: Ancient Hohokam (*Huhugam*, "Those Who are Gone"), Pima (*Akimel O'odham*, "People of the River), Apache (*Ndé*, "The People"), Tonto Apache (*Dilzhę'é*, "People with High Pitched Voices), San Carlos Apache (*Tiis Zhaazhe Bikoh*, "Small Cottonwood Canyon People"), and Southeastern Yavapai (*Enyaeva pai*, "People of the Sun").

Contents

Acknowledgments	ix
Preface	xiii
I. Journeys of Discovery	**1**
1. My First Bivouac	3
2. A Journey in the Footsteps of the Vanished Ones	9
3. Tracking the Ghost Trail of Adolph Ruth	24
II. Welcome to the Superstitions	**55**
4. Peeking In, Before You Go	57
5. Native Peoples	77
6. Natural History	87
III. Adventures in the Superstitions	**109**
7. The Apache Trails: Through Apache Land	111
8. Weavers Needle: Locus for the Lost Dutchman's and Peralta's Gold	143
9. Superstition Mountain: Where the People Turned to Stone	155
IV. Trails and Tales of The Mystery Mountains	**171**
10. Trails of the Superstition Mountains	173
–Lost Dutchman State Park	174
–Superstition Wilderness	176
–Lost Goldmine Trail	177
11. The Peralta Trail	181
–Abbey's Road	184
–Peralta Trail Head Hikes and Treks	188
–Needle Canyon/Weavers Needle Trail	189
–Miners Needle Trail	192
–Coffee Flat Mountain Trail	194

12. Superstition Mountains Transect	203
13. The Dutchman's Trails	211
–First Water Ranch Trail	212
–El Viejo's Wild Bunch Trail	212
–Grand Enchantment Trail	214
–Joaquin Murrieta and the Spanish Racetrack	219
–Massacre Grounds Trail and the Perralta Mine	221
14. Adventure Challenge Discovery Traverse	227
Appendix: Death Stalks the Superstitions	239
Selected Bibliography, Maps & Filmography	259
Glossary	277
Photography & Illustration Credits	291
About the Author	293
Maps of the Superstitions	296

Acknowledgments

SPECIAL THANKS TO THE APACHE MEDICINE MEN, (*Di'Yih*, "One Who Has Power"), Robertson Preston, and *Di'Yih* Leroy Kenton; Sheena Goseyun and family; Wanda Smith and family; Wendsler Nosie Sr., former San Carlos Apache Tribal Chairman; the San Carlos Apache people who welcomed me and my family to their sacred ceremonial ground; students who trusted me to lead them on one of the first ridgeline traverses of Superstition Mountain, Chris May, and Michael Thomas, who later accompanied me, Lance Laber, Director, and Christine Hubbard, Art Director, DeGrazia Gallery in the Sun, and Native speakers Alejandrina Sierra and Lucinda Bush. Also thank you to proofreader Jeanine Habscom. This book was made possible by my editor Jay Cassell and assistant editor Veronica Alvarado at Skyhorse Publishing.

"There is something in a treasure that fastens upon a man's mind. He will pray and blaspheme and still persevere, and will curse the day he ever heard of it, and will let his last hour come upon him unawares, still believing that he missed it only by a foot. He will see it every time he closes his eyes. He will never forget it till he is dead—and even then . . ."

—Joseph Conrad, *Nostromo* (1904)

Preface

"Nobody gets in and out of the Superstition Mountains completely untouched. Even the most hex proof infidels cannot escape the power of such a magic name, the glamour of the sinister reputation, the occult touch of all those bored and restless haunts, the spirits of the place."

—Edward Abbey, "The Mountains of Superstition" (1972)

FEW MOUNTAINS ON EARTH HAVE PROVEN TO BE more treacherous, hauntingly beautiful, and deceptively enchanting as North America's Superstition Mountains, located in what author Edward Abbey called, "A Dry Corner of the Continent," and what Spanish explorers cursed as a *despoblado*, "uninhabited land," that vast nothingness of the Ninety Mile Desert that once stood between Sonora, Mexico's San Xavier del Bac Mission, and the foot of Arizona Territory's Superstition Mountains. The 29,029-foot Mount Everest (*Sagarmāthā*) ranks above all other mountains in altitude, supernal beauty, and the number of climber's and Sherpa's lives it has claimed (295 people as of this writing). Tibet's 21,778-foot Mount Kailāśa (*Gangs Rin-po-che*) is perhaps the earth's most revered and elegant mountain, attracting thousands of Buddhist, Hindu, and other devote pilgrims of other faiths each year on sacred journeys to the holy peak that date back several millennia. The Seven Summits (including Everest) of Argentina's 22,838-foot Aconcagua, Alaska's 20,310-foot Denali, Tanzania's 16,100-foot Mount Kilimanjaro, Russia's 18,510-foot Mount Elbrus, New Guinea's 16,024-foot Puncak Jaya, and Antarctica's 16,050-foot Mount Vinson, have the distinction of being the highest summits on each of the world's seven continents, among other attributes. Yet, Arizona's 5,057-foot Superstition Mountains, which some might consider too lowly to be included among the world's notable mountains, stands apart from all others for the sheer number of lives it has claimed.

As the ancestral ground of the Western Apache who called the mountains *Wee-kit-sour-ah*, "The Rocks Standing Up," and sacred heights to the neighboring Pima, who knew it as *Kakâtak Tamai*, "Crooked Top Mountain," no other mountain range in the United States has proven to be as perilous as what sixteenth century Spanish explorers called the *Sierra de la Espuma*, "Mountains of Foam." Once a primeval Sonoran Desert biosphere of towering saguaro cactus forests, desert wildflowers, golden eagles, bighorn sheep, mule deer, Sonoran pronghorn antelope, cactus wrens, jackrabbits, and desert tortoise, the Superstition's innocence was lost, and its sublime natural history was overshadowed, when the advance parties of Spanish conquistador Francisco Vázquez de Coronado ventured north into *Nueva España*, "New Spain," from Mexico City in search of the mythic Seven Cities of Gold in 1540. The march of history and lust for gold changed perceptions of what once was the bountiful hunting-and-gathering domain of indigenous desert dwellers to that of a wild country under siege that was overrun with heavily-armed Euroamericans who knew little about the Sonoran Desert, and less about the traditional lifeways that sustained the Pima, Western Apache, and Southeastern Yavapai and the respect they had for their hallowed land.

Prospectors and forty-niners who went bust after the 1849 California Gold Rush turned their attentions to Arizona Territory in 1863, and discovered the rich placer gold on Lynx Creek and Walker Creek that gave birth to the mining boomtown of Prescott, and Antelope Hill near Wickenburg where $7,000 in a "float" of gold nuggets was picked up off the ground before breakfast. Mexican miners were among Tennessee mountain men and scouts Paulino Weaver's and Captain Joseph Walker's prospecting parties. Word got out about a rich mine owned by a Mexican family named Peralta located in the Superstition Mountains. And the genii got out of the bottle. The timing could not have been worse. The United States had declared war against the Apache and other "hostiles" who tried to protect their homelands against the tide riding and rolling west "from sea to shining sea" under the call of Manifest Destiny, the Homestead Act, Indian Removal Act, and Indian Appropriation Acts. Deadly conflicts and brutal massacres encircled and spilled over into the Superstitions creating a dreaded landscape of soaring cliffs, dead-end box canyons, and eerie hoodoos of stone that was the last place on earth many should have tread, a cursed domain of Diamondback rattlesnakes, Gila monsters, cactus spines and plants and animals that stick, sting, or bite, gun-wielding soldiers, pioneers, prospectors, dry-gulchers, and renegades, and, what one territorial newspaper opined, "snakes and other plaguery things . . . [that] grow, thrive, and erect their dangerous terror-inspiring heads."

Though difficult to imagine for most first-time visitors driving to the trailheads in the picture postcard scenery, the Superstition Mountains have claimed the lives of what by conservative estimates may be 654 or more people. Some died of thirst in the brick-oven heat, others froze to death in the icy rain, still others vanished without a trace never to be seen or heard from by loved ones again. Many were murdered—a single bullet to the head—or massacred wholesale. There are a hundred ways to die in what some called the "Killer Mountains," America's deadliest wilderness area. Almost to the man, woman, and child, most died on the ghost trails of Spanish gold and the Lost Dutchman Mine.

Since I first roamed the Superstition Mountains alone with my dog, and later as a wilderness guide, my adventures and journeys of discovery formed my foundation for understanding the Superstition Mountains. I viewed the Sonoran Desert's remarkable beauty through innocent eyes evoked in the prose of writers like Mary Hunter Austin who roamed her own beloved desert:

> For all the toll the desert takes of a man it gives compensations, deep breaths, deep sleep, and the communion of the stars. . . . Wheeling to their stations in the sky, they make the poor world-fret of no account. Of no account you who lie out there watching, nor the lean coyote that stands off in the scrub from you and howls and howls.

I prepared for the Superstitions' dangers by making sojourns across the desert that stretched from my family's home to twin hummocks of pink stone where I camped with my dog in a wonderful cave overlooking the Valley of the Sun and across the night sky that was streaked with comets and twinkling stars.

I was not influenced by the myriad books, and tall tales too tall to believe, which had been written about Superstitions' lost treasures that shaped the perceptions and changed the reality of many who had visited the range.

By Grand Canyon standards, the 249.6-square-mile Superstitions Mountains Wilderness is dwarfed by the canyon's 1,900 square miles of mile-deep chasms, and is more comparable in size to Utah's Zion National Park and Florida's Biscayne National Park. Yet, the Superstitions' extreme summer heat and rugged topography rivals West Texas's captivating and forlorn Big Bend National Park. Moreover, consider that nearly five million people live on the front range of the Superstition Mountains presents the dilemma of accessibility. Step out of your car or truck, and there's a thin line between comfort and safety and a raw wild thornscape of cliffs and canyons that too often prove unforgiving for the unprepared.

I've been inspired to write this book to impart my experiences and explorations, and the lessons I've learned traveling alone and while guiding others, with an eye toward informing, entertaining, and keeping you safe. This new book, *Exploring the Superstition Mountains: Tales and Trails of the Southwest's Mystery Mountains*, has been written for beginning day hikers, backpackers, ramblers, seasoned trekkers, adventurers, desert rats, and treasure hunters. It's also been written for armchair adventurers, sophisticated travelers, winter snowbirds, and lost treasure aficionados. If you don't want to scour the remote canyons and mesas looking for Spanish symbols highlighted in this book that some believe will lead to the "cave of the gold bars," you can stay in the comfort of camp, tent, trailer, lodge, resort, or home, and delve into the early exploits of prospectors, treasure hunters, claim jumpers, cutthroats, Mexican miners, cowboys, Spanish aristocrats, artists, writers, pioneer photographers, and indigenous Pima, Western Apache, and Southeastern Yavapai.

To ensure the accuracy of the trail and route descriptions, I've only described those areas that I've personally day hiked, backpacked, traversed, canyoneered, climbed, or run. I've cross-referenced each trail and route descriptions with my maps, field notes, hikes, and treks, 7.5 minute topographical maps, and trip reports. I've devoted special attention to researching primary sources, historical surveys and accounts, scientific papers, and ethnographies to uncover, sift through, and glean nuggets of truth and insight in a genre that's rife with hearsay and misinformation beyond the bounds of imagination. The discoveries are included in each trail description, historical overview, and mileposts, which also feature directions, geological, historical, cultural, and scenic highlights. Of special interest: If you're inspired to search for the X on your map, I've provided Spanish treasure maps and Spanish/English translations, along with the clues and directions to hidden mine locations as I've understood them. Also included is a trilingual glossary, and the detailed appendix, *Death Stalks the Superstitions,* which features the dates, circumstances, locations, and names, where known, of the 654 victims who perished or vanished without a trace.

Segueing into the heart of the book are the accounts of three journeys of discovery I made on foot I've penned to help establish the Superstition Mountains' Sonoran Desert setting that will provide insight into the people, the time, the place, and the irresistible lure the Superstitions still hold over many.

Stay safe above all else, dig deep, and enjoy your journey of discovery and adventure by walking the trails or reading the tales.

—John Annerino
. . . somewhere out there in the Great Southwest, 2017

I
Journeys of Discovery

One of Coronado's Children on the trail of Spanish gold. Copyright © John Annerino Photography.

1

My First Bivouac

"The very air here is miraculous, and the outlines of reality change with the moment. The sky sucks up the land and disgorges it. A dream hangs over the whole region, a brooding kind of hallucination."

—John Steinbeck, *The Log from the Sea of Cortez* (1951)

AS A TWELVE-YEAR-OLD BOY, I HAD NOT YET READ OF John Steinbeck's mesmerizing journey among the deserts, seas, and indigenous people of Baja California and mainland Sonora, Mexico, but I had discovered what desert rats, mystics, indigenous peoples, scientists, hermits, naturalists, and adventurers already knew about the world's great deserts: You will either flee this hot, dry, and empty ground at first sight, or you will be drawn into it, captivated by the elements of sun, wind, sand and rock, your perceptions shaped by the illusion of time, distance, and space. Once you are drawn into a desert place, however, there is no escaping it—you will spend the rest of your life trying to unravel its mysteries.

Most likely you will try to do this one of several ways. You will study and classify its plants, animals, stones, or bones. You will get to know, where possible, the indigenous people who still live where modern man would likely perish. You will try to capture the marvel with your camera, paintbrush, or pen. Or you will simply need to cross the desert because it stands between you and the horizon line. . . . And, when by day's end, you have not yet reached that distant point, you will need to sit and contemplate your journey in front of a crackling campfire, as the dark heavens unveil the star fire of the cosmos.

That's how I came to know the desert as a boy. Two red stone monoliths loomed high above the Sonoran Desert in the eastern horizon outside my bedroom window. I knew this because whenever I climbed up on the rooftop, which was often, I could see the colossal red stones shimmering through the distant heat waves, as dust devils whirled across the desert floor. They loomed as large in my mind's eye as photographs I'd seen in grade school of Ayer's Rock (*Uluru*) in Australia's Red Centre desert. I had to go to them. I did not know why. But to reach them, I had to cross the desert that stood between my parents' home and the beguiling red stones.

The journey from our doorstep led my dog and me down a busy thoroughfare that was used by horse and wagon riders at the turn of the last century to travel between the distant Arizona settlements of Phoenix and the Pima Indian Reservation. In what seemed like an interminable mile, this paved wagon road eventually gave way to the desert *bajadas*, "lowlands," which fanned out from the base of the red stones. These rolling *bajadas* were covered with saguaro cactus that towered above us with bizarre looking trunk-shaped arms.

The city and traffic behind us, I unleashed my white shepherd and watched in delight as he vainly tried to run down black tailed jackrabbits that exploded from beneath the creosote bushes and left him gasping in the distance. Whirring coveys of white wing doves and Gambel's quail flew from palo verde to palo verde tree as the futile chase continued. When my dog finally retreated, he was limping, his long tongue was wagging from exhaustion, and his pelt was covered with golden burrs of needle-tipped cholla cactus.

After removing the spiny clusters from his black paws and tawny white coat with my comb and tweezers, we continued our journey across the desert toward the red stones. They loomed higher and higher as we approached. I soon discovered, though I could not articulate it, that we were crossing a mysterious, indefinable line that separated civilization from the magic and mystery of going deeper and deeper into a desert place. Nor did I know the names of many of the odd-looking plants—that would come much later—but I was held rapt by the sight of ocotillo waving their long thorny arms in the warm spring breeze, as roadrunners sped after lizards that scurried along our rocky path.

Named for the indigenous Papago (known as the *Tohono O'odham*, "People of the Desert"), who dwelled in the vast desert lands to the south, the 1,663-foot-high red stones were called Papago Buttes by most, and by 1914 they formed the heart of Papago Saguaro National Monument. Until Congress rescinded that designation in 1930, this desert hideaway covered 4,000 acres of lush Sonoran Desert that stood on what was then the outskirts of cowtown Phoenix. When we finally reached the foot of Papago Buttes, my dog and I faced an exposed rock climb to reach a large black cave I had eyed from the distance. But first I gathered firewood from beneath a palo verde tree and stuffed the dead gray branches into my canvas pack.

Comprised of copper-colored conglomerate rock geologists have identified as Tovrea Granite, and estimated to be five million years old, Papago Buttes were as mystifying and exciting to me as the plants and animals that thrived around them, because here wind, but mostly rainwater, sculpted wide shallow caves called *tafoni*, and they also overlooked the sprawling Valley of the Sun.

Three rivers converged in the Sonoran Desert basin below Papago Buttes: the Gila, the Salt, and the Verde Rivers. They were surrounded by black mountains and red peaks that floated in the dreamy distance.

Long before anyone could remember, an ancient desert people called the Hokokam, once flourished around the red stones much the way Australia's aboriginal Pitjantjatjara people hunted and gathered around Uluṟu. In the Piman lexicon, *Hohokam* has been variously translated to mean "those who have vanished." Once my dog and I negotiated a perilous stretch of rock to reach our lofty bivouac cave, I felt we, too, had disappeared from the rest of civilization. I could not imagine a more remote or exciting place. Off in the distance, another cave had eroded to the point it created a hole-in-the-rock that was used as a prism through which the Hohokam viewed the summer solstice.

My bedroll was a simple wool blanket that I rolled out on the rocky floor of the cave. My canteens were stainless steel one-quart surplus Army that we drank from whenever the ice melted enough to give up another swig of cold water. And our meal was a can of pork and beans that continually spilled and hissed in the coals of our little campfire. But for a twelve-year-old boy and his dog, there was no better camp to watch the sky suck up the land that decades later would fall to the blade of a civilization that was said to rise from the ashes of the Hohokam. A dream hung over the red stones because here, as night fell across the crimson desert, constellations climbed over the distant black ridges of a mountain I would later come to know as the *Sierra Estrella,* "Mountains of the Star." My dog dozing alongside of me, his ears perked when coyotes yelped and howled on the desert floor below us, as my dreams and eyes were lulled deeper into the burning red coals.

In the years that followed that formative desert journey, the names of the deserts and bivouacs would change, as did the lessons I learned. But the allure of the desert never diminished. It grew stronger. It nearly always enraptured me. It drew me deeper and, at times, I thought closer to reaching the vanishing horizon that always seemed just out of reach.

The desert cast a lifelong spell on me. I sometimes cursed this spell, but I never broke it because I was drawn to explore the desert at nearly every turn in my life. Living in someplace as rugged and sublime as the American West, it was difficult to limit those journeys to the trackless sand-covered expanses that typically define the popular image of the desert.

I was drawn not only to Death Valley and the Mojave Desert in California, and *El Gran Desierto* in the frontier of Sonora, Mexico, but to explore the yawning desert chasms and burning rimrock of the Grand Canyon and Colorado Plateau of the Four Corners region; the rugged summit crests of imposing desert sierras like Picacho del Diablo in Baja California Norte; the Sierra Kunkaak on Tiburon Island in the Sea of Cortés; and the Sierra del Carmen, which soared above the Rio Grande's Big Bend frontier of Texas and the Mexican states of Chihuahua and Coahuila. Yet, as far as those desert journeys have led me from Papago Buttes—by foot, raft, rope, camera, and pen—and as seductive a mistress as some of those adventures have been, the Superstition Mountains stood waiting to beckon me over the horizon.

Barren mountains rear up out of the silent wilderness that was forsaken by the Hokokam. Copyright © John Annerino Photography.

2

A Journey in the Footsteps of the Vanished Ones

> "From the Superstition mountain rose the Eagle;
> From the sluggish-moving Gila rose that
> Hawk . . . There I am going; there I am going."
>
> —*VIrsak VáI-I,* "Hawk Flying,"
> 1904 Pima festal song (1904)

I STOOD ALONE AT FOOT OF THE GREAT PEAK BALANCing myself with two wooden crutches. The summit seemed impossibly far away, but I needed to reach the distant perch to see if I could once again return on foot to the mysterious mountains of my teens.

In the beginning, before the time of myths and legends, no one was here to see this primal land that was roamed by longhorn bison, bow-tusked mammoths, herbivorous mastodons, dire wolves, five-hundred-pound lions, and Pleistocene jaguars.[1] Paleo Indians had not yet migrated to North America where they hunted the late Pleistocene-aged mega beasts with wooden spears tipped with hand-fluted lanceolate projectile points. The lush desert that formed between eight and fifteen million years ago had not yet been called Sonoran. And the

---

[1] Bison (*Bison latifrons*), Mammoth (*Mammuthus columbi*), Mastodon (*Mammut americanum*), Dire wolf (*Canis dirus*), Lion (*Panthera leo atrox*), Jaguar (*Pantera onca*).

Valle de Sol, "Valley of the Sun," was not thought of as paradise until Paleo Indians, Archaic Peoples, and the Hohokam vanished from the face of the earth. The silence and stillness of the crisp clean air was broken by summer monsoon thunderstorms and violent micro bursts that flooded rivers, streams, and dry arroyos and nourished an arid landscape that thirsted for torrential rain. During times of drought, windborn dervishes spun across the sun-seared desert floor, twisting and whirling through virgin forests of emerald green cacti that one day would be called saguaro.

The mountains encircling the Valley of the Sun, and the wild waters they bore—the Salt, Gila, and Verde Rivers—once knew names that were lost to modern knowledge. In time, the mountains that stood before me would be called *Vainom Do'og,* "Iron Mountain," by the indigenous Akimel O'odham. Formed nearly fourteen million years ago, Vainom Do'og was a dark 2,608-foot pyramid of schist and quartz that soared out of desert seas that stretched to the horizon in every direction. It was roamed by fleet-footed ancestors of the Akimel O'odham. They were remembered as the *Huhugam,* "Those Who Have Gone" and "Those Who Have Vanished." Hunters and gatherers from the ancient desert culture climbed the rugged peak in braided yucca fiber sandals. They sought out its stony flanks to harvest sweet red fruit from towering *Ha:sañ* (saguaro cactus) they gathered using long sun-dried poles of saguaro ribs, and there they also dug up and rooted out the succulent hearts of agave to roast in stone hearths. Here, too, they hunted desert bighorn sheep and mule deer, and made sacred offerings to the sun, moon, and stars. From AD 600 to 1450, the desert river valley encircling Vainom Do'og was the hub of their great civilization that was said to peak at forty thousand Hohokam inhabiting thirty-eight thousand square miles of lower Sonoran Desert during the early 1300s. Using stone hoes fashioned from flakes of schist, tough digging sticks shaped from ironwood, and shovels fire-hardened from cottonwood, the Hohokam dug hundreds of miles of twelve-to-fifteen-foot deep canals they burrowed through the burning black malpais, sand, mud, and cement-hard caliche, constructing an irrigation network on a scale that was said to be unrivaled in the Western Hemisphere. Descending one-to two-feet per mile, the ingenious hand-tapered forty-five-foot-wide channels carried mesmerizing streams of cool water that coalesced and carried silt-laden flood-water irrigation that rumbled under the blazing yellow sun, providing the Hohokam with bountiful agrarian harvests of cotton, maize, tepary beans, and cushaw squash. Pioneer city engineer Omar A. Turney wrote that the Hohokam had "450,000 acres under ancient cultivation . . . the largest single body of land irrigated in prehistoric times in North or South America." But after nearly a millennia, the Hohokam disappeared and the Valley of the Sun once again became the desert first viewed by Paleo men, women, and children.

Some anthropologists speculated the mysterious Hohokam fled to higher ground in the Tonto Basin and beyond, where visions of fertility could be realized closer to the source of the life-giving Salt, Gila, and Verde Rivers that gave birth to their civilization and created the Valley of the Sun. Other scholars said they'd journeyed south, as they had been doing for centuries, on ritual vision quests to the Gulf of California to collect the shells of marine bivalves *(glycymeris gigantea)* used for trade and jewelry.

Find the "Lost City" old-timers said of the phantom Hohokam village glinting in the broiling salt pan along what became the treacherous *El Camino del Diablo*, "The Road of the Devil"—that claimed the lives of hundreds of hardy prospectors, *gambusinos*, and forty-niners trying to reach the California Gold Fields—and you will discover an ancient encampment far from the nearest drop of any living water. Evidence of their artistry suggests many generations of Hohokam had been carving, etching, and polishing the saltwater clam shells at Lost City for hundreds of years, crafting bracelets, necklaces, finger rings, bird and animal jewelry, and turquoise and beaded pendants they wore with ceremonial copper bells and tropical bird feathers. Their trade, shell expeditions, and hypnotic desert journeys were not easy. Between Vainom Do'og and the Gulf of California in northwest Sonora, Mexico they traveled on foot along pathways that led from trail shrine to trail shrine two-hundred miles through searing creosote flats, scorching black lava, and shimmering desert pavement across *El Gran Desierto,* the largest sand sea and starkest no-man's land in North America. Along the way, they paid homage at petroglyph shrines of shells and mystifying figures they'd pecked into the black basalt and granite stones and boulders that overlooked the "great bend" of the Gila River, and precious catchments of rain water called *tinajas* that sustained them in the austere landscape. Others insisted the Hohokam perished from the "Aztec Plagues," epidemic diseases of *zahuatl* (smallpox) and *cocoliztli* (hemorrhagic viral fever) carried twelve-hundred miles north from the Mesoamerican center of Teotihuacan by ancient Toltec and Aztec traders who first brought them maize, copper, turquoise, and green, red, yellow, and blue macaw feathers.

    Whatever befell the pre-Columbian Hohokam, they reemerged as a new people, the desert-dwelling *Akimel O'odham,* "People of the River," (Pima), *Tohono O'odham,* "People of the Desert," (Pápago), and *Hia Ced O'odham,* "People of the Sand," (Sand Pápago), who believe they are the true descendants of these remarkable people. Their ancestors abandoned clan castles, sun-temples, ball courts, platform mounds, and the caliche-covered adobe dwellings and settlements of *Casa Grande,* "Great House," once called "America's first skyscraper," *Los Muertos,* "the dead," named for human remains archaeologists unearthed, Snaketown, *Ska-kaik,* "many rattlesnakes," in Hohokam Pima National Monument which opened the secret door to understanding the Hohokam as a people, and *Pueblo Grande,* "Big Village," on the Salt River where one can still marvel at the remnants of their engineered waterways. These, and other Hohokam settlements, inspired contemporary Phoenix architecture and buildings that were said to rise from the ashes of the Hohokam. In time they would surround Vainom Do'og, which soared above the adobe-style homes and palaces nearly three times higher than the Great Pyramid of Giza. "When they forsook their last cities," Turney wrote in his 1929 study, "Prehistoric Irrigation," "all remained untouched: ollas and axes, bracelets and beads, votive and funerary offerings . . . dedications to the ruling forces of nature. All suffered and all became fugitives alike; the barren mountains and drought-stricken valley again became a long silent wilderness."

Many barren mountains reared up out of the silent wilderness that was forsaken by the Hokokam. To the west there was the 4,512-foot *Sierra Estrella,* Spanish for "Mountain of the Stars," called *Vialxa,* "Berdache Mountain," in O'odham. To the south, there was 2,526-foot South Mountain, *Muhadagi Do'ag,* which bore no indigenous translation; and beyond was 1,660-foot Pima Butte, *Vii Vav,* or *Viva'va,* "Solitary Mountain." To the east there was 2,832-foot Red Mountain, *S-wegi Do'ag,* whose name still remains a mystery. And far beyond soared the lofty ramparts of the 5,057-foot Salt River Range, known today as the Superstition Mountains, that were called *Wikwaxa,* "Greasy Mountains," in O'odham. In Pima festal songs, the mountains were also sung to life as *Kakâtak Tamai,* "Crooked Top Mountain." According to Columbia-educated anthropologist Leslie Spier, "They [the Pima] thought of these . . . mountains as their own because they lived between them. They were not safe beyond these limits." Standing in the midst of this ring of mountain peaks and ranges was the rough uncut black diamond of Vainom Do'og.

Italian missionary explorer Padre Eusebio Francisco Kino was one of the first Europeans to see the lone mountain when he gazed upon the Salt River during his seventeenth century *entrada,* "entry," and named it *Río Salado,* "Salt River." Between 1693 and 1701, the indefatigable Jesuit priest traversed 7,500 miles of "unexplored trails" on foot and by horseback among the O'odham in quest of souls, to forge indigenous missions, and to herd cattle from Mexico across the desolate deserts to provide food ". . . to nourish the Indian converts . . ." of *Pimería Alta,* "Upper Pima Lands."

Long after the "Padre on Horseback" rode into legend, a hardscrabble trail was hacked into the jagged schist of Vainom Do'og to reach an eight-foot deep vein prospectors dynamited into a small notch below its summit to test for copper and gold fever-inducing ore. It may have been the site of the Discovery No. 1, Seal Rock mining claim that was noted in March 1916. Records are sketchy. But years after the glory hole's surprising yield of quicksilver (mercury) played out, Valley of the Sun residents began hiking up the mountain for their health. They called it Squaw Peak. Most did not know it was a disparaging term for indigenous women adopted by English colonists from the Plains Cree's, *iskwe'wiwin,* and Powhatan's, *usqwausum.* Befitting the times, the US Board of Geographic Names changed the name to Piestewa Peak in honor of Lori Anne Piestewa, the first Native American woman who sacrificed her life in modern combat. Her family still remembers her by the Hopi name, *Köcha-Hon-Mana* (or *Qotsa-hon-mana*), "White Bear Girl." Today, one thousand or more Phoenicians make pilgrimages up Piestewa Peak each day. Many refer to it as "the peak" or "the mountain" or "up the trail" because it is the most important destination in their daily lives. Seen from the distance, the Peak could be mistaken for a mountain of daunting proportions. It is dark, angular, and brooding, yet it is always captivating. For those it has touched it remains sacred—a Sonoran Desert Mount Kailāśa—beckoning many others who approach it.

    For many, the peak was both a testing place and a training ground en route to more sublime and distant destinations like Mount McKinley (*Denali*), the Grand Canyon, and the Superstition Mountains, which beckoned me from the distance. As I struggle up the stony trail with my crutches, I realize I had come full circle. The peak was now my testing place if I were to return to the Superstitions of my teens when I explored the mysterious mountains alone with my dog, shouldering a canvas pack filled with canned beans, beef jerky, and dog food, and carrying surplus Army canteens and my trusty pocketknife and compass. I gasp for breath and stare at the distant summit of this ancient Hohokam refuge. It is far beyond my feeble reach. So I resign myself to seeing how far I can get before turning back.

    Forged with picks, shovels, and prybars into the steep rocky flanks of this craggy peak, the old miners' trail climbs and weaves twelve-hundred vertical feet through prickly saguaro, ocotillo, barrel cactus, mesquite, ironwood, and palo verde trees, chuckwallas, occasional rattlesnakes, and rare lucky-to-see Gila monsters in a little over one mile. To ascend so abruptly, the trail angles steeply, frequently zigzagging back and forth on itself in a series of switchbacks stacked atop one another, which climb high above the tallest saguaros. As soon as I reach the first set of the steep switchbacks, my progress slows to a crawl. I stop, ease into a sitting position, and stick my left leg out in front of me across the trail. I lean back against the warm black rock and catch my breath as hikers carefully step around me.

    Recovered, I get up and tackle the next series of switchbacks with as much momentum as I can muster. But I am lucky if I can match the slow determined pace of a desert tortoise for a few dozen yards before I sit down, catch my breath, and rest again. To the Chemehuevi, *Nüwüwü,*

"The People," of California's Mojave Desert far to the west the desert tortoise, or *aya*, was revered for its "will and ability to endure." Fearing someone will trip over my leg cast, I struggle to my feet again and resume my journey to see if I have the ability to endure.

I am sweating profusely, just as I had the last time I climbed Superstition Mountain along a faint half-century old mule trail that lead to the saddle and summit passage between a hidden cave some called Robber's Roost and another cavern that was believed to be the lair of *Haskay-bay-nay-ntayl*, the "renegade" Apache Kid and tracker who served under Chief of Scouts Al Seiber during the United States Apache Wars. The rocky path I'm following now winds through spring blossoms of golden poppies, yellow brittlebush, and purple lupines. I breathe in the sweet scent of spring. I listen to the pleasant hum of bumble bees flying from flower to flower. And I watch white wing doves scurry effortlessly back and forth across the rocky trail in front of me coo-cooing, "hooo-hooo-hooo . . ." For a few moments, the pain falls away.

The next switchback tops out on a small vista. It's a good place to sit down and rest. White quartz litters the ground near flakes and slabs of shiny black schist. I wondered if it was a Hohokam shrine. No one knows for certain, but Omar Turney wrote that the Hohokam used ceremonial caves in the Phoenix Mountains, one cave altar was located at the foot of the terra cotta stone pyramid of 2,706-foot Camelback Mountain, *Cew S-wegiom*, a descriptive name said to mean "long red." Further south, the Hohokam and the Akimel O'odham made offerings of beads, shells, sacred cloth, and creosote branches near the hundred-foot long intaglio of a human figure outlined with stones on the desert floor called Hâ-âk Vâ-âk, Hâ-âk Lying in the 3,010-foot San Tan Mountains. And atop the foothills of Mummy Mountain to the north, the Hohokam built a solar observatory from native stone and aligned the chamber door to view sunrise the first morning of summer solstice.

Portrait of Pima man, Panhop, 1902, Sacaton, Arizona.
Frank A. Russell, black and white glass plate negative.
Courtesy: National Anthropological Archives,
Smithsonian Institution

    I ease into a sitting position and lean back on a vertical slab of black rock. My head is spinning. I close my eyes. And I see the pebble and stone figure of Hâ-âk Vâ-âk, Hâ-âk Lying tended to by a Pima shaman. The *Kúlañ O'odham,* "Medicine Man," is shaking a gourd rattle, holding an eagle feathered-prayer stick, chanting and fanning ceremonial tobacco smoke over the sacred giant who stopped to sleep on his mythic journey to the secret cave of Hâ-âk Teia Hâk in the Ta-atûkam mountains. I open my eyes. I take a deep breath. And the spinning stops. A warm breeze fans my sweat-soaked t-shirt, and a red tail hawk soars on a spring thermal. The raptor drifts aloft, sweeping back and forth in the blue sky in mesmerizing concentric circles, searching for pocket gophers it will pluck from the rocky cactus-studded slopes in the clutch of its sharp talons. The feathers of the *Víshúk,* "hawk," were used by Pima shamans to invoke spiritual power and visions. I hoped it was a good omen for me.

North of this mountain-high vista, I can see the trail snaking its way along a serrated ridgeline. *I can rest on that stretch,* I muse, before it climbs again, swing-and-hop step up the next set of switchbacks, catch my breath again, then crawl the last quarter-mile if I have to. For the first time, I can actually see the summit up close. The thought of somehow reaching it makes me struggle to my feet.

I crutch on in the soothing desert breeze that caresses my face and arms, slowly, methodically, one swing-and-hop step at a time, up one switchback then another, until I finally reach the summit horn of black rock. A short scramble from the end of the trail up a chimney-like gully will put me on top of the mountain. I put both crutches in front of me, hop up, and grab the black rock with one hand. I push the crutches up the rock overhead and reluctantly let go of them, fearing I might slip, fall, and catapult down the rocks without them. I grab the rock overhead with both hands, and I stand squarely on the toes of my right foot. I hold my left leg out in the air. I hop up to the next little foothold. I push the crutches up again, caress the next hold, one hand at a time, and hop up again. I repeat the painful, awkward process until I can't go any higher. Suddenly, I can see over the other side. I am on the summit. I slide across the summit rock on my right hip, lever the crutches beneath me, and struggle up.

I stand up with my crutches and sway in the gentle buffeting breeze. I'm overcome with exhaustion and joy. Tears and sweat sting my eyes and sunburned lips, but I'm on top of the world. "I made it!" I whisper. Crimson stone hoodoos called "Fingers of Fire," that some believe were "people-turned-to-stone" during the Great Flood, crown Superstition Mountain which calls out to me in the distance: "From the Superstition mountain rose the Eagle; From the sluggish-moving Gila rose that Hawk . . . There I am going; there I am going."

* * *

SUPERSTITION INTERLUDE

Many moons have orbited my world since I first crutched up and down the Hokokam's black peak of Vainom Do'og.

  Not long after, I hired a horseshoe-less mustang to carry me into the Superstition Mountains to take me where I couldn't possibly crutch and stumble alone. Still hobbled by a full leg cast, I needed to resume guiding and teaching my students as I'd been scheduled to do, come hell, high water, or the broken cinch on my saddle that dumped me on the floor of La Barge Canyon. Much earlier, I had led a different band of adventurers on what we believed was the first contemporary traverse of the hoodoo-crested ridgeline of Superstition Mountain from Carney Springs across the skyline to the foot of Siphon Draw. In the company of many other students, I had the good fortune to guide them on a climb and sometimes a bivouac atop the mythical Peralta Gold and Lost Dutchman compass point of 4,553-foot Weavers Needle perhaps two dozen times during the course of my tenure as a rock climbing instructor. I had also lead a ten-day "challenge discovery" adventure for young teens whose parents said they were "troubled." They were normal, healthy young people who just needed a good dose of the wilderness, and we agreed to hike through the 249-square-mile "look alike" terrain of the Superstition Mountains Wilderness from Fish Creek Canyon beneath the shadow of Weavers Needle where we picked up and traced the footsteps of environmental essayist Edward Abbey down Peralta Canyon to the trailhead. No less compelling was the route of artist Ettore "Ted" DeGrazia I traced from First Water Ranch through the labyrinth of cliffs that led to Angel Springs where the renowned painter burned $1.5 million dollars in paintings. Much later, I culminated my early explorations of the Superstitions by threading the maze of canyons leading north from Apache Leap, past J. F. Ranch, to the 7,667-foot summit of the Mazatzal Mountains the Yavapai called

Wikedjasa, "Chopped-up Mountains," during a month-long journey run from Mexico to Utah. On occasion, oftentimes out of the blue, I was hired to guide tinhorns, treasure seekers, and get-rich-quick "prospectors," some armed, some not, on their search for the fabled Lost Dutchman's treasure, one pair promising me a 50 percent-50 percent split for whatever they found; and others, like two New Jersey gold seekers who paid real money to horse pack them in and out of Needle Canyon three years running. These adventures and journeys of discovery formed my foundation for understanding the Superstition Mountains; it's remarkable Sonoran Desert environment, beauty, and dangers, not the myriad books that had been written about its lost treasures that changed the perceptions of many who visit the range.

Many came to believe, or were enticed about what they'd read about the Superstition Mountains. Early writers described it as "The Other World," where "The most terrible things told are the swinging stones that turn out from the walls of the canyon and crush the passerby . . . trees that reach out their branches and entangle all who come near them . . . wild animals by the thousands that come right out of the solid rocks. Fishes with legs come from the lakes and drown all within their reach. Fire and smoke and horrible groans and howls fill the air on all sides."

The region encircling the mythic Superstitions was, indeed, "another world," an area of the globe where the wildest tales imaginable are believed by some to be gospel: Take the young logger who reported seeing "a fire in the sky" before he was abducted by aliens in a forest clearing on the edge of the Mogollon Rim north of the Superstition Mountains on November 5, 1975. Or imagine being one of ten thousand people who were reported witnessing the mile-wide V-shaped UFO formation of the "Phoenix Lights" flying over Phoenix and Vainom Do'og (Piestewa Peak) west of the Superstitions on March 13, 1997. And there was an astute Lost Dutchman treasure seeker who photographed what he reported was ectoplasm (paranormal) spirits in a hidden cave in S-wegi Do'ag (Red Mountain), northwest of the Superstitions in 1997. If these incidents weren't enough of a stretch into the realm of fantasy, a Minnesota native reported seeing Big Foot—yes, a Sasquatch—at the ancient Hohokam desert settlement of Painted Rocks on the Gila River southwest of the Superstitions in May of 1988. Among the eight hundred recorded carvings at the proposed Great Bend of the Gila National Monument are two petroglyphs that archaeologists reportedly said were ". . . picturegraphs [that] represent a half-man, half-beast creature!" that substantiated the Minnesotan's claim to the Phoenix television station that interviewed him in Bigfoot's desert hideway. Missing from the Channel 3 News "Searching for Bigfoot Team" 2013 broadcast was a detailed physical description of the bipedal, grizzly-sized *Gigantopithecus blacki*, "giant ape," and whether or not the snow-birding Bigfoot was wearing sunglasses, a straw hat, and a xxxxxxxxxx-sized t-shirt stenciled with a sunbathing, cocktail-sipping skeleton reclining next to a saguaro cactus parroting, "Yeah, but it's a dry heat."

Measured against my personal experience and travels on foot throughout the range, reports that defy everyday reality, and the myths, tales, and legends of the Superstition Mountains, no journey I'd embarked was stranger or more unsettling than reopening a cold case to follow the ghost trail of Washington, DC prospector Adolph Ruth.

A Spanish treasure symbol looms over Buff Springs Mountain and points toward the legendary Peralta's Gold landmark of *El Sombrero*, Weavers Needle, (distant right). Copyright © John Annerino Photography.

3

Tracking the Ghost Trail of Adolph Ruth

"I met a prospector with two burros loaded with camping equipment. And I shot him without giving him a chance to explain . . . I killed him. I unloaded the equipment, set fire to it, then drove the burros away."

—Jacob Waltz, "The Dutchman" on his Phoenix deathbed, October 25, 1891

THE WARM SPRING WIND WHISPERS THROUGH THE hoodoos as I trace the serpentine path along a shimmering creek that winds through mesmerizing mountains still haunted with dread. Two grim-faced revolver-toting wraiths whisk past me hell bent on crossing over Parker Pass before it turns into a furnace. One mutters, "Peters Mesa," under his breath without explaining and presses up the stony trail like he's being hunted. The sun climbs higher. And the morning chorus of white wing dove, Gambel's quail, and cactus wrens gives way to the incessant buzz and whine of cicadas. Deer flies and no-see-ums swarm me. I swat at them with my bandana and continue searching among saguaro, prickly pear, and chain fruit cholla cactus, palo verde trees, and boulders for any movement. I narrow my focus and scan the dusty trail in front of me, cutting for sign as it twists and turns through rocky bluffs, jojoba bushes, and dense skin-tearing brush. The trail I'm following is seventy-five years old and there's little chance of discovering new physical evidence to a cold case that's puzzled investigators since Washington, DC treasure hunter Adolph Ruth vanished without a trace in a hellish maze of cliffs and canyons in the American West while searching for the Dutchman's trove of fabled riches. To my alarm, I soon discovered it was a tale of greed and deception, treachery and murder, where God and goodness ceased to exist.

I push on past high noon, climbing up the boulder-strewn creek bed until I finally reach the site of Ruth's only known camp at Willow Springs. It's 2:40 p.m. I'm hot. I'm dehydrated. And my sweaty pack is smothering me. I peel it off, set it on the ground, and glance up at the imposing terrain. Corralled by an avalanche of boulders choking West Boulder Canyon, the daunting, seemingly inescapable cliffs, ramparts, and serrated ridgelines of Superstition Mountain loom overhead. Willow Springs lay in what cowboys tracking maverick cattle call a "box canyon." For most, there was only one way into, and one way out of, the shadeless and forlorn spring-fed bedrock tank. It was nestled among cattails, bulrush, a lone willow tree, stone corral, prospector diggings, and a Spanish petroglyph etched with the word *oro*, "gold." Nearly disabled by a painful leg injury, Ruth ventured into this unforgiving wilderness hoping to find the X on his Spanish treasure map and wound up with what looked like a bullet in the head. Willow Springs marked the beginning of my quest to retrace Ruth's last days to his open grave that many claimed lay in Needle Canyon, three thousand miles from home.

I peer into the pool of water I once viewed from the hoodoo-feathered ridge tops of Superstition Mountain a half-mile above. The sight of dragonflies alighting the surface at the edge of the gray rock tank underscores the thin line between life and death Ruth faced alone in this desolate canyon. On June 14, 1931, he wrote:

My dear Wife and Children,

Yesterday, Saturday, June 13th, Mr. Purnell and Jack Keenan and I rode 3 burros and two carried my tent, bedding, fifty pounds of flour, 10 pounds of sugar, coffee, etc. I rode my burro until we got to this water. I didn't get off because I was afraid I could not stand on it [my bad leg] again . . . .

Love A. Ruth

Little did Ruth know at the time, but six months after he wrote his loved ones, a search party's bloodhound would discover his skull in La Barge Canyon, three-quarters of a mile distant from where they would later find his skeletal remains. Searchers contemplated their find, huddled around a campfire with their remuda of pack horses and black and tan hunting dogs, unnerved by the sight of the fire-lit skull they hung in a canvas bag from the branches of a sycamore tree. What puzzled me most was the fact that both sets of remains were scattered far from Ruth's camp at Willow Springs, where two cowboys had abandoned a helpless old man carrying a map to America's most fabled treasure—the Lost Dutchman Gold Mine some believed was the Peralta Gold Mine. That's where I was headed, through one of the West's most beautiful tracts of Sonoran Desert into a cold case mystery I wanted to investigate. I wanted to walk the seven tortuous miles Ruth endured in leather street shoes in the same blistering heat to decide for myself whether he had fallen victim to the merciless desert sun as Maricopa County Sheriff J. D. Adams had claimed, or whether he'd been killed, as I'd long suspected, with a .44 caliber pistol, or a .45 caliber bullet fired from a US Colt Single Action Army revolver.

I stand up and shoulder my pack. I am still cramped, stiff, and dehydrated. I had no reason to be. I'm fit, acclimated, and packing far more water than Ruth had. I'd cached another gallon of water beneath a palo verde tree several miles below. In spite of the gallon of water I'd consumed following the trail of Ruth's burro train into Willow Springs from First Water Ranch, I did something I'd never considered doing before. I've limited my fluid intake in order to level the playing field to that of a frail old man limping down the brutal course of West Boulder Canyon in the searing June heat, carrying little more than a cane, a Spanish treasure map, and a metal thermos of hot water to slake his thirst and moisten his parched lips.

Dust whirls as I slide down the steep embankment and start boulder-hopping down a river of gray stones rimmed with green slime and white-washed with alkali. The canyon temperature hovers above 100 degrees Fahrenheit. I am light-headed. And my cumbersome load of water, cameras, and gear sways from side to side like a pack saddle as I pick my way from boulder to boulder. They move and turn underfoot like huge marbles, waiting to snap an ankle like a twig or wrench a knee like a green stick. I climb out of the boulder-strewn creek bed and try following an old trail overgrown with jojoba bushes, bear grass, and mesquite trees. My map calls it the "West Boulder Trail," but it's a figment of the cartographer's imagination. It dead ends in a dense thicket of thorn scrub, spindly ocotillo called *El Bastón del Diablo*, "The Devil's Walking Stick," and poison spine-tipped century plants cursed as "Spanish Daggers." They can easily puncture and immobilize a foot or a leg with numbing pain from steroidal saponins. I backtrack into the creek bed, and methodically hop, step, and jump from one loose boulder to the next. Sweat rolls down my forehead, burning my eyes with salt.

The sun bears down on me, the spring goes out of my step, and I slowly teeter from boulder to boulder until I slip and drop in my tracks. I lay on the hot stones for a few moments recovering as gnats buzz around my head, face, nose, and ears.

During the height of the Mexican Revolution in 1913, Adolph Ruth's son, Erwin C. Ruth, made a pact with imprisoned insurrectionist Juan J. González to provide safe passage for his family from their hacienda in Monterrey, Nuevo León, Mexico across the US/Mexico border to Laredo, Texas. At the time, the borderlands was a hotbed of conflict, bristling with warring factions of bandolera-strapped soldiers, revolutionaries, and *soldaderas*, "women soldiers," armed to the teeth with Winchester saddle rifles, German Mauser rifles, Japanese Arisaka arms, Colt revolvers, Browning machineguns, and "Long Tom" canons, and pitting revolutionary José Venustiano Carranza's *Carrancistas* and General Francisco "Pancho" Villa's Northern Division of *Villistas* against Mexican President José Victoriano Huerta's Federal Army, Rurales, and Militia of forty thousand to seventy thousand men and women. Under the command of El General Carranza, Señor González was executed by a firing squad. The *insurrecto's* widowed wife Señora González, a Peralta family member, their daughter Mercedes, and stepson crossed the borderlands' fields of fire safely. And Erwin, an American doctor and veterinarian who worked for Carranza to eradicate tick fever from his stolen cattle before selling the herds in Texas, was paid off with a set of treasure maps he carried across the border "next to his flesh." The most telling of these maps was the *Perfil Mapa* or *Mapa del Desierto*, "Profile Map" or "Map of the Desert" that was called the González-Peralta Map. (See map page 190). The second map a bit more vague was the González "locator map." On face value, they were deceptive. Both maps needed to be reversed—or held up to a mirror—in order to decipher the topography and crack the code to locating the secret mine by identifying and matching the named features on the González-Peralta Map with the Superstition Mountains' landmarks. The original González-Peralta Map that Erwin wrote was an "incomprehensible old map," and several versions of it still puzzle gold seekers today.

Conflicting accounts profess the González-Peralta Map view looks south up Needle Canyon toward Weavers Needle, others believe the map view looks east through La Barge Canyon, still others confess it looks north toward 3,648-foot Miners Needle, while the biggest detractor from the Needle Canyon view purports the map focuses on Red Mountain twenty miles distant from the Superstition Mountains. The mysterious Spanish landmarks on the crude line-drawing González-Peralta Map include: *El Sombrero* (The Hat), *Caverna con Casa* (Cave with House), *Agua* (Water), *S[ur] Cima* (South Top, or summit), *Hoyo* (Hole), *Escardada* (Hoed), *Tunel*, (Tunnel), and *Sierra Mas Alta en Medio* (Highest Range in Between). A third map that was also given to Erwin reportedly showed the location of the González family's California gold mine. Erwin and his father crossed the desolate reaches of *La Palma de la Mano de Dios*, "The Hollow of God's Hand," in California's Colorado Desert and used the González California map, along with the 1916 Thurston Road Map, to navigate the Mojave Desert's rugged Anza Borrego Badlands where they searched for El Dorado in a Model T Ford. Erwin wrote that the González map was "correct even to the location of the smaller canyons," and his marks on the Thurston Road Map indicated the González mine was located near Grapevine Canyon in the vicinity of mountain man, path finder, and prospector Thomas Long "Pegleg" Smith's 1860s-era lost gold mine. But the father and son came back empty-handed. During their last prospecting trip to the Mojave Desert in 1919, Adolph walked off the edge of the desert, tumbled into a deep ravine, broke his right femur, and lay stranded in the Borrego Badlands where his son frantically searched for him day and night. Serenaded by howling, yipping, and barking coyotes, the frail old man moaned and whimpered alone in the desert for three days and nights without food or water until he was finally rescued by a local homesteader. When San Diego, California surgeons riveted Ruth's brittle leg bone back together

Adolph Ruth nearly perished in Anza Borrego Badlands in 1919 during his search for the González family's California gold mine.
Copyright © John Annerino Photography.

with a metal plate, they shortened his right leg two inches and reportedly warned him that if he ever fell again, he'd die.

I crawl to my feet, brush off the sand and gravel, and slowly stand. My left leg is rigid with a deep, painful cramp. I try to shake it out, but I'm too dehydrated. I weave and peg-leg down the cobble stones toward my water cache. It's only a quarter-mile away, but it takes forever in the monotonous pall of heat and the unblinking glare of the sun.

I stop for a few minutes in the warm shade of a big palo verde tree before picking up my cache of water, canned fruit, and stove fuel. I make camp a half-mile beyond at 6:35 p.m. I unshoulder my pack, and drain a quart of warm water before drinking another quart as I walk a quarter-mile back upstream to a rank bedrock pool of stagnant water. I replenish a gallon and half of water, straining it through my sweat-stained bandana before treating it with powdered chlorine, and walk back down to camp. I am weary, but refreshed, and I spend the evening gazing at the starlit heavens contemplating the fate of Ruth.

Twelve years after his brush with death in the Borrego Badlands, Adolph Ruth resumed his search for lost gold after discovering another map in Erwin's trove, the González-Peralta Map. The two wealthy Mexican families made their fortunes mining gold and were related through marriage. Their map profiled the canyons and landmarks encircling the pinnacle on their map named *El Sombrero* that many believed was Weavers Needle. It was the compass point many gold seekers used to begin their futile lifelong quest for what they believed was the Peralta's Gold, Dutchman's Gold, and Lost Jesuit Gold.

On January 13, 1895, writer and treasure hunter Pierpoint C. Bicknell broke a major story on page one of the *San Francisco Chronicle* that unveiled the location of what would become the world's most infamous tale of lost treasure:

It lies within an imaginary circle whose diameter is not more than five miles and whose center is marked by the Weaver's Needle, a prominent and fantastic pinnacle of volcanic tufa that rises to a height of 2,500 feet among a confusion of lesser peaks and mountainous masses of basaltic rock . . . the first gorge on the south side, from the west end of the range . . . [Jacob Waltz, "the Dutchman," and his partner Jacob Weiser] found . . . a monumented trail [Peralta Trail] which lead them northward over a lofty ridge, [Fremont Saddle]; thence downward past Sombrero butte into a long canyon running north [East Boulder Canyon], and finally to a tributary canyon [Needle Canyon] very deep and rocky, and densely wooded with a continuous thicket of scrub oak." (See Lost Dutchman Peralta Locality Map page 296).

Against his family's advice, Adolph Ruth bought a two-door V-6 Essex and drove across country from Washington, DC with an unidentified stranger, carrying two suitcases, Bicknell's newspaper account, and the González-Peralta Map. Ruth reached the Quarter Circle-U Ranch east of Apache Junction near the Peralta Trail on May 13, 1931. Ruth expected to be guided by Tennessee-born ranch owner William A. Barkley, but "Tex" was reluctant to pack the old man into the desert in the infernal heat. The no nonsense steel-eyed cattleman asked Ruth to wait a few days while he herded his cattle to the railhead at Florence Junction, Arizona. But Ruth was chomping at the bit. Convinced he could find the mine with little trouble, Ruth drove to Barkley's First Water Ranch and, unbeknownst to Tex, brokered a deal with his cowhands Jack Keenan and Leroy F. Purnell to guide him. Why Keenan and Purnell packed Ruth into the godforsaken depths of Willow Springs seven miles distant from a vantage point that resembled the terrain on the González-Peralta Map looking up Needle Canyon toward Weavers

Needle was the first of many red flags that went up when I reread a 1932 letter purporting to substantiate Ruth's death from natural causes.

I break camp at 7 the next morning. It's cool. I'm rehydrated, and I'm well rested. I continue dogging the ghost trail of Ruth and make the steep 500-vertical-foot climb to Bull Pass. Some writers believe Ruth continued his fateful rendezvous with destiny on foot from West Boulder Canyon to Bull Pass. This is where the second red flag went up. I cache two quarts of water beneath the sparse shade of a jojoba bush for my return and enjoy the long winding descent into Needle Canyon, where the third red flag went up. How on earth could the slight, five foot tall, 125-pound Ruth have possibly limped down West Boulder Canyon, staggered over Bull Pass, and hobbled down this rocky trail into Needle Canyon in the cloudless June heat dressed in a sweltering wardrobe of a long pinstripe coat, full-length trousers covering a metal leg brace, a short-brimmed Homburg hat that absorbed the sun like a cast iron skillet, and sweat-smudged wire rim glasses, carrying a cane and a one-quart thermos of dwindling hot water? Moreover, when Ruth wrote his wife Clara at Willow Springs, he said: "I was afraid I could not stand on it [my bad leg] again." Which begged the question, how did Ruth make it back down West Boulder Canyon?

The sound of running water beneath the shade of a young cottonwood tree in Needle Canyon is music to my ears. I make what I presume will be a brisk two-mile detour through La Barge Canyon to Charlebois Spring in order to locate what some treasure seekers call the "Peralta Master Map." One book I'd studied for clues stated, "They [the petroglyphs] are on a south-facing cliff at ground level." I spend too much precious time in the burning sun fruitlessly examining the south facing cliffs and boulders a quarter-mile upstream and downstream from Charlebois Spring.

I lay up in the shade of a mesquite tree swatting flies, *comiendo moscas*, "eating flies," as Mexican miners working Peralta's mine no doubt often repeated, until the heat begins to abate around 4:00 p.m. What was I missing? I shoulder my pack, disregard the directions, and follow my hunches. There, on a *southwest*-facing cliff *above* the creek bed 150 yards south of Charlebois Spring, about where La Barge Canyon makes a dogleg turn southeast through the canyon narrows, was the Peralta Master Map. Or was it?

The ancestral *Salado*, (People of the Salt), inhabited Salt River Canyon and its tributary creeks and canyons in the Tonto Basin north of here from AD 1250 to 1450. On the edge of the Superstition Mountains at the foot of a steep saguaro cactus-covered hillside, the Salado had painstakingly built a forty-room, three-story cliff dwelling in the hollow of a conglomerate stone cave sixty feet deep and eighty feet high that offered stunning vistas of the Salt River. The agriculturalists, potters, and builders left their indelible mark in the Superstitions, as well, crafting the small adobe-mud cave dwelling of Angel Springs. It's been called the "real treasure of the Superstitions." Here, too, at the cottonwood and sycamore tree-shaded oasis of Charlebois Spring, French Canadian cowman Martin Charlebois built a wooden cabin, ran cattle, and tended a garden during the 1890s. Nearby, the Salado used a hammerstone and flint to etch puzzling symbols on their stone canvas. Early writer Bernice McGee went to great lengths to explore the Superstitions on foot, motorbike, and horseback, and studied the site in 1963. Upon arrival, her seasoned guide and pack string wrangler Tom Daly told her, "There's your master map." McGee initially ascribed the drawings to "an archaic form of a topography map . . . [that showed] water, favorable campsites, and migration routes." But after drinking two canteens of cool spring water in the broiling heat, McGee added: "The Peraltas were known to use La Barge Canyon as an entrance into the mountains . . . The opportunity to document the authentic route to the now hidden Peralta Gold Mine was ours."

Charlebois Spring's ancient Salado petroglyphs, or what some treasure seekers believe is the "Peralta Master Map." (Note: This photo has been flipped to see if it mirrors the 1753 Peralta map next page). Rotate book clockwise to compare the similarities. Copyright © John Annerino Photography

1753 Manuel Alejandro Peralta map, Cuento de Oro del Río Salado del Norte, "Legend of Gold of the Salt River of the North."

Standing at the foot of what felt like a brick oven, I studied the symbols that some professed was an ancient Salado map of the stars and constellations. On the left side of the panel, a desert bighorn sheep was paired with a spiral maze. Petroglyphs and pictographs of bighorn sheep are common figures seen throughout the Southwest and are said to signify hunting grounds or spirit animals. A spiral maze is also a familiar symbol on Hohokam petroglyph shrines that some archaeologists believe to represent a journey similar to the Man in the Maze, a spiritual and cultural icon of southern Arizona's Tohono O'odham said to be their Creator, *Se:he* "Elder Brother," entering the Labyrinth. Was the desert bighorn about to enter a labyrinth of canyons where Salado hunters tracked them down for food to sustain their families and clans? Along the right side of the spiral maze, I trace and count eighteen circles carved into the patina-covered granite wall, and compare them to other petroglyphs I've viewed and noted before. They might be Salado clan lines, but they could also represent waterholes linked by trails. Three of the concentric petroglyphs I see on the burning rock are grouped together, two others are linked by a line, and thirteen other rings are connected by a network of lines that might also conceivably be trails. Six of these rings are punctuated with center dots that seem to say, "This is the spot." Some "Dutch hunters," as Lost Dutchman Gold seekers often call themselves, agree with McGee that this is the "Peralta Master Map" that reportedly shows the locations of nine to eighteen mines, tunnels, and diggings that Mexican miners worked in the Superstitions when it was still located on the northern periphery of *Alta Sonora*, "Upper Sonora," Mexico. That was before the 1848 Treaty of Guadalupe Hidalgo and the 1853 Gadsden Purchase effectively moved the Mexican border nearly two hundred miles south of the Superstition Mountains. These circles and trails, I see, resemble a Spanish symbol hidden on Black Top Mesa I hoped to find.

However these mystifying etchings are interpreted, their similarities are striking when compared to the 1753 Manuel Alejandro Peralta map, "Cuento de Oro del Río Salado del Norte," or the "Legend of Gold of the Salt River of the North," if, indeed, the map is authentic. It arouses my wonder and suspicions. The chart did not surface in the United States until 1966 when it was reportedly found in the back of an "old book," and brought to light by the "Chicago group," identified as Errnie Saviano, Basil Zircardi, and Hank D. Anelea. So far as is known, the title of the book was never disclosed publicly. So who's to say whether or not the map was authentic, as it was reported to be, or a Goldfield grifter sketched a rendition of the Charlebois petroglyphs to create another "Lost Dutchman Treasure Map" to barter with unsuspecting prospectors for their precious little "brag bottles" of gold dust and placer gold that proved to them they were on the Dutchman's trail and about to strike it rich? Authentic or not, the Alejandrro Peralta Map has a common trait with the González-Peralta Map and the Peralta Locator Map. In order to compare the Alejandro Peralta Map to the petroglyph lines and circles, you need to flip the map over, hold it up to a mirror, or face down over a pool of water, then rotate it right to approximately 314 degrees in order to match the symbols. If Ruth intended to compare the petroglyphs to the maps he got from his son Erwin, he didn't live long enough to say. (See photo and map page 36).

I retrace my footsteps through a verdant grove of cottonwood trees that tower above La Barge Creek between Charlebois Spring and Needle Canyon. The warm breeze rustling through flickering green leaves is soothing and the two-mile stroll along the perennial creek is captivating. There's no place better to be today. On the rugged grass-covered slopes of 4,152-foot Bluff Spring Mountain soaring above my left shoulder, the late treasure seeker Charles L. Kenworthy pinpointed what he claimed was the Lost Dutchman Mine and the Peralta Mine in his book, *Treasure Secrets of the Lost Dutchman* (1997). High above my right shoulder a trove of artifacts had been discovered atop the remote hardscrabble fault-split tablelands of 3,765-foot Peters Mesa. The remarkable find that ended in 1989 included a weathered strongbox holding a rusty 1846 Paterson Colt .44 caliber five-shot revolver, an extra fully loaded cylinder, and 7.75 ounces of gold; mining picks, pry bars, hand tools, canteens, and hobnail boots; diggings that indicated sixty to seventy men had worked a Mexican or Spanish drift mine at the "salt flats" over the course of six months; a hidden cache of nearly twenty pounds of gold and quartz concentrate that yielded 11.45 pounds of gold ore assayed at 996 fine; and a fully-dressed skeleton, Mexican clothing, and a cowhide bag containing one pound of high grade gold ore that was first discovered by Wm. Edwards of the 1st Arizona Volunteers in 1866. These and other intriguing signs, artifacts, and hand-dug glory holes confirmed for many that Peters Mesa still held hidden caches of gold, lost mines reclaimed by nature, and untold secrets. Why Keenan and Purnell didn't pack Ruth into the canyon oasis of Charlebois Spring so very near his destination raised the fifth red flag for me. Or did they?

Where *did* Adolph Ruth go after he was reported missing on June 14, 1931? His doting wife Clara and son Erwin needed answers and results. They offered a $200 reward to anyone who found the missing government pensioner, dead or alive. The exhaustive month-long search in 110-degree heat was led by a Mexican tracker named Gabriel Robles who guided search parties beneath soaring cliffs in the Dutch oven heat, and through deep canyons where one misstep could cripple a man or a horse. Fatigued from their efforts, Robles told the party, "Soon we will look up in the hope of seeing vultures which will guide us to the body." The vultures never appeared. Still they came looking with hope they'd find Ruth alive, the missing body that would bring closure to a page one mystery that riveted the nation, or evidence of what befell the treasure hunter.

Ranchers, homesteaders, horseback posses, and hounds searched high and low, trailing burros loaded with ten-gallon wooden kegs of drinking water led by Mexican cowhands carrying ropes for probing fissures, tunnels, and caves. Everyone came searching, but "The Indians," the *Arizona Republic* reported, "having in mind an ancient legend, were inclined to believe gods had avenged themselves on the mere mortal who presumed to enter the sacred and dangerous recesses of the Superstitions." Erwin ramrodded the tenacious search efforts that included Maricopa County Sheriff J. R. McFadden, Deputy Sheriff Jeff Adams, sun-creased Tex Barkley, and prospectors Ray Howland and George Holmes. Together the ground searchers continued probing nooks and crannies in rocks too hot to touch, and dry arroyos that offered only sand, stones, and dust instead of sweet water. Meanwhile Phoenix pilots Charley Goldtrap and Carl Knier braved fickle winds and violent down drafts to search the impossible terrain by air, wary of the fact the Superstitions offered no place to land in event of an emergency, or if they spotted the tiny figure of Ruth waving his arms in the mirage far below. "We had to keep at an altitude of two thousand feet to prevent dropping out of control in an air pocket," Knier said. "At that altitude the mountain looked like a huge pile of broken glass and we saw no sign of life." Nor would any of the searchers.

"Scorching heat, Indian legends and a limited knowledge of a mysterious mountain, combined yesterday in defeating the efforts of those hunting in the Superstition range for A. Ruth, 65-year-old gold seeker, who disappeared a fortnight ago," read the page one June 28, Sunday morning, *Arizona Republic* headline. Another *Arizona Republic* headline read, "The furnace-like heat of the Superstitions mountains brought an end today of formal efforts to solve the disappearance of Adolph Ruth, amateur prospector of Washington D.C." For their tireless efforts in the appalling heat, the weary sunburned searchers discovered few signs of Ruth; a handkerchief, piece of paper, a small square bullion cube tinfoil wrapper that Ruth may have left as trail markers, tracks in clay that disappeared in the rocks and boulders, and Ruth's handwritten journal he'd left on his camp cot at Willow Springs. Ruth's entry for June 14 read, in part: "It was cool last night. It is now 2 p.m. and 94. I am sitting under a big willow tree, water in front of me and water behind me . . . sometime tomorrow morning I will prospect some." Willow Springs was likely the last water Ruth would ever see before he met his fate in search of the Golden Fleece. No one knows for certain what Ruth's final thoughts or dying words might have been, whether he was murdered for the Gonzalez-Peralta maps some searchers had suspected, fell to his death off a cliff or into prospector's crumbly mine shaft, died of thirst or heat stroke, was bitten by a rattlesnake or scorpion, or got lost and simply went mad in the maze of cliffs that imprisoned him. One way in, no way out.

* * *

It's twilight when I cross the low divide separating La Barge Canyon from Needle Canyon. I stand there for some time contemplating Ruth's deathbed scenarios. Six months after Ruth vanished, his skull was found in La Barge Canyon on December 12 by a beefsteak-stealing and eating, black and tan mountain lion hunting hound named Music three-quarters of a mile from where his skeleton was later discovered on the slopes of Black Top Mesa on January 8. George "Brownie" Holmes guided the five-man, eleven-packhorse Arizona Republic-Phoenix Archaeological Commission's Expedition into the Superstition Mountains. The expedition breakfasted on bacon, beans, and black coffee on cool rainy mornings and included leader and *Phoenix Gazette* photographer Edward D. Newcomer, horseman and guide Richie Lewis, *Arizona Republic* writer Harvey L. Mott, and Pueblo Grande Museum director and archaeologist Odd S. Halseth. When Music broke away from the pack train and made the surprising discovery, Holmes retrieved the skull from beneath a palo verde tree while expedition members tied up their mounts and pack string. Halseth studied the "green" skull and noticed it still had flesh on it, gave off a pungent smell, and attracted flies. That raised three more red flags for me. How did Ruth manage to stumble cross-country and climb 574 vertical feet up from Bull Pass to the top of 3,356-foot Black Top Mesa with a right leg that was two inches shorter than his left leg and encased in a metal brace? How did Ruth's skull travel more that 1,000 vertical feet from Black Top Mesa down into Needle Canyon and cross a linear distance of 3,937 feet? This wasn't the slick rock canyon country of southern Utah where deadly flashfloods travel far and fast carrying heavy stones, broken timbers, and debris flows; it was a rugged volcanic boulder-strewn cactus-studded Sonoran Desert hillside where a deadeye professional bowler would have a difficult time throwing an eight-pound ball partway into Needle Canyon. And how did the skull climb seventy-five feet up over the divide between Needle Canyon and drop 160 feet into La Barge Canyon where it was found more than fifty feet above the high water line? It defied credibility. Yet, many claimed a flashflood carried the skull down the craggy mountain, or coyotes dragged it a way, perforating it with two bullet-sized holes, without damaging the delicate nasal bones and zygomatic arch.

 Cradling the skull in his bare hands while Newcomer photographed him, Holmes reportedly commented he thought Ruth had been shot. That evening expedition members concurred that "Ruth who by many here is believed murdered." Archaeologist Halseth later shipped the skull to the Science Service in Washington, DC, which routed it to the laboratory of Smithsonian Institution physical anthropologist Dr. Ales Hrdlicka. In his January 1931 report Dr. Hrdlicka wrote: "Holes in the skull . . . indicate a strong possibility that the man was shot to death by a shotgun or a large caliber rifle." Dr. Hrdlicka later clarified that point when he reportedly told author Sims Ely the murder weapon was a .44- or .45-caliber old Army revolver. The fact that the skull was found in a picture-perfect upright position beneath a palo verde tree also raised my suspicions. Most of the craniums I had observed or photographed while working as a photojournalist in the Southwest's borderlands were found lying on their side, often with their mandible scattered several feet or more away. Oftentimes, javelina, vultures, or coyotes had carried the skulls further away from the skeletal remains, which for me dispelled speculation that Ruth had been decapitated.

In that light, and other considerations such as natural direction finding and routes of travel, Ruth's death troubled me for some time. The dots weren't connecting and the pieces weren't fitting together. Could Ruth have died of thirst as Maricopa County Sheriff J. D. Adams concluded in the January 25, 1932 letter he wrote to US Senator Carl Hayden, without benefit of having examined Ruth's skull? "Mr. Ruth left his camp provided with a one quart thermos bottle which was found empty, at the season of the year when there was no water to be found in the mountains and you know that a crippled man walking six miles over rugged rough mountainous country for six miles under the burning heat of an Arizona sun in the month of June would absolutely perish of thirst," Adams wrote. I didn't dispute that. But Ruth wouldn't have covered the distance on foot and made it as far as Needle Canyon. If you're fit, prehyrdated, and acclimated to the extreme heat, I'd learned in the borderlands, one quart of water will sustain two to three miles of foot travel across level desert pavement. Add in other factors such as difficult terrain, elevation gain and loss, dehydration, heat-induced dizziness or loss of perception, and a restrictive leg brace, and the distance decreases correspondingly. If Ruth died of thirst trying to negotiate the boulders beneath his Willow Springs camp on a leg he ". . . could not stand on it again . . ." West Boulder Canyon would have done him in.

How then did Ruth and his remains reach the confluence of Needle and La Barge Canyons? I began to suspect foul play. He was murdered for the González-Peralta map, which was not found among his remains. His body was moved from the crime scene. And the physical evidence either was tampered with, stolen, moved, or covered up.

The sound of water trickling alongside my camp in Needle Canyon calmed me throughout the night, and the cool desert breeze kept the mosquitoes at bay as I drifted off to sleep with a bandana covering my face and ears. This was not the mysterious desert sanctuary I relished in my teens, or enjoyed exploring with students as an outdoor education instructor in my twenties. That was a time when we were held rapt by the mystifying scenery we traveled through and the storybook setting of roadrunners chasing lizards, black-tailed jackrabbits bounding through the brittlebush ahead of us, cactus wrens feeding their nestlings in saguaro cactus hollows, *remolinos,* "dust devils," spiraling like mini-tornadoes across the bajadas, trails shrouded with desert wildflowers bursting open with color each spring, Old West sunsets hanging over our campfires, and coyotes still howling at the moon. Ruth's was another time and place when a dead man's trail snaked through perilous mountains stalked by a rogues gallery of two-legged varmints that took the lives of unwary victims who, once they were hypnotized by the Lost Dutchman's Gold Mine, never escaped its clutches. When prospector Travis Marlow, a fictitious name by his account, told the *LIFE* magazine reporter who accompanied him into the Superstitions in 1964 to examine Spanish symbols and strange carvings on saguaros, he said: "I've run into characters up there packing rifles, six-shooters and knives." A Western revolver tucked in a leather holster that hung like a taunt from his right hip, the mystery character warned, "Brother, look out. They could kill you off, throw you over a cliff and who would ever know? You go into those mountains loaded for bear, shoot first and wonder later."

Bewitched by the tales, or overcome with gold fever, many people have devoted their lives—and subsequently lost their lives—in search of untold riches they thought was theirs for the taking if they could just find the Lost Dutchman Gold Mine. It was long said to be cursed by Apache "Thunder Gods," but that claim was never substantiated by traditional Apache elders nor anthropologists who studied their myths, tales, ceremonial songs, and lifeways. I never bought into the Dutchman's story because nothing was ever really clear-cut in the tale of greed, tragedy and murder. And once I started digging in hopes of discerning irrefutable facts from primary sources, I discovered it was a land of smoke and mirrors, where "eye-witness" reports, as-told-to accounts, misinformation, rumors, hearsay, red herrings, "Chinese Whispers," moonshine-fueled campfire rants, bold face lies, and collusion masqueraded the truth about clues, physical evidence, landmarks, and mine locations to preserve personal legacies, maintain the status quo, and the lost treasure *Illuminati*. Why give up the secrets if you have the inside track and discovered how to locate Peralta's hidden caches sometimes called the "caves of the gold bars," you can secretly plunder, ferret out of the Superstitions, and broker to private collectors, or smelt down in kiln-fired ingot molds, cash out, and hide in offshore accounts? Greed.

Unfortunately, Ruth was a newcomer. For outsiders and the uninitiated who were often buried in deep debt, unearthing a pot of gold seemed like the only solution. Historian Clay Worst wrote of their options: "They turned to a succession of fortune tellers, clairvoyants, mediums and sundry other wizards to whom the desperate seem to turn."

Among the desperate were Adolph Ruth, Jacob Waltz, and a lineup of other characters, suspects, and nameless prospectors who went "toes-up" during the Old West and Depression era saga.

During his death bed confession to maverick cattle wrangler and cowboy Richard "Dick" Holmes, Jacob Waltz reportedly admitted to killing seven men: three Peralta descendants he'd claim-jumped for the mine, his own nephew who'd traveled from Germany to help Waltz, two soldiers he later found working the "Dutchman's" mine, and a lonely prospector with two burros. "I shot him without giving him a chance to explain," Waltz confided to Richard Holmes in the wee hours of October 25, 1891. "I unloaded his equipment, set fire to it, and drove the burros away."

If Dick Holmes's as-told-to, twice-removed account to his son Brownie is credible, this was not the fuzzy, white-bearded "Dutchman" who clicks his heels waving a miners pick and tossing a fist-sized gold nugget in the air as the cheery mascot for the million dollar Arizona lottery, bearded prospector character actors working Old West family tourist towns, or whimsical legends and children's books. It's the tale of a greedy, cold-blooded European immigrant who shot first—and never asked questions later.

That was one school of thought. The other was that of a quiet unassuming German who immigrated from Württemberg, Germany, became a naturalized American citizen, and traveled west with the Forty-niners to work the goldfields in California's Mother Lode Country. Waltz was said to be a "Day late, and a dollar short," and pushed on to Arizona Territory's Bradshaw Mountains where he tried his hand prospecting the Walker Mining District in Prescott. Once again, his efforts "didn't pan out." Moving on, Waltz homesteaded a quarter-section (160 acres) on the banks of the Salt River in Phoenix in 1868 where he began anew his unrequited search for gold. How Waltz and his partner Jacob Weiser came into possession of a Peralta map is vague speculation and as-told-to hearsay. It was reported that while prospecting somewhere in Mexico, Waltz and Weiser visited a gambling tent, and noticed a Mexican rancher named Don Miguel Peralta being cheated. The pair stepped in and saved the unrepentant gambler's life before he was stabbed. The map and $60,000 changed hands twice between Peralta and Waltz. In the final deal, Waltz got the map and rights to the Peralta mine, and Peralta paid off his heavy gambling debt. So it was recounted through "Chinese whispers," a popular chidren's game of whispering a message from one person to another until the original story becomes unrecognizeable

A far more graphic, and perhaps reliable account, has Waltz traveling from Globe, Arizona in 1868 across the Superstitions to the US Army outpost of Fort McDowell when he was waylaid by "Apaches" and lost his outfit and pack animals. Traveling alone on foot through the wild mountains, Waltz sought refuge in hidden caves where he hid out while traveling back to the fort. Crossing open ground between the caves, Waltz discovered three Mexican miners working a claim. Waltz befriended them, and for a time worked as their guard, until they showed him their diggings. The Deutschländer, who spoke little English or Spanish, could not believe what he saw: an eighteen-inch wide seam of quartz streaked with a six-inch vein of pure gold. Stricken with gold fever, Waltz realized the Mexican miners had no legal claim to the mine and decided to take it from them. Lowering his double-barrel, breech-loading shotgun, he pulled the trigger and the muzzle roared with a load of Civil War "blue whistlers" that hit the first miner in the back and cut him down. He shot the second miner with another load of buckshot that opened his chest and blew him backward off his feet through the air. Waltz reloaded, bided his time, and waited until nightfall to ambush the third victim with a shot in the back that dropped him cold. The grim and gruesome account, by a respected historian, speaks of Waltz dragging the bodies into a ravine, burning their outfits, and cutting loose their burros before continuing to Fort McDowell and back to Phoenix.

Waltz reportedly traveled to the Superstitions twice a year when there was water in the canyons, journeying from his Phoenix homestead to the Board House at what would later become the Quarter Circle U Ranch. There, he stocked up with flour and bacon before heading into mountains to work two small holes and one large hole in a "coyote tunnel." Presumably they were caches of Peralta's gold because they required little more than tough pick and shovel work to unearth the lodes before Waltz reburied his tools and recovered the "mine." According to the as-told-to account Holmes relayed to his son, Brownie, who later transcribed it, Waltz told the senior Holmes from his deathbed: "In the mine you will find about $75,000 dollars already dug out . . . ." Holmes pressed Waltz, "Did you dig all the gold out or is there some left?" Waltz reportedly said, "There is enough gold to make twenty men millionaires."

Pure sleight of hand and musical chairs. After Salt River floodwaters destroyed Waltz's adobe and homestead in 1891, the pneumonia-stricken Dutchman was carried to Julia Thomas's home storeroom, where his neighbor and friend cared for him until the end. Thomas owned a bakery near her home and at one point found herself $2,000 in debt. Waltz cashed out fifty pounds of gold ore at the Wells Fargo Bank and paid off Thomas's debt for sugar and flour. She sat at Waltz's bedside until his final moments, when she stepped outside and announced, "Come quick, Jacob Waltz is dying," before running off to get the doctor. Stepping through the doorway were Richard Holmes and Gideon Roberts. Among the men who reportedly stalked Waltz into the Superstitions, only to lose his elusive trail, were Holmes and Roberts. When Waltz laid eyes on the pair, he said, "Follow me again and I'll kill you." Waltz was said to have a miner's candle box stored under his bed that held forty-eight-and-a-half pounds of gold ore that was 33 percent pure and was assayed at 5,500 ounces to a ton! Waltz had reportedly promised the gold to Thomas to take care of her after he was gone. But when she returned from fetching the doctor, Holmes told her Waltz had given the gold to him. What was a "mulatto" woman, as she was described at the time, to do staring at two hardened territorial cowboys? So began a Hatfield and McCoy-type feud that began when Waltz drew his last breath and spanned the next six generations.

Peralta's Curse? If there was a lost cache of Peralta gold, it was not mine for the taking. There's a saying in the colonial silver cities of Guanajuato, Zacatecas, and San Luis Potosí, Mexico about cursed silver and gold: *Ni para mí, ni para el diablo,* "If I can't have it, the devil can't have it either." Viewing the grim toll of deaths I'd compiled, the harbinger of death and misfortune hung over the Superstition Mountains since the Peralta Massacre. The Peralta maps, and the hundreds who perished following their dodgy trails, deceptive clues, and strange-looking landmarks, begged the question: Had the maps been cursed by an indigenous *brujo,* "witch," or *hechicero,* "sorcerer," in the forgotten sierras of Sonora, Mexico? Had one of the Peraltas summoned a powerful Ópata *brujo* to hex the maps in order to protect the family's fortune?

* * *

Early the next morning, I climb from my camp in Needle Canyon up to my water cache in Bull Pass. No one had found it, so I continue hiking cross-country to the top of Black Top Mesa to search for the Spanish symbols I'd first discovered in a special collections vault. I've packed in two gallons of water from Needle Canyon, so I can endure the hot day, hopefully locate and study the Spanish symbols, and bivouac in relative comfort. I set my pack down in the shade of a boulder and start crisscrossing the high point on the southern end of the mesa. I was looking for anything that stood apart from the natural Sonoran Desert environment, or didn't fit the "What's Wrong with This Picture" newspaper puzzle I studied as a child. Roaming back and forth across the mesa I narrow my focus on a stone garden of basalt set among stark-looking century plants.

There's an odd saguaro or two, and beguiling strands of dollar-joint prickly pear cactus adorned with round pancake-shaped pads protected by needle-sharp gray spines. I go back to the stones, and start examining them one by one until I discover the symbols. There they are, hidden right out in the open, etched in shiny carbon-colored veneered basalt. I'm stunned by what I see. At my feet, clear as day, is the symbol of a rising sunburst over the capitalized Spanish word ORO, "gold," and a P petroglyph stone. Immediately above it to the left is a large, sharp flint-shaped broken boulder with a sunburst scrawled across the face of it. Viewing the terrain in the distance, the directional stone points southeast toward Bluff Saddle at the head of Needle Canyon between Weaver's Needle on the right and Bluff Spring Mountain on the left, about where Jacob Waltz may have dry-gulched three Peralta descendents. The scenery below the directional stone over Needle Canyon is stunning, and the find seems too good to be true. So I climb down behind the stone, wary a rattlesnake den may lurk in the shade below. I scratch the ledge with my tripod, poke the legs in the crevices, and fortunately there's no response. On the backside of the flint stone marker is a hidden Spanish symbol that resembles one of the circles and trails found on the Charlebois Spring petroglyphs. I balance on the backside of stone with one hand to take a photo with the other, then climb back up to more solid footing. I circle around the pointed stone marker and locate a petroglyph of what resembles a seventeenth-century Jesuit cross. Many treasure hunters believe such symbols represent the Southwest's legendary tale of Lost Jesuit Gold, but historians have long refuted such stories and scholars have pontificated Jesuits never mined or processed gold. That is, until 1986. That's when four savvy treasure hunters discovered a Jesuit cross symbol carved on a stone high atop the southern

Arizona's 5,736-foot Tumacácori Mountains on the US-Mexico border. Encircling the cross were eight stone markers bearing strange symbols they later discovered were Mayan numerics. They converted the vigesimal numerals to feet, aligned the stone markers around the Jesuit cross, started digging, and unearthed eighty-two pounds of Jesuit gold bars they cashed for $410,000. Not too distant was the site of the legendary *Planchas de la Plata*, "Ledges of Silver," lode that was discovered by explorer and trail-blazer Captain Juan Bautista de Anza. On January 7, 1737, Anza wrote Bishop Benito Crespo the following: "Toward the end of last October, between the Guevavi Mission and the ranchería called Arizona, some balls and slabs of silver were discovered, one of which weighed more than one hundred arrobas (2,500 pounds), a sample of which I am sending to you, Most Illustrious Lord."

I go back to ORO rock and examine it and the surrounding view more closely. In April of 1949, Phoenix surveyor Clay Worst used the intriguing stone as a triangulation point when he reworked what was called the 1924 Perfecto Salazar Survey. At the time, Salazar was shown maps and black and white wet-plate photographs of *El Sombrero* (Weavers Needle) by seventy-two-year-old Cristóbal Peralta. Born in Mexico and living in Spain, Peralta sought documents for the Peralta family's mining claim that ultimately proved unsuccessful. Knowing what the future bode, the Peraltas made one last furtive effort to work their mine before the Gadsden Purchase. During the winter of 1853-54, they returned to the Superstitions, uncovered their hidden mine, hand-cobbled as much rich gold ore as they could, and recovered the mine. As insurance to protect their mine, they surveyed the location so they had evidence to file a future claim if they became naturalized American citizens. Cristóbal Peralta surveyed the line on the precise date of April 13, 1854, and referenced Polaris, the North Star, to pinpoint the hidden mine's exact location.

Enter Bernice McGee. After studying the Peralta Master Map at Charlebois Spring, McGee was guided to the summit of Black Top Mesa by her wrangler Tom Daly. McGee and her horseback party located the sunburst Oro petroglyph and what she wrote was a "Spanish land measure sign meaning 50 *varas*—33 1/3 inches to a vara." Following the secret signs and her instincts 150 feet to the southeastern edge of the mesa, McGee discovered a mine tunnel fifty feet below the Spanish symbols. Fast forward to October 5, 2008. Two ambitious hikers search atop Black Top Mesa on foot, then by air, on four consecutive occasions, when they locate what presumably is the same mine tunnel explored by McGee they estimated was 100 varas from the Spanish symbols. Was this one of Peralta's mines in the area where Jacob Waltz claim-jumped one of their hidden caches of gold, the rumored "cave of the gold bars?" Before Waltz died, he whispered several clues: "The rays of the setting sun shine into the entrance of my mine." The rays of the setting sun shine into the entrance of the tunnel on Black Top Mesa. The rays of the setting sun shine into the entrance of the cave on west side of Bluff Spring Mountain seen to the east from Black Top Mesa. The rays of the setting sun shine into the entrance of the cave in . . .

Late that afternoon, a dark dusty menacing-looking storm rolls in from the south and hangs over Weavers Needle and Bluff Spring Mountain. By evening the advancing lightening strikes force me off the mesa in dwindling light. Two weeks after mining engineer Vance Bacon fell to his death from the summit of Weavers Needle, McGee wrote: "Black Top Mountain is the most dangerous area of the Superstitions." The feeling that something happened here, that "*this* is the spot," is almost palpable as I head off the mesa. *What about Ruth*, I start wondering again as twilight slowly turns to darkness. Far below, I see searchers huddled around a campfire as Ruth's bullet-shattered skull dangles near a roaring campfire. I see his white bones scattered like rock salt below the black cliffs beneath my feet. And I see the silhouettes of Tex Barkley and cowhand Tom Dickens heaving Ruth's body over the edge of the mesa.

More and more, I suspect locals had a hand in the killing. Set against this backdrop, and the sudden poverty of the 1930s depression that drove many over the edge, Adolph Ruth was a marked man the moment he mentioned his treasure map.

Inspired by Ruth's tragic tale, San Francisco chef William Gassler became a confirmed "Dutch Hunter" in 1934. He befriended Tex Barkley and later wrote: "Tex claims the guide put the gun to the side of Ruth's head and told him to get going. He must have gotten excited and pulled the trigger, took the map and disappeared . . . He said the killer had the pistol actually right to his head—flush. Then he pulled the trigger so it knocked Ruth sideways and he died that way and laid that way. That's what made me think he actually found the body shortly after death." According to Gassler's account, Barkley and Dickens put Ruth's remains in a burlap sack then packed them on a mule from Peters Mesa to Black Top Mesa so he'd be found there. Several years earlier throngs of people had scattered Barkley's "Cattle to Kingdom come—clear up to four peaks," after someone claimed they'd found the Lost Dutchman Gold Mine, and it took extra cowhands two months to round up his strays and mavereick cattle. How then did Ruth get from West Boulder Canyon to the top of Peters Mesa? Was he abducted, hog-tied to a burro against his will, carried over Bull Bass, through Needle and La Barge Canyons, led through Pistol Canyon above Charlebois Spring to the top of Peters Mesa, and forced to pinpoint the clues on his map along the way? What were Barkley and Dickens doing on Peters Mesa? Was Barkley's an eyewitness or an as-told-to account? Who was the guide who shot Ruth, Purnell or Keenan, or one of Barkley's other cowhands? And did the killer use the 1846 Paterson Colt .44-caliber revolver that was discovered in the hidden strongbox on Peters Mesa?

I hurry down off the dark mesa toward Bull Pass. Before McGee's party headed off of Black Top Mesa, she wrote: "It was hard to imagine anyone walking around out here after dark, because when the sun sets it seems to takes the moon with it. It is blacker than Satan's heart." I spend an eerily dark, damp, and silent night bivouacked alone in Bull Pass. I have everything packed, my running shoes are laced on my feet, and I'm sleeping with one eye open in case someone else steps into this bad dream and levels a Peralta gold-style *El último tiro de gracia*, "final blow," as I lay in the rocky saddle. Officially, Purnell, Keenan, and Barkley all had bullet-proof alibis and were exonerated. Case closed. Who else then had the motive, the means, and the opportunity to bushwhack Ruth? The unidentified man who drove with Ruth from Washington, DC? A mysterious, machete-wielding "renegade" that's been reportedly seen over the years? Desperate Goldfield, Arizona miners sifting through meager diggings who didn't much like the idea of a pin-striped Easterner driving off into the sunset in his fancy two-door Essex with "their" mother lode of lost treasures?

Two other red flags kept me tossing and turning throughout the night as I counted down to first light when I could walk out of Adolph Ruth's nightmare. A month after the December 13, 1931 edition of the *Arizona Republic* newspaper published the headline, "Skull Believed to be That of Missing Prospector Found in Mountains, Possible Murder of A. Ruth, Aged Easterner, Seen," Ruth's skeletal remains were "discovered" by Tex Barkley and Sheriff Adams who'd also been searching the area for the Dutchman's gold. Thirty-five years later, private investigator Glenn Magill interviewed Jack Keenan's widow, and she reportedly told him: "You know, my husband and his partners never were able to find the mine, even with Mr. Ruth's maps."

Blue whistlers, Chinese whispers, follow the trails and tales and see where they lead—if you dare.

II
Welcome to the Superstitions

A hiker balances himself on a precipice for a better lookout over the eastern Superstition Mountains. Copyright © John Annerino

4

Peeking In, Before You Go

> "Mystery, a mystery as luminous and yet as impenetrable as its own mirage, seemed always hanging over that low-lying waste. It was a vast pit dug under the mountain bases. The mountains themselves were bare crags of fire in the sunlight and the sands of the pit grew only cactus and grease-wood."
>
> —John C. Van Dyke, *The Desert* (1901)

IF THIS IS YOUR FIRST HIKE IN THE SUPERSTITION Mountains, or the Sonoran Desert, you can acquaint yourself with the wonders of the desert, its strange-looking and beautiful plants and animals, and the lay of the land by hiking up the Peralta Trail to Fremont Saddle for the iconic vista of Weavers Needle, or walk one of the many short trails in Lost Dutchman State Park at the foot of the imposing front range of the Superstitions.

More than 200 miles of routes, including a network of 170 miles of trails, crisscross the 250 square miles wilderness area. The best way to get in shape to hike is to hit the trail and put one foot in front of the other and walk as far as is reasonably comfortable for you, enjoy the scenery, a snack and water at a rest stop, and then return the way you came.

If you want to venture beyond the short park walks, or if you need to get in shape to hike up Peralta Canyon to Fremont Saddle, or beyond, you should consider simulating seven principles in your daily walking or running schedule wherever you might live: Distance, Elevation Loss and Gain, Altitude, Weight Carried, Surface Footing, Time Spent Traveling, and Environmental Readiness. For the roundtrip Peralta Canyon to Fremont Saddle hike, you'll be walking two miles one way (four miles roundtrip), climbing 1,360 vertical feet (and descending 1,360 vertical feet back to the trailhead), hiking at a reasonable altitude, carrying an eight- to ten-pound day pack with a minimum of three to four quarts of water and a snack or lunch, walking on uneven bedrock, loose stones, and creek gravel, and hiking for three to four hours or more through a spectacularly rugged and beautiful hoodoo-rimmed Sonoran Desert canyon. You can adapt this same training principle for any hike or trek you plan to embark upon in the Superstition Mountains, including the more challenging Superstition Mountain Skyline Traverse characterized by desert wanderer John C. Van Dyke's description. It's more than double the elevation gain and loss total of 5,314-feet both ways, triple the roundtrip distance of the Peralta Trail to Fremont Saddle trek of eleven miles point-to-point, and largely off-trail. If you're a local, or visiting the area for a few days before you hike, the popular 1.1-mile long hike and 1,200 vertical foot climb up Piestewa Peak in Phoenix is also a good place to train or get ready. (See page 14). Check with your physician before you start training or hiking, and monitor your fitness, diet, health, water consumption, and energy level.

Fluid Requirements

My experience trekking the US/Mexico border's 130-mile long *El Camino de Diablo*, "The Road of the Devil," during the midsummer, and the hot weather training for other adventures, is this: It takes a *minimum* of one gallon of water to run or trek eight to ten miles in 100 to 110 degree Fahrenheit on level trails. That is, as long as I prehydrate beforehand to make certain I'm not in a fluid deficit even before I start. Use two to two-and-a-half per quart, or eight to ten miles per gallon of water as a guide for warm weather hiking, but experiment in your own training beforehand to determine your personal fluid requirement minimums before you head up Peralta Canyon or deep into the Superstitions. You'll need more or less drinking water depending on your fitness level, acclimatization, season, weather, temperature, body weight, hiking distance, elevation gain and loss, altitude, weight carried, surface footing, time spent traveling, and environmental readiness.

Hiking Seasons

Stay out of the Superstition Mountains during the summer. Period. Many hikers and treasure hunters have fallen victim to the merciless Sonoran Desert heat. A twenty-five-year-old hiker died in 107-degree heat while day hiking the Peralta Trail with a friend during a heat wave that claimed three hikers in Phoenix and Tucson and made national news in June 2016. Spring is the best time of the year, when the desert blooms with colorful wild flowers, as are the clear sunny skies of fall and winter when migratory snow birds can be observed delighting in the balmy weather. The summer monsoons and mile-wide dust storms are incredibly spectacular, but they pose deadly hazards of violent flashfloods, booming thunder, and hair-raising lightening strikes. Hike smart. Even the tough seasoned gold seeker, Jacob Waltz, "The Dutchman," limited his prospecting sojourns to the fair weather window of winter and spring when the "canyons had water."

National Weather Service

Stay safe with up to date weather reports by visiting: www.weather.gov/psr/

Local Weather Advisory

"If the zarape is wet,
It is raining
If the zarape is stiff,
It is freezing
If the zarape is moving,
It is windy
If the zarape is faded,
It is sunny
If the zarape is gone,
It's been stolen"

—Don Joseph P. Berumi

Communication

Cell Phones

Don't bet your life relying on cell phone coverage alone in the Superstition Mountains. (See Superstition Mountain page 155).

Satellite Phones

If you need communication that you can depend on with your life, I suggest leasing a satellite phone for the duration of your journey. Numerous services offer rental and leasing for dependable Iridium 9505A satellite phones. Or you can opt to stay off the grid altogether. I've done both. I almost always choose the latter, relying on preparation, experience, and knowledge. How often do you untether yourself, rely on your skills and judgment, and enjoy the solitude and beauty of nature?

Satellite Messaging, and Tracing

A growing number of hikers, high altitude climbers, sea and ocean crossing sailors, and a diverse array of adventurers are using services like Spot.

I haven't used the service, so I can't share a personal field-tested experience. But the statistics on their *Find Me Spot* website, which amounts to 5,057 rescues as of this writing, are convincing. Visit: www.findmespot.com

PLANNING

Refer to the Superstition Trails section to see which trail engages you most that you're physically fit, acclimated, and mentally prepared enough to embark upon. Once you've studied the list, compare it to your previous (recent) Superstition Mountains, or Sonoran Desert, hiking experiences, training, and the corresponding trail descriptions, then decide your trail preference and adjust your training accordingly. (See Superstition Trails page 173). The following resources will further assist your planning and preparation.

Pinal Country Search and Rescue

"The SAR Unit conducts day and night mobile SAR operations, sometimes during adverse weather conditions, in both urban and wilderness environments. The SAR Unit searches for children, the elderly, vehicles, lost hunters and downed aircraft. Deputies are on call 24 hours a day, 365 days a year, and at a moment's notice to provide assistances in a crisis.

"The SAR Unit is specialized in rope rescue services, including high and low-angle rope rescue, and swiftwater rescue. Deputies also have extensive training in human and vehicle tracking for law enforcement or civilian applications. The extensive training required for these highly skilled services ensure our SAR deputies are prepared to help those that find themselves in a life threatening situation. The SAR Unit coordinates with the Pinal County SAR Posse, made up of dedicated volunteers who respond day and night to assist with search and rescue call outs." *Source:* Pinal County

Phone Numbers
Emergencies: 9-1-1
Non Emergency: 520-866-5111

Pinal County Sheriff's Office
971 N Jason Lopez Circle, Building C
Florence, AZ 85132

SAR Sergeant: Doug Peoble (520) 866-5111 doug.peoble@pinalcountyaz.gov

SAR Posse Civilian Lieutenant: Louie Villa (520) 705-7511 louie.villa@pinalcountyaz.gov

US Board of Geographic Names:

The domestic locations and spellings in this book conform to US Board of Geographic Names standards. Visit: https://geonames.usgs.gov/ for more information.

Superstition Wilderness Topographical Maps

Printed Topographical Maps

All of the 7.5-minute quadrangles named at the end of each trail description can be ordered from the US Geological Survey. Visit: www.usgs.gov

- Goldfield 7.5 Minute Quadrangle, USGS: 2004, ID: o33111d4, Maricopa County, Arizona, Scale: 1:24000, Size: 24" × 36"
- Weavers Needle 7.5 Minute Quadrangle, USGS: 2004, ID: o33111d3, Maricopa County, Arizona, Scale: 1:24000, Size: 24" × 36"
- Iron Mountain 7.5 Minute Quadrangle, USGS: 2004, ID: o33111d2, Maricopa County, Arizona, Scale: 1:24000, Size: 24" × 36"
- Horse Mesa Dam 7.5 Minute Quadrangle, USGS: 2004, ID: o33111e3, Gila County, Arizona, Scale: 1:24000, Size: 24" × 36"

- Mormon Flat Dam, 7.5 Minute Quadrangle, USGS: 2004, ID: o33111e4, Maricopa County, Arizona, Scale: 1:24000, Size: 24" × 36"

Resources, Online, and Print

TopoZone and TopoQuest Maps

These online sources are convenient and easy-to-use for studying and printing US Geological Survey-based topographic maps. The elevations used in this book were sourced from these sites and printed USGS topographical maps. Visit: www.topozone.com and www.topoquest.com

Printed Highway and Road Map

The Benchmark Maps *Arizona Road & Recreation Atlas,* displays detailed mileages, interstate, state highway, all weather and four-wheel drive roads, and features color topographical landscape and public lands maps. Available at both brick-and-mortar bookstores and online retailers.

Printed Tonto National Forest Superstition Wilderness Trail Map

Includes numbered Forest Service roads and hiking trails, trailheads, 400 feet topography, waterproof.

Order online from the US National Forest Map Store.

Visit: www.nationalforestmapstore.com/product-p/az-18.htm

Piestewa Hiking Trail Map and Descriptions
Hiking and training in the City of Phoenix Trails and Desert Preserves
Visit: https://www.phoenix.gov/parks/trails/locations/piestewa-peak/hiking-trail-map

Fees

Entrance Fees

There are no entrance or camping fees to hike and camp in the Superstition Wilderness.

Activities

Sight seeing, birding, day hiking, backpacking, trekking, back country camping, horse back riding, rock climbing, exploration, adventure, and treasure hunting.

Treasure Hunters and Gold Seekers

If you're searching for the Peralta's Gold, Lost Dutchman Gold Mine, Lost Jesuit Gold, or Cave of the Gold Bars, you can check permit availability and regulations under the following official categories for the Superstition Wilderness: Prospecting, Gold Panning, Metal Detecting, Mining, and Treasure Trove Hunting.

Visit:www.fs.usda.gov/detail/tonto/specialplaces/?cid=fsbdev3_018726

Prohibited Activities

The Wilderness Act, Public Law 88-577 (16 US C. 1131-1136) 88th Congress, Second Session, September 3, 1964 prohibits the use of "... motor vehicles, motorized equipment [motor cycles], or motorboats, no landing of aircraft, [helicopters, drones, hang gliders], no other form of mechanical transport [mountain bikes, wagons, carts], and no structure or installation within any such area."

TRAVELERS, HIKERS, LODGING, CAMPING, AND AREA SIGHTS

Lodging and Resorts

For the best deals on lodging and resorts in Apache Junction and Goldfield, which are in close proximity to the Superstition Wilderness trailheads visit www.hotels.com or your preferred booking service.

Lost Dutchman State Park, Open Year Round

Easy Day Hiking, Tent Camping, Glamping, and RV sites
Visit: https://azstateparks.com/lost-dutchman

Superstition Mountain Museum Lost Dutchman Museum

Exhibits, Bookstore and Gift Shop, Events, Elvis Chapel, Movie Studio. Also featuring artist Ted DeGrazia's "Prospectors & Pack Animals" Exhibit. Visit: http://superstitionmountainmuseum.org/

Mining Camp Restaurant & Trading Post

Family Dining, Dinner Shows, Gift Shops, Events
Cowboy Steak Dinner, Gold Strike Burger, Prosecutors Stew, Dutchman's Prime Rib
Visit: www.miningcamprestaurant.com
A favorite stop after the Superstition Mountain Skyline Traverse

Goldfield Ghost Town, Est. 1893

"Gateway to the Legendary Superstition Mountains"
Mine Tours, Mammoth Steakhouse & Saloon, and Shops til' You Drop
Visit: http://goldfieldghosttown.com/

Boyce Thompson Arboretum

Sonoran Desert Guided Walks, Birds, Butterflies, Plants, Animals, and Cacti
Visit: https://arboretum.ag.arizona.edu/

Car Touring

Scenic Drives

One of the beauties of hiking the Superstition Mountains are the scenic drives into the trailheads, as well as the paved highway and backcountry road tours that skirt its flanks. From Apache Junction, you can drive northeast up the historic Apache Trail (Highway 88) to Roosevelt Dam (see page 128), or you can drive southeast up the Gila-Pinal Scenic Road (Highway 60) to Apache Leap, Devils Canyon, Top of the World, Oak Flat (*Chich'il Bildagoteel*), and Globe. These outings require little more equipment than a good spare tire, jack, and ample refreshments and snacks.

Vehicle Survival Kit

When you follow the dirt roads that branch off these two main highways and drive into both the accessible and remote Superstition Wilderness trailheads, you should check your radiator hoses and fan belts before you leave home and consider packing along the following items in your vehicle survival kit in event of an emergency: Two good sources of light, first-aid kit, reliable communication to call for help, (satellite phone or messaging), one or two three-to-six gallon water containers (depending on the season), extra food in your storage box or ice chest, lighters and matches, tools, reliable jack, at least one full-sized spare tire, tire plugs and tire inflation kit, a sturdy jack, shovel, jumper cables, a tow rope or chain, compass or GPS (be wary of false directions leading to "Death by GPS"). **Hot Weather Warning:** Stay out.

GEAR

Day Hiking

Day pack, hat, bandana, polarized sunglasses, water, fruit, snacks or food, sunscreen, chapstick, small first-aid kit, insect bite treatment, headlamp, pocket knife, and a comb, tweezers, adhesive tape for removing cactus spines and hairs called glouchids, and whatever additional items you want to carry to keep you safe.

Ultra Light Backpacking, Trekking, and Camping

Except for the day-pack, you'll want to include all of the above in an internal frame backpack. Keeping in mind ultra light backpack and camping, you'll want to pare down additional items to include only essential items that will keep you safe and comfortable: Water, food, waterproof matches, lighter, and flint, topographic map, emergency communication, whistle, signal mirror, water purification pump or potable purification tablets, compass and/or GPS, extra headlamp batteries, whistle, thirty-foot length of six mm or larger perlon cordage for hauling and lowering packs, stove, fuel, cook pot or camp cup, spoon, sleeping bag and mat, Betadine surgical skin cleanser, bandages, surgical adhesive tape, moleskin, elastic bandage, safety pins, and space blanket. Depending on the season and the weather, you may want to include a light-weight tent for shelter, or a tarp for shade.

Water Containers

Sturdy recycled one-quart sports drink containers, and rinsed screw-cap one-gallon milk containers. In hot weather traveling, I carry two to four quarts of water inside my pack, and two one-gallon containers looped together with a bandana behind my shoulders between the pack.

Clothes

Dress for the season and the weather. Be mindful you need to protect yourself from the wind, wetness, cold that can lead to hypothermia, and direct sunlight, extreme temperatures and refracted solar heat that can lead to to heat exhaustion or heat stroke. Pack only what you want to carry and actually need to stay safe and comfortable.

Once You're In, Make Sure You Get Out
Route Description

If you're hiking solo, or in a pair, it's imperative you prepare a detailed route description, including your point of entry from the highway, planned route of travel from the trailhead, itinerary, and map. Carefully review your plans with someone you can trust with your life and leave a copy with them. In the event of an emergency, or delay, searchers will know exactly where to start looking. **Warning:** If you deviate from the route, and it's a critical emergency, the Superstition Mountains have proven that search delays caused by inaccurate information can cost you your life.

Stay Found! Take a Mental Picture, Before You Take Another Selfie

If you're hiking out and back on a new trail or route, stop every now and then to turn around and take a mental picture of the canyon, or country, you've just walked through. That way, upon your return, the mental postcard pictures will look familiar to you and not seem strange, or confusing: "Did we come this way?!" said one lost hiker to the other. "I don't know, what do *you* think?"

Don't Bet Your Life On It
Rattlesnakes

Don't put your hands or feet where you can't see. You may startle a rattlesnake and get bitten which you want to avoid at all costs! If it looks like a stick lying across the trail, stop to make sure it's not a snake. If it is, give the ectothermic (cold blooded, meaning it regulates its own body heat) pit viper a wide berth.

Flashfloods

Do not ignore flashflood weather alerts and posted warning signs. Don't underestimate the power and fury of a flash flood and try to drive across flood-swollen creeks and arroyos. These crossing attempts had become so dangerous and problematic in the state of Arizona that the legislature passed the "Stupid Motorist Law," Arizona Revised Statures 28-910, which compels stranded motorists to pay for towing and rescue costs, assuming they survived their folly. Likewise, don't try to ford flashflood swollen creeks and arroyos on foot.

Terrain

If you're trekking off trail, follow the natural, easiest, and safest line of travel. If your route involves exposed scrambling or climbing reconsider your route, look for a safer route, and make sure you can reverse the route safely so you don't get "cliffed out" on a precarious or dangerous perch. Avoid cholla cactus stands!

Warning: Stay Safe, Be Prepared, or Don't Go!

(See the appendix Death Stalks the Superstitions page 239)

Hiker Deaths/United States

https://skyaboveus.com/climbing-hiking/Whats-Killing-Americas-Hikers

Wilderness Etiquette

Stay on the Roads

All weather, primitive, and two-wheel tracks. The Superstition Wilderness may look tough, but it's a fragile environment that bares the scars of careless off-road drivers for many years.

Off Trail

Don't cut trail switchbacks, which create scars that carry rain runoff and floodwater that cause trail damaging erosion.

Camping

Don't camp within a quarter mile of any perennial spring, stock tank, or guzzler that birds, animals, timid desert bighorn sheep, livestock, and other hikers depend upon.

Your Campsite

Don't camp on fragile soils. If you carried it in, carry it out. Be meticulous, clean up your campsite, and leave it cleaner than when you found it. Use existing fire rings. Don't burn plastic.

Your Cat Hole

"He went to see a man about a horse." Uh-huh. Dig your cat hole six to eight inches deep and bury waste one quarter mile away from springs, water sources, and other fragile desert areas. Carry out your paper or use a smooth creek cobble.

Be a Good Samaritan

If you encounter someone else who's in trouble, help them however you can, but don't become the "second victim."

Native American Antiquities and Historical Sites

Leave them where and how you found them.

Group Size

Keep it small, and keep it quiet so you can listen to nature speak. Nobody wants to encounter a parade of noisy backpackers deep in the wilderness.

Water

Assuming you're fit, acclimated, and prepared for your day hike, excursion, or adventure in the Superstition Mountains, nothing will be more important than the air you breathe, common sense, and good judgment than water. You need to carry enough water, and you need to study the locations of the Superstition's reliable water sources beforehand and plan your hike or trek that goes from one water source to the next. In the Sonoran Desert and the Superstitions water sources are known as streams, creeks, springs, *arroyos*, (dry creek beds that offer seasonal water), *tinajas* (stone rain water catchments), ephemeral water pockets, and *charcos*, (mud holes). Don't camp within a quarter mile of perennial springs.

Barrel Cactus Myth. It's largely a myth that you can tap a barrel cactus like an old-fashioned wooden water keg and use it as an emergency water source. Caught by a rising thermometer during an end-to-end skyline traverse of the Sierra Estrella, I can attest it's difficult to cut open a fishhook spine-covered barrel cactus and eat enough hot, acrid stomach-turning pulp to replenish your fluid deficit. Even the Seri, *Comcáac*, "The People," of the Gulf of California coast of Sonora, Mexico, perhaps the most resilient and highly adapted desert peoples of North America, sometimes grew ill when they were forced to chew and swallow barrel cactus juice: "Possible deleterious effects were avoided if barrel cactus juice was taken on a full stomach; when taken on an empty stomach it was said to cause diarrhea." Diarrhea is the last thing you need if you're hot, dehydrated, and a barrel cactus starts looking like a wooden keg of water to you. The key word in the Seris' life or death remedy is juice, not pulp. For most it's difficult to drink enough water that's taken on the outside air temperature of 100 degrees plus Fahrenheit to stay ahead of the dehydration curve let alone eat enough cactus pulp, or take the time to mash it into juice, when you're tired, dehydrated, and heat stressed.

Remember the Rule of Threes: Three **minutes** without oxygen, three **hours** without warmth, three **days** without water (if you remain inactive, you're in a shaded cave, and you're lucky!), and three **weeks** without food.

Seasonal Springs, Bedrock Tanks, Pools, and Stream Flows Used and Reported

Water: Angel Spring seasonal spring.
Water: Charlebois Spring reliable spring and seasonal pools.
Water: East Boulder Canyon seasonal bedrock pools and stream flows.
Water: First Water seasonal pools and stream flows.
Water: Fish Creek Canyon seasonal pools and stream flows.
Water: La Barge Spring cattle trough spring and seasonal pools and stream flows.
Water: La Barge Spring No. 2 seasonal spring.
Water: Mud Spring piped cattle trough spring.
Water: Needle Canyon seasonal pools and stream flows.
Water: Peralta Canyon Spring and seasonal bedrock pools and stream flows.
Water: Piñon Camp seasonal spring, bedrock tanks and stream flows
Water: Rodgers Canyon seasonal pools and stream flows.
Water: Rodgers Spring piped spring, seasonal pools and stream flows.
Water: Tortilla Spring seasonal spring and stream flows.
Water: Upper Fish Creek Canyon seasonal pools and stream flows.
Water: Upper La Barge Box seasonal pools above the trail crossing.
Water: West Boulder Canyon seasonal pools and stream flows.
Water: Whiskey Spring seasonal spring and pools.

Superstition Wilderness Water Report Late Spring April 2017

Always carry at least one gallon of water per person per day.

Rating Comments: (>>). (Scale Description below)

Source: Tonto National Forest

West End

- Bluff Spring, Trail 104: Slow steady flow from pipe >> (3)
- Charlebois Spring, Trail 104: Good water >> (4)
- Hackberry Spring Slow steady flow from pipe, clear pool behind pipe >> (4)
- Kane Spring, Trail 105: Good water >> (4)
- La Barge Spring, Trail 107: Good flow >> (4)
- Second Water Spring, Trail 236: Good water at spring >> (4)

East End

- Campaign Creek, Trail 256: Good pools with good flow along trail >> (4)
- Reavis Creek, Trail 109 (AZ Trail): Very good water >> (4)
- Roger's Spring, Trail 212: Tubing has steady flow >> (3) *See note below
- Walnut Spring, Trail 119 (AZ Trail): Good water, box nearly full >> (3)
- Pigeon Springs, Trail 134 (AZ Trail): Good water in top section >> (3)

Remember:

- Purify all water to be certain it is safe for drinking.
- Do not contaminate the water with leftover food, soaps, sunscreen, or lotion.
- Respect wildlife and camp at least a quarter mile from water sources! (A.R.S. 17-308. Unlawful Camping).
- Do not camp within a quarter mile of a natural water hole containing water or a man-made watering facility containing water in such a place that wildlife or domestic stock will be denied access to the only reasonable available water.

Note: Tubing cut; is now running 160 yards from the trough. East on TR 212.

Scale Description: Water availability throughout the year in Tonto National Forest
  0: Not reliable
  1: Seasonal or "iffy"
  2: Probable
  3: Fairly Reliable
  4: Reliable

Adorned in sacred corn pollen and beaded buckskins, a young woman comes of age in the sacred *Na ih es*, "Getting her ready," Sunrise Ceremony to embody the spirit of White Shell Woman. Copyright © John Annerino Photography.

5

Native Peoples

"I am a full-blooded Apache [Yavapai] Indian born about the year 1866 somewhere near Four Peaks, Arizona Territory. For five years I lived in a most primitive state with my people—a band of about one hundred and fifty souls. I was captured by the Pima Indians in the month of October 1871 from the plateau known as Iron Peak . . . On this elevated Plateau our camp was raided at midnight. Thirty or more were killed and about 16 or 18 children taken captive. I was one of that number and . . ."

—Carlos Montezuma, *Wassaja,* (1871)

AMONG THE NATIVE PEOPLE WHO ROAMED THE SUPERstition Mountains in the footsteps of the ancestral Hohokam, Salado, and Mogollon peoples were distinct bands of Pima, Western Apache, and Southeastern Yavapai. They adapted their cultures and traditional lifeways to the nuances and extremes of their environments that often proved challenging. In the lowest reaches of the Sonoran Desert the Pima used *ak chin,* or floodwater, farming at the mouths of dry arroyos to grow corn, beans, squash, and melons. Elders recorded their history and traditions on wooden saguaro ribs called *Oos:hikbina,* "stick cuts upon," or calendar sticks, they daubed with natural blue and red pigments mixed from clay and charred wood. The calendar sticks were hand-carved and notched by weathered hands that meticulously incised lines, dots, figures, and symbols of the sun, animals, warriors, and lightning that sometimes resembled petroglyph figures. Each carving represented a life-changing event on calendar sticks that spanned the course of decades: a meteor falling from the sky, a Salt River flood, the death of two medicine men, a battle with the Apache, "black vomit... that killed them by the hundreds," lightning strikes, and rattlesnake bites that took victims in the blink of an eye, and marathon-length desert bighorn sheep hunting journeys from their Blackwater village to *Kakâtak Tamai*, "Crooked Top Mountain."

So, too, did the Western Apache and Southeastern Yavapai recall their oral histories of tracking the craggy calderas and peaks of the Superstitions for bighorn sheep they also hunted, skinned, cooked, and ate. Living in close proximity to one another, the Tonto Apache sometimes intermarried with the Southeastern Yavapai. They also hunted mule- and whitetail deer, javelina, cottontails, jackrabbits, and ground squirrels, and gathered important food at *Chich'il Bildagoteel* (Oak Flat) such as *Chí'chil* (Emory oak acorns), and *chí* (hematite) they used for ceremonial paint, and *dotl'izhi* (turquoise) for adornment and trade. The Superstitions offered Native Americans a bounty of mescal, or agave hearts, that were dug up, roasted in underground stone ovens, and eaten; saguaro and prickly pear fruit that were the sweet delight of summer, along with fermented saguaro wine they used in ceremonies to beckon summer rains; and mesquite trees, "the tree [singular] of life," which provided shade, wood for building dwellings called *jacals* and ceremonial *vatto* (rarmada), making weapons, stoking long-burning camp and cook fires, leaves and sap for making curatives, malleable bark for cordage and cradleboards, and nutritious mesquite beans that were winnowed and ground with a mortar and pestle to make flour and bean cakes. Life was tough, and for many generations it was good.

In their own language the Pima would call themselves the *Akimel O'odham*, "People of the River"; the Tonto Apache—a disparaging Spanish term—*Dilzhę'é*, "People with High Pitched Voices," and the San Carlos Apache, *Tiis Zhaazhe Bikoh*, "Small Cottonwood Canyon People"; and the Southeastern Yavapai, *Kwevkepaya*, "People of the East." Each tribe fought to the death to preserve their families and their lifeways, sometimes amongst one another, but principally against Euroamerican settlers, pioneers, immigrants, and prospectors who, along with the US Army that protected them, came to homestead, stake their claim, graze cattle, and mine all the gold they could find. An early observer, J. P. Dunn, wrote "although these Indians committed atrocities that devils alone would be capable of, they have [also] been subjected to atrocities that devils might blush to commit."

Among the slaughter of innocents was the Camp Grant Massacre south of the Superstition Mountains in Aravaipa Canyon: On April 30, 1871, the 146-man contingent of Tucson's "Committee of Public Safety," including forty-two Mexicans, ninety-two Papagos, and six Americans, killed, scalped, and burned 144 Pinal (*T'iis Tsebán*) and Aravaipa (*Tséjìné*) Apache, and auctioned twenty-nine children into slavery. The Skeleton Cave Massacre was no less heinous. On December 28, 1872, thirty Apache Scouts under the command of General George Crook, led 120 5th Cavalry Troops, and ninety Pima to the edge of a bluff overlooking a large shallow cave hidden north of the Superstition Mountains in Salt River Canyon. It was the refuge of ninety-seven Kwevkepaya Yavapai who were reportedly mistaken for Apache they were hunting. The roar of heavy caliber, breech-loading Sharps and Spencer rifles broke the icy morning stillness. An avalanche of boulders and stones was rolled into the shallow cave, followed by deadly volleys that ricocheted off the ceiling and walls of the cave that cut down seventy-six to ninety-six Kwevkepaya Yavapai elders, men, women, and children. "Screams of the dying pierced the dust, rising high in the air. Only echoes responded. The death chant was quiet. No rifle spoke. The cave was the house of the dead," so wrote soldier and diarist Captain John Bourke who penned General Crook's diary, *On the Border with Crook,* and was known among the Apache as *Nantan Lupan,* "Grey Wolf."

Among the Native People who survived the depredations of war, famine, kidnapping, slave trading, and fusillade of long range 50–70-caliber bullets that also decimated the American buffalo was a six-year-old Yavapai boy named *Wassaja* who lived with his people atop 6,056-foot Iron Mountain. That changed overnight when the Pimas launched a stealthy midnight attack against the Yavapai encampment and took them by surprise. Thirty people were murdered around the horrified child, and more than a dozen children were taken into slavery. Wassaja, which meant "Signaling" or "Beckoning," was among the captives who were forced to walk out of the eastern Superstition Mountains. "Two days of travel over the hot desert brought me to what is known as Black Water Camp," Wassaja wrote later. "After waiting a week with these Pimas, they took me away on horse-back to sell or barter." In a telling entry for 1871–72 on the Pima calendar stick that was inscribed by elder Juan Thomas, and translated years later, it noted, in part: "In the fall the Pima went on a war campaign to the Globe Mts [Iron Mountain]. They came to the Apache camp where they fought the Apaches at night. The Pimas killed many Apaches and take many captives. Among the captives was a boy, now Dr. Montezuma."

If redemption was to be found after the deadly ambush in the Superstitions, Wassaja was purchased on the south bank of the Gila River in Adamsville, Arizona for thirty silver dollars. Carlo Gentile, a globe-trotting Italian photographer, was roaming the American West in search of adventure, gold, and stirring images of its native inhabitants. The goateed and bespectacled Napoletano found everything he wanted, except the trove of gold that eluded him when he joined the three hundred-man prospecting expedition called the Mogollon Mining and Exploration Company that went bust in the scorching August heat of Salt River Canyon in 1871. If there was goodness to be found in the Superstition Mountains, Gentile gained it with his adopted son, Wassaja, whom he renamed Carlos Montezuma. Gentile home-schooled Carlos on the road while traveling amongst the Pueblo people in New Mexico, and touring with Buffalo Bill's Wild West show, until settling down in Chicago. Gentile's brilliant son Carlos earned his medical degree and eventually returned to Fort McDowell, as Dr. Carlos Montezuma, to help his people establish a reservation that became the Fort McDowell Yavapai Nation.

Wassaja was not the only one among the Pima, Apache, and Yavapai who may have been touched by the benevolent *Gáán*, "Mountain Spirits," who still dance in the fire lit canyons of Chich'il Bildagoteel carrying the prayers of the *Ndee*, Apache "People." Born on the North Fork of the White River in the evergreen forests of Arizona's 11,409-foot *Dził Łigai*, "White Mountains," Alchesay, was an Apache Scout who rode under the command of General George Crook. Chief of the White Mountain Apache, Alchesy was described by Captain Bourke as "a perfect Adonis in figure, a mass of muscle and sinew of wonderful courage, great sagacity, and as faithful as an Irish hound." That did not impress Geronimo, *Goyaałé*, "one who yawns." Sergeant Alchesy met the infamous Chiricahua warrior and medicine man on March 27, 1886 when Geronimo surrendered for the first time at Cañon de los Embudos, Sonora Mexico. "Once I moved about like the wind," Geronimo said. "Now I surrender to you and that is all," Geronimo

White Mountain Apache Scout, Sergeant William Alchesay, April 12, 1875, Medal of Honor Recipient. 1888, Globe, Arizona Territory, Andrew Miller sepia-toned cabinet card photograph.

shook General Crook's hand, then asked Alchesy to speak on behalf of the captive Chiricahua. "They have surrendered," Alchesy said. "They are all good friends now . . . because they are all the same people—all one family with me." Alchesay earned Geronimo's lifelong respect and was later awarded the Medal of Honor for bravery and "Gallant conduct during campaigns and engagements with Apaches."

Geronimo had escaped earlier and some professed he hid out in "Geronimos Cave" off the Peralta Trail in the Superstition Mountains. According to author Angie Debo's definitive history, *Geronimo: The Man, His Time, His Place* (1976), there's no record of the fleet-footed warrior and superb horseman entering the Superstitions. The closest records place the *Bedonkohe Chiricahua*, "In Front of the End People," at San Carlos, Arizona when he "jumped the reservation" with 134 Chiricahua followers on May 17, 1885. Enter Lydian Perrine. The full-blooded Chiricahua Apache woman was reportedly born in East Boulder Canyon in 1860 on the west side of Weavers Needle. According to the deathbed story she told her grandson, Walter Perrine, she lived at the base of Weavers Needle with a small band of Apaches until she was around ten years old. The nugget of the as-told-to-account was this: "Just prior to the Apaches sealing up the entrance, she was asked if she wanted to see what was inside. She said yes, and was lowered down into the cave. She said she saw a pile of gold bars, that was almost shoulder high to her, and went far enough back into the darkness, that she could not see the end of it." According to the map drawn by gold hunter John McComb, the mine that became known as "Walter Perrine's Cave of the Gold Bars," was located on the east side of Black Top Mesa beneath the "Spanish Marks." However, the hand-marked dot on the accompanying topographic map places it on the west side of the mesa in proximity to the tunnel Bernice McGee explored in 1963 and was rediscovered by two hikers in 2008. (See page 52).

Born in Sacaton, Arizona, Ira Hayes was a bilingual Pima and English speaking young man who lived within sight of the Superstition Mountains. It's not known if Hayes followed in the footsteps of his father or grandfather to hunt desert bighorn sheep in the Superstition's lofty ramparts. But he was undoubtedly told about his ancestors who climbed the mythic mountain to escape the great flood. Sitting on the south bank of the Gila River, Hayes was sheltered by a traditional *vatto* (ramada) built from stout, forked-mesquite poles roofed with a cordage-bound lattice of ocotillo limbs lashed to cross-braces of wooden saguaro ribs. The women deftly threaded strands of bear grass with sharp deer-bone awls and continued weaving basket designs of the Man in the Maze, *Se:he* "Elder Brother," the O'odham's Creator, as the elder recounted the story to the children, families, and friends:

> When Earth Doctor stuck his staff into the ground to cause the flood, and water covered the earth, most of the people perished, but some escaped and followed White Feather, who fled to the top of Superstition Mountains. The water rose, covering all the valley until it was as high as the line of white sandstone which is a conspicuous landmark . . . After [White Feather] had sung four songs he raised his hand and seized the lightning and with it struck the stone which he held. This broke into splinters with a peal of thunder and all his people were transformed into the pinnacles of stone which can now be seen projecting from the summit of one of the peaks of the Superstition Mountains.

Hayes climbed another far more dangerous mountain that has never been forgotten by Americans everywhere. On February 19, 1945 the US Marine paratrooper, code named "Chief Falling Cloud," was one of six Marines from the Third Platoon of Easy Company that raised the American flag atop Mount Suribachi during the Battle of Iwo Jima that killed thousands of valiant soldiers. Memorialized by a prize-wining, black-and-white photo, bond posters, war memorials, ballads, movies, and a cluster of medals and ribbons that adorned his chest, the quiet spoken Hayes retreated to the less tumultuous surroundings of his homeland. In what might have been his last heroic effort, Hayes reportedly walked and hitchhiked 1,300 miles from his home within sight of the storied Superstitions to Weslaco, Texas to notify the parents of Harlon Block that their son was one of the courageous unidentified flag bearers.

Falling Cloud's deeds were undoubtedly etched in the time worn "stick cuts upon" tradition of *Oos:hikbina* he watched elders notch when he was a child.

The Superstition Mountains remain a hallowed landscape for Native Peoples. But for conquistadors, Spanish and Mexican miners, Americans and European immigrants, soldiers, prospectors, bushwhackers, artists, writers, pioneer photographers, naturalists, hikers, and treasure hunters they viewed the same mountains with very different eyes.

Saguaro sunset, a landmark of the Sonoran Desert, Superstition Spanish treasure hunters, and indigenous peoples who survived on their bounty. Copyright © John Annerino Photography.

6

Natural History

"I brought home the bleached bones as my symbols of the desert. To me they are as beautiful as anything I know. To me they are strangely more living than the animals walking around—hair, eyes, all with their tails switching. The bones seem to cut sharply to the center of something that is keenly alive on the desert . . ."

—Georgia O'Keeffe, "About Myself" (1939)

THE STONY MOUNTAINS CLAW OUT OF GREAT DESERT seas, bristling with forests of cactus, palo verde, and mesquite, nurturing a magnificent ark of raptors, song birds, lizards, and snakes that thrive amongst bighorn sheep, mule deer, and mountain lions who also lie in wait for black-tailed jackrabbits, head feather-plumed quail, and white wing doves. One and all, they form the fragile web of life in an undeniably harsh but bountiful domain sustained by dust storm-driven rains that roar down the boney flanks of lonely mountains and sheet-flooded alluvial bajadas, bringing to life fields of wild daisies, lupines, lilies, and poppies adorned with vibrant golds, reds, purples, and whites that burst out of rocky soils each spring. To me, the bones of distant mountains are as beautiful as anything I know, as great as anyone who has galloped across, run free, or walked upon. To me, they are strangely more alive than cities that continue to march across them, sweeps of a living desert breathing with the mysteries of time, solace, and space. One such desert is the home of the Superstitions. "It was not an unknown land to them and yet it had its terrors," wrote desert vagabond John C. Van Dyke. "Tradition told that the Evil Spirit dwelt there, and it was his hot breath that came up every morning on the wind, scorching and burning the brown faces of the mountain-dwellers."

Before the time of myths and legends, the Superstition Mountains were lost in the mirage of what would later be described as the American Desert, known today as the Great Basin Desert, Painted Desert, Mojave Desert, Chihuahuan Desert, and Sonoran Desert. Straddling an ethereal transition zone in the Basin and Range Physiographic Province that's defined by climate, geography, geology, soil, and plant and animal distribution, the small 250-square-mile Superstition Mountains are located in the Sonoran Desert. An otherworldly landscape for many city dwellers, the Sonoran Desert encompasses an estimated 106,000 square miles that covers most of southwestern Arizona, a slip of southeastern California, half of Sonora, Mexico including the Midriff Islands in the Sea of Cortés, and most of the eight hundred-mile-long Baja Peninsula. Of North America's five wildly diverse desert biomes that stretch south from Oregon to the state of Nayarit, Mexico, the Sonoran Desert is the hottest, arguably the most lush, and comprised of incomparably rugged mountain islands that soar above desert seas and radiate the illusion they are much higher than the reality of 1890s-era surveyors' chains, compasses, transits, theodolites, levels, and solar compasses.

Since Spanish conquistadors first called them the *Sierra de La Espuma*, "Mountains of Foam," and pioneers came to know them as the Salt River Range, the Superstition Mountains stood among the Sonoran Desert's craggy desert peaks and sprawling desert valleys that became known more for their blood-stained history, enchanting and evil myths, and difficult cross-country travel by horse, mule, wagon, and foot. They included the 1,000-foot-high porphytitic felsite dome that caps the 7,734-foot Baboquivari Mountains to the south, the supernal dwelling place of the Tohono O'odham's Creator, *Se:he* "Elder Brother," on the US/Mexico border. Far to the west a perilous day's march short of the lower Colorado River, the granite canyons of the 2,764-foot Tinajas Altas Mountains cupped precious rainwater-filled tinajas that beckoned thirst-ravaged forty-niners struggling across the merciless *El Camino del Diablo*, "The Road of the Devil," to reach the California gold fields. Traveling northeast along the prehistoric Indian trade route that traced the Gila River to the Hohokam settlements of Snaketown and Los Muertos, and coursed beneath the jagged saw-crests of the 4,512-foot *Sierra Estrella*, "Mountains of the Stars," at times the daunting landmark forced Spanish missionary explorers, Butterfield Overland Stage drivers and Pony Express riders, and surveyors and pioneers to cross the dangerous "Forty Mile Desert" in order to cutoff the great bend of the Gila River that looped around the northern terminus of the Sierra Estrella. Spaniards called the waterless *jornada* (journey) the *Jornada de los Esrellas*, "Day's Journey of the Stars," because the toll exacted was thirst, torment, heat, and privation that inflicted men, women, children, horses, and livestock. Directly east across the Valley of the Sun, the Superstition Mountains cleaved the blistering blue skies and star-filled heavens between the Salt River to the north and the Gila River to the south.

Twenty to twenty-five million years ago, geologists tell us, the Superstition Mountains was a fiery landscape of volcanic calderas spewing 2,500 cubic miles of molten lava, stones, and ashes that created the sheer cliffs and benches of dacite tuff, basalt, rhyolite, and deeply-eroded precambrian Ruin Granite. Encircling the imposing eastern front of the 5,057-foot resurgent dome of Superstition Mountain was an 180-degree arc of broad alluvial fans cut and gouged by sheetfloods that thundered with seasonal runoff down creeks and arroyos that often evaporated or disappeared like a phantom in the sand long before a drop of water could ever reach the Gila or Salt Rivers. Thrusting out of its puzzling tangle of interior canyons and hogback ridges for 1,763 vertical feet was treasure hunter Pierpoint C. Bickernell's ". . . fantastic pinnacle of volcanic tufa . . ." that geologists determined was the "erosional remnant of indurated volcanic tuff" of the twin-summated 4,553-foot Weavers Needle. And in the highlands beyond, the rising sun winked over the blue mountains called Iron where ancient mountain dwellers adorned with turkey-feather headdresses once danced day and night in a great circle of stones, illuminated by torches and campfires that lit up forests of piñon, juniper, and ponderosa that sang with primal winds that combed and whistled through the treetops.

The Superstition Mountains are more than the mythical bones of sleeping giants, hoodoos of "People Turned to Stone," and bedrock and boulders that impeded travel by foot, mule, and horseback at nearly every bend in the canyon where death or misfortune often met those in search of an elusive dream that would never be theirs. Peer beyond the peek-a-boo tales and haunts, and you'll unveil and discover a Sonoran Desert biosphere that few can imagine and the aromatic spell-binding fragrance of creosote that still beckons city dwellers into the desert when it rains.

Following are featured lists of the Sonoran Desert's signature life forms that can still be discovered with wonder and awe. Many were utilized, hunted, or gathered for food, curatives, and adornment by ancient Hohokam, Salado, and Mogollon peoples. Almost all can be seen and touched—if you dare. Some remain hidden from all but the most inquisitive eyes, and others should be avoided or given their pass.

THE EDIBLE DESERT

Warning: Do not eat, drink, ingest, or use any of the entries listed in this section without prior knowledge, personal experience, and being informed of wilderness laws, environmental ethics, cultural traditions, and dangers, or you may encounter a recipe for disaster.

> ". . . perhaps the most remarkable, of all desert birds—namely a road runner—nearly two feet of relentless energy from the tip of his wicked bill to the tip of the long, expressive tail . . . Nearly everybody is curiously cheered by the sight of a road runner. Inevitably such a creature is the center of many legends. There seems to be no doubt that he takes the killing of rattlesnakes in his stride . . ."
> —Joseph Wood Krutch,
> *The Voice of the Desert: A Naturalist's Interpretation* (1954)

Agave and Yucca

An estimated three hundred species of agave have been utilized by indigenous people, from the Aztec (*Náhuatl*) in Central Mexico to Native Peoples throughout the Great Southwest, including the Pima, Western Apache, and Southeastern Yavapai who harvested the life-sustaining agave and yucca hearts in the Superstition Mountains and the desert homelands surrounding them. Some species of both agave and yucca have been nicknamed "Spanish Dagger" or "Spanish Bayonet" for their long pointed barbed-leaves.

Century Plant (*Agave Americana*), or Maguey. Arizona Agave (*Agave Arizonica*), Endangered Species; and Goldenflower Century Plant (*Agave chrysantha*). Century Plant Uses: Edible roasted hearts, cut and dried flower stalks, *aguamiel*, "honey water," agave syrup, and agave sap for making fermented pulque, and mezcal for distilling tequila.
Warning: The thick needle-pointed spines of the Century plants can

cause a deep puncture wound, and secrete toxic sap that contains calcium oxalate crystals and steroidal saponins that immobilize hands, feet, and limbs with swelling pain and a variety of other symptoms.

Backstory: After summiting Weavers Needle, one of my students, a healthy high school PE coach, was joking with several students when he stumbled on a rock, fell on the ground, and punctured his wrist on a century plant trying to catch himself. We cleaned, compressed, and bandaged the wound, and gave him aspirin, but the numbing pain and cramps immobilized his arm. We put his arm in a snug sling, and lowered him with his free hand sliding down the rope overhead three pitches (rope lengths) down off the Needle and walked back out to the trailhead together carrying his pack and water. A doctor treated him and he was back climbing with us the following weekend. Fortunately, it was the only mishap in my years of backcountry wilderness guiding.

- Yucca (*Yucca baccata*), "Banana Yucca." Uses: Edible seeds, delectable banana-shaped fruit, and stalks that bloom fleshy white flowers.
- Sotol (*Dasylirion wheeleri*). Uses: Edible roasted hearts and stems, fermented ceremonial beverage, and distilled stomach-burning Sotol. Leaves used for weaving baskets. Blooms white and yellow tufted lilies.

Cactus/i

A recorded 1,750 species of cacti have been identified around the world. Following are popular cacti seen throughout the Superstitions.

- Arizona Hedgehog (*Echinocereus arizonicus*), Endangered Species; and Engelmann Hedgehog (*Echinocereus engelmannii*). Arizona Hedgehog Uses: Edible fruit that can no longer be gathered and eaten because of its protected status. Blooms orange-tinted, red claret-cupped flowers

- Barrel Cactus (*Feroocactus wislizeni*): Uses: Edible fruit. Blooms yellow and orange flowers. (See page 71, Barrel Cactus Myth).
- Buckhorn Cholla (*Cylindropuntia acanthocarpa*). Uses: Edible flower buds roasted for food. Blooms red-tinted orange flowers.
- Giant Saguaro (*Carnegiea gigantean*), pronounced "sah-WAH-ro." Uses: Red fruit for food, fermented ceremonial wine, and seeds ground and roasted for food; wood for calendar sticks, roof lattices for ceremonial ramadas, and fences. Blooms white flowers.
- Pincushion (*Mammillaria microcarpa*): Uses: Edible "wild strawberry"-tasting fruit. Blooms lavender to pink flowers.
- Prickly Pear (*Opuntia engelmannii*), and Dollarjoint Prickly Pear (*Opuntia chlorotica*), Black Top Mesa. Prickly Pear Uses: Despined edible red fruit (*tuna*), syrup, and jelly; and pads (*nopales*) eaten raw in salads, cooked in a variety of foods. Split pads used for poultices, salves, and medicine. Spines used for needles. Blooms yellow and red tulip-shaped flowers.
- Teddy Bear Cholla (*Cylindropuntia bigelovii*), "Jumping Cactus." Uses: Despined edible cholla buds, flesh cooked and eaten, or eaten raw as a palatable emergency source of moisture. You'll need to figure out the simple and easy manner to remove the tenacious spines and glouchids. Blooms yellow-tinted-to-lime green flowers. **Warning.** Cholla cactus spines are anteriorly-barbed like an arrowhead and they are tipped with a fungal organism called *Alternaria tenuis* that, apart from the mechanical injury, can elicit painful allergic reactions and produce granulomas and lesions that should be treated by a physician—assuming they know cactus. Backstory: Working on assignment in the US/Mexico borderlands, I was changing a blown-out tire when I accidentally kicked a cholla burr. I carefully removed it with a comb from

the joint of my big left toe and shook it off. No big deal. When I got home, my foot started to swell, and by the next morning it looked almost twice its normal size and was too painful to stand on. I called every doc and podiatrist in town, but no one knew how treat it. I called a friend at a desert museum and he suggested I call a professor in San Diego, an acanthochronologist, who specialized in cactus and succulents. Fortunately, he took my call. I explained my symptoms, and before I could finish, he told me to call my family doctor and ask him to prescribe a short, three-day blast of RX, and it should clear up in days. It did.

Trees

- Alligator Juniper (*juniperus deppeana*), Oneseed juniper (*Juniperus monospermous*), and Redberry Juniper (*Juniperus coahuilensis*). Alligator Juniper Uses [single species]: Edible berries for food, cakes, tea, distilled gin, and also ceremonial smoke, curative remedies, firewood, and dwellings.
- Arizona Sycamore (*Platanus wrightii*). A perennial water source indicator plant. Uses: Limbs used as roof beams for Salado cliff dwellings.
- Arizona Walnut (*Juglans major*). Uses: Edible walnuts (*nogales*) gathered for food.
- Blue Palo Verde (*Parkinsonia florida*), and Foothill Palo Verde (*Parkinsonia microphylla*), *Palo Verde*, "green stick." Uses: Edible seeds eaten raw, cooked, dried, or pounded into flour for cakes and gruel. Wood used for a variety of utensils and tools. It provides a canopy of desert shade and serves as a nurse plant for young saguaro. Blooms vibrant yellow flowers called *Lluvia de Oro,* "Rain of Gold," when they fall on the ground. Some locals are allergic to Palo Verde blossoms.

- Desert Willow (*Chilopsis linearis*). Uses: Flowers used for tea, and for coughs, poultices, and anti-fungal curatives; wood used for hunting bows, thatched roofs, and houses. Blooms funnel-shaped lavender to burgundy petals.
- Emory Oak (*Quercus emoryi*), and Gambel Oak (*Quercus gambelii*): Uses: Edible acorns gathered for food, pounded into flour for cakes and gruel. Wood used for long-burning firewood, and construction.
- Fremont's Cottonwood (*Populus fremontii*). A perennial water source indicator plant. Uses: Bark used for making curatives and weaving intricately-designed baskets, wood for making tools and ceremonial drums, and roots for Arizona's Hopi to carve sacred *Katsina* (spirit beings), or Kachina dolls.
- Ironwood (*Olneya tesota*), *Palo Fierro*. Sonoran Desert indicator plant. It's the second-hardest wood on the continent, it does not float, and it's too dense to cut for practical use for firewood or construction. The Seri of the Gulf of California coast of Sonora, Mexico developed an art form of machete and axe sculpting, hand filing, and polishing life forms of the Sonoran Desert and Sea of Cortés region they inhabited, including: desert bighorn sheep, road runners, rattlesnakes, quail, owls, ospreys, whales, sharks, dolphins, leatherback and green sea turtles, harpoons tips, and spiritual totems of men and women. Blooms light-purple to lavender flowers.
- Piñon Pine (*Pinus edulis*), Pinyon. Uses: Edible piñon nuts have been a major food source for Native Americans throughout the West dating back 10,000 years. The protein and fat rich seeds were eaten raw, toasted and stored, or winnowed and ground into flour for pine nut soup or meal mixed with juniper berry cakes.

- Ponderosa Pine (*Pinus ponderosa*). Uses: Edible oil-rich seeds were eaten raw, or crushed into flour, patted into cakes, and cooked; inner bark was peeled and eaten, boiled, or pounded into flour; pine needles were used for tea and sweat baths; pine pitch was used for curatives, torches, waterproofing moccasins and water jugs; and the wood was used for camp and ceremonial fires, wind breaks, sweat houses, and construction.
- Velvet Mesquite (*Prosopis velutina*), Western Honey Mesquite (*Prosopis glandulosa Torr*), and Screwbean Mesquite (*Prosopis pubescens*). Uses: Edible mesquite seeds, beans, and pods, and provides a canopy of desert shade.

Plants, Bushes, and Shrubs

- Beargrass (*Nolina microcarpa*). Uses: Edible fruit, boiled stalks, and seeds ground into meal. Serrated leaves used for making sleeping mats, cordage, thatching, and weaving baskets. Blooms stalks of cream-white to yellow flower sepals and petals.
- Brittle Bush (*Encelia farinose*), *Incienso,* "Incense." Uses: Resin used as glue, oral curatives, fire starter, and burned as incense in Great Southwest Spanish missions. *Note:* Resin may provoke an allergic reaction in direct contact with bare legs. Blooms stemmed, yellow, sunflower-like blossoms.
- Bursage (*Ambrosia deltoidea*), nurse plant of the saguaro. Uses: Sweat baths. Blooms small petalless yellow-tinted green flowers.
- Catclaw Acacia (*Acacia greggii*), Wait a Minute Bush. Uses: Edible pods eaten fresh or ground into meal for food, cakes, and soup; unripe seeds roasted, ground into meal, or stored for future use. Blooms spikes of fragrant creamy-white flowers that attract butterflies like catnip. **Warning:** Don't get in a cat fight with

the Devils Claw, also called *Uña de Gato's*, "cat claw's," curved skin-tearing, clothes-ripping thorns.
- Creosote Bush (*Larrea tridentate*), Greasewood. The oldest living plant on earth is reportedly a creosote bush discovered in the Mojave Desert named the King Clone, and radiocarbon dated to be 11,700 years old. Many of the creosote bushes you'll observe in the Superstitions are a bit younger and may be only hundreds or thousand of years old. Uses: Curatives, antiseptics and emetics used for treating wounds, rheumatism, stomach, gastrointestinal, and respiratory ailments. Blooms fuzzy seed pods and small yellow flower petals.
- Crucifixion Thorn (*Canotia holacantha*), *Corona de Cristo*, "Crown of Christ." Uses: Edible berries used by the San Carlos Apache for fruit and food. Blooms green-tinted-white to yellow-tinted white flower sepals.
- Jojoba (*Simmondsia chinensis*), pronounced "ho-HO-ba." Uses: Edible acorn-shaped nuts. The wax from the oil-rich nut is prepared as a skin salve, hair conditioner, and to tan deer and other animal hides. Now commercially harvested for cosmetics and industrial lubricants. Blooms small green-tinted yellow flower sepals.
- Mormon Tea (*Ephedra trifurca*), Indian Tea. Uses: Edible, leaves boiled for tea, and used as a curative for colds, asthma, and other ailments. Blooms stems of seed cones sprouting yellow flower whorls.
- Netleaf Hackberry (*Celtis reticulata*). Uses: Edible sweet red berries used for food, cooked for jelly, ground into meal with seeds, caked, and eaten, or dried and stored. Bark used for sandals, sticks and leaves for dye, wood for campfires and axe handles. Blooms small green-tinted flowers.

- Ocotillo (*Fouquiera splendens*), *El Bastón del Diablo*, "The Devil's Walking Stick." Uses: Edible sweet red flower nectar, pealed bark used for curative tea. Dethorned limbs used for making fences and roof lattices for ceremonial ramadas. Blooms vibrant red tubular flowers at the end of each limb.
- Pointleaf Manzanita (*Arctostaphylos pungens*). Uses: Edible berries eaten ripe for food, ground into meal, and for making cider. Blooms drooping clusters of pink flowers.
- Shrub Live Oak (*Quercus turbinella*), *Chaparro*, "Live Oak." Uses: Edible acorns eaten fresh, or ground into meal mixed in stew, caked and eaten, or for making unleavened bread. Blooms tiny drooping yellow-tinted green catkin flowers.
- Wolfberry (*Lycium* spp). Uses: Edible orange-tinted red berries eaten ripe, sun-dried and eaten, or made into jam. Blooms small bell-shaped purple-tinted lilac flowers.

Wildflowers

Few sights bring the Sonoran Desert and visitors to life better than the sight and scent of spring wildflowers.

- Blackfoot Daisy (*Melampodium leucanthum*). Blooms white flower petals and yellow pistils.
- Desert Hyacinth (*Dichelostemma capitates*). Blooms lavender flower petals and yellow crowned stamens.
- Desert Lupine (*Lupinus sparsiflorus*). Blooms blue to violet flower petals.
- Desert Marigold (*Baileya multivariate*). Blooms yellow daisy-like flower petals.
- Globemallow (*Sphaeralcea ambigua*). Blooms bright orange flower petals.

- Golden Poppy (*Eschscholiza Mexicana*). Blooms orange cup-like flowers with red-tinted interiors.
- Firecracker Penstemon (*Penstemon eatonii*). Blooms scarlet-red tubular flowers.
- Mariposa Lily (*Calochortus nuttallii*). Blooms white-to-lavender tulip-like flowers.
- Prairie Spiderwort (*Tradescentia occidentlis*). Blooms blue-violet flower petals and six yellow crowned stamens.
- Sacred Datura (*Datura wrightii*). Blooms a purple-tinted trumpet-shaped white flower.

Warning: Do not ingest.

Mammals

- Black Bear (*Ursus americanus*). Rarely seen, may be observed in the eastern end of the Superstition Wilderness. Body Length: five to six feet; Diet: Berries, carrion, roots, and small mammals. Revered Native American spirit animal, taboo to eat for many. Avoid close contact, especially a sow with her cubs.
- Badger (*Taxidea taxus*). Body Length: eighteen to twenty-two inches; Diet: Rodents. Revered Native American spirit animal, taboo to eat for many. Avoid close contact.
- Black-tailed Jackrabbit (*Lepus californium*). Body Length: seventeen to twenty-one inches; Diet: Green vegetation, including tree leaves.
- Bobcat (Lynx rufus). Body Length: twenty-five to thirty inches; Diet: Small mammals, rabbits, squirrels, and birds. Consider yourself lucky if you see one.
- Coyote (*Canis latrans*). Body Length: thirty-two to thirty-seven inches; Diet: Small and large mammals, birds, berries, nuts, and fruit. Revered Native American spirit animal, taboo to eat God's

Dog or The Trickster, which appears in many Native American ceremonial songs, chants, myths, and stories. The coyote's howl and silhouette against a full moon is an iconic symbol of the American West, long-featured in "Wile E. Coyote and the Road Runner," that got a bad rap in recent cell phone television commercials: "You don't want to be out here at night, 'cuz of the coyotes." "Uh rrru, uh-uh, uh-rrruuuuuuuu!"

- Desert Bighorn Sheep (*Ovis canadensis nelsoni*), Sensitive Species List. Size: Rams (male) 150 to 200 pounds, Ewes (females) seventy-five to 130 pounds; Diet: Browse, grasses, jojoba, and pincushion and saguaro cactus. Extirpated from Superstition Mountains by poachers during the 1930s, bighorn sheep have been successfully reintroduced to the Superstitions. The translocated sheep, however, suffer from predation by native mountain lions and the tightening noose of civilization's din, lights, and encroachment.
- Desert Cottontail (*Sylvilagus Audubon*), Cottontail Rabbit. Body Length: twelve to seventeen inches; Diet: Grass, fruits, and nuts.
- Gray fox (*Urocyon cinereoargenteus*). Body Length: twenty-one to twenty-nine inches; Diet: Rodents, birds, eggs, fruits, and nuts. Consider yourself lucky if you see one.
- Javelina (*Tayassu tajacu*), Collard Peccary. Body Length: thirty-four to thirty-six inches; Diet: Prickly pear pads, flowers, mesquite beans, grubs, and roots. Javelinas are often noisy, invasive, pungent smelling, and run in packs of twelve to eighteen animals. Avoid close contact, especially with a near-sighted sow and her offspring. How fast can you shinny up a saguaro?!
- Jaguar (*Panthera onca*), Mexican Jaguar, Near Threatened Species. Body Length: 3.7 to 6.1 feet, Tail: eighteen to thirty inches; Diet: Black bear, mule deer, whitetail deer, small mammals, and birds.

Reportedly extirpated from the Superstition Mountains when an unsubstantiated account reported: "The last Mexican Jaguar (*El Tigre*) was killed near the Reavis Ranch around 1913." According to the page 5, Monday, June 29, 1903, *Arizona Republic* account another jaguar was hunted near the J. F. Ranch: "W. D. Tanner and W. L. Pinney returned yesterday morning from their week's outing at John F. Fraser's ranch among the pines in the Superstition mountains, about sixty miles east of Phoenix. Some of their friends thought the report that they were going after bear and lions was a joke, but last Tuesday with the aid of dogs they tracked a large mountain lion several miles over the mountains and canyons and killed him. No bears were seen, and the balance of the time was spent in trying to locate a huge jaguar that has been killing cattle there lately, which effort was not successful."

- Mule Deer (*Odocoileus hemionus*). Body Length: 3.75 to 6.5 feet; Diet: Flowering plants, grasses, and woody vegetation. Principal Predator: Mountain lion.
- Mountain Lion (*Felis concolor*), Cougar. Body Length: forty-two to fifty-four inches, tail thirty to thirty-six inches; Diet: Primarily mule deer, white-tailed rear, mammals including bighorn sheep, small mammals, and birds.
- Porcupine (*Erethizon dorsatum*). Body Length: eighteen to twenty-two inches; Diet: Inner bark of trees, buds, and cacti.
- Raccoon (*Procyon lotor*), *Mapache*, "racoon, thief." Body Length: eighteen to twenty-eight inches; Diet: Acorns, nuts, fruit, insects, and frogs
- Ringtail (*Bassariscus astutus*), Ringtail Cat. Body Length: fourteen to sixteen inches; Diet: Lizards, small mammals, fruit, and insects.

- Rock Squirrel (*Otospermophilus variegatus*). Body Length: ten to eleven inches; Diet: Nuts, seeds, leaves, and fruits.
- Sonoran Pronghorn Antelope (*Antilocapra americana sonoriensis*), "prairie ghosts," Endangered Species. Body Length: four to five feet; Diet: Grasses, herbs and cactus, Speed: Up to sixty miles an hour. Reportedly extirpated from the Superstition Mountain bajadas in 1903. Stage coach drivers and passengers traveling the Phoenix, Mesa, Florence and Globe Stage Line during the mid-1890s reported seeing ". . . large herds of antelopes on the desert plains southeast of Superstition Mountain . . ." each spring.
- White-tailed Deer (*Odocoileus virginianus*). Body Length: 4.5 to 6.75 feet; Diet: Green plants, acorns, and woody materia; Principal Predator: Mountain lion

Avifauna

- American Bald Eagle (*Haliaeetus leucocephalus*), Endangered Species. Length twenty-seven to thirty-five inches; Wingspan seventy-one to eighty-nine inches, Diet: Fish (from the Salt River), frogs, tadpoles, jackrabbits, cottontails, squirrels, lizards, snakes, small birds, rodents, and insects. Revered Native American spirit animal, taboo to eat. The sacred feathers and plumes were gathered and used by Native Americans for ceremonies, shrine offerings, adornment, and prayer sticks.
- Black Hawk (*Buteogallus anthracnose*). Body Length: twenty-one inches; Wingspan fifty inches; Diet: Frogs, fish, lizards, snakes, rodents, small birds, and insects.
- Cactus Ferruginous Pygmy Owl (*Glaucidium brasilianum cactorum*), Endangered Species. Body Length: seven inches; Wingspan twelve inches; Diet: Mourning dove, lizards, and rodents.

Natural History

- Cactus Wren (*Campylohynchus brunneicapillus*). Body Length: 8.5 inches; Wingspan: eleven inches; Diet: Insects and fruit.
- Canyon Wren (*Catherpes mexicanus*). Body Length: 5.5 inches; Wingspan: 7.5 inches; Diet: Insects and spiders.
- Cardinal (*Cardinalis cardinalis*). Body Length: 8.75 inches; Wingspan: twelve inches; Diet: Seeds, fruit, insect larvae.
- Common Raven (*Corvus corax*). Body Length: twenty-four inches; Wingspan: fifty-three inches; Diet: Omnivorous scavenges nuts, berries, and fruit, rodents, small mammals, reptiles, birds, carrion, and your unprotected snacks and food.
- Costa's Hummingbird (*Calypte costae*). Body Length: 3.5 inches; Wingspan: 4.75 Inches;Diet: Nectar, insects.
- Elf Owl (*Micrathene whitneyi*). Body Length: 4.9 to 5.7 inches; Wingspan 10.5 inches, Diet: Insects, moths, scorpions, and centipedes.
- Gambel's Quail (*Callipepla gambelii*). Body Length: ten inches; Wingspan: fourteen inches; Diet: Seeds, leaves, and insects. The sudden sound of a covey of quail taking flight at your approach may surprise you.
- Gila Woodpecker (*Melanerpes urophyialis*). Body Length: 9.25 inches; Wingspan: sixteen inches; Diet: Insects, fruit, seeds, bird's eggs, and lizards.
- Golden Eagle (*Aquila chrysaetos*). Body Length: twenty-six to forty inches; Wingspan seventy-one to eighty-four inches; Diet: Black-tailed jackrabbits, cottontail rabbits, desert tortoises, foxes, squirrels, and rodents.
- Greater Roadrunner (*Geococcyx californianus*). Body Length: twenty to twenty-four inches, Wingspan seventeen to twenty-four inches; Ground Speed: Up to twenty miles an hour; Diet: Rattlesnakes and other snakes, lizards, scorpions, tarantulas,

black widow spiders, small birds and mammals, rodents, and insects. Revered Native American spirit animal, taboo to eat.
- Lesser Goldfinch (*Carduelis pstaltia*). Body Length: 4.5 inches; Wingspan: eight inches; Diet: Seeds.
- Peregrine Falcon (*Falco peregrinus*), Sensitive Species List. Body Length: thirteen to twenty-three inches; Wingspan twenty-nine to forty-seven inches; Diet: Principally medium-sized birds, falcons, ravens, woodpeckers, white wing dove, mourning dove, swifts, swallows, larks, shorebirds, and small mammals and reptiles.
- Redtail Hawk (*Buteo Jamaicans*). Body Length: eighteen to twenty-six inches; Wingspan: forty-three to fifty-seven inches; Diet: Principally rodents, and jackrabbits, cottontails, doves, quail, turkeys, reptiles, snakes, lizards, and other raptors.
- Turkey Vulture (*Cathartes Aura*), Turkey Buzzard. Body Length: twenty-six inches; Wingspan: sisxty-seven inches; Diet: Carrion.
- Warbling Vireo (*Vireo gilvus*). Body Length: 4.7 inches; Wingspan 8.7 inches; Diet: Seeds, berries, and insects.
- White-throated Swift (*Aeronautes saxatalis*). Body Length: 6.5 inches; Wingspan: fifteen inches; Diet: Insects.
- White Wing Dove (*Zenaida asiatica*), and Mourning Dove (*Zenaida macroura*). White Wing Dove: Body Length: eleven inches; Wingspan seventeen inches; Diet: Seeds, cactus fruit, and wild berries.

Reptiles

- Banded Gecko (*Coleonyx variegatus*). Body Length: four to six inches; Diet: Scorpions and insects, Mimics: Scorpions by raising its tail.

- Chuckwalla (*Sauromalus ater*). Herbivorous. Body Length: fifteen to twenty inches; Diet: Annual wildflowers, especially yellow brittlebush, cactus fruit and flowers, leaves of perennial plants, and insects. Formerly captured and eaten by Native Americans who hunted them with pointed sticks when they sought refuge in rock cracks and crevices.
- Desert Iguana (*Dipsosaurus dorsalis*), Herbivorous. Body Length: eighteen to twenty-four inches; Diet: Pincushion cactus, creosote flowers, and ironwood tree seeds, leaves, dried flowers, and other flowers and fruits. Formerly captured and eaten by Native Americans who hunted them with pointed sticks when they sought refuge cracks and crevices.
- Desert Tortoise (*Gopherus agassizii*), Herbivorous. Threatened Species. Body Length: ten to fourteen inches; Diet: Primarily grasses, herbs, annual wildflowers, new growth cactus, fruit, and flowers, and shrub.
- Gila Monster (*Heloderma suspectum*), Poisonous. Venom: Neurotoxin. Iconic symbol of the Sonoran Desert. Body Length: nine to twenty inches; Diet: Eggs, small mammals, nestling birds, and carrion.
- Horned Lizard (*Phrynosoma solare*), Horny Toad. Body Length: three to five inches; Diet: Harvester ants, insects, and spiders. Camouflages itself from predators and reportedly squirts blood from its eyes. Backstory*:* I handled many horny toads as a child growing up in the Sonoran Desert, and kept one as a pet for a few days in an open-lidded shoe box before letting it go in the desert where I'd found it. I never witnessed such a thing.
- Sonoran Collared Lizard (*Crotophytus bicinctores*). Body Length: 2.5 to 4.5 inches; Diet: Insects, spiders, centipedes, scorpions, lizards, snakes, rodents, and plants.

Snakes

- Arizona Black Rattlesnake (*Crotalus Cerberus*). Poisonous. Venom: Hemotoxin. Body Length: 15 to 65 inches. Color: Black-scaled with white, yellow, or orange pinstripes. Indicator: Tail rattle, but don't expect it to warn you. Diet: Amphibians, reptiles, rodents, small mammals, birds, and eggs.
- Arizona Coral Snake (*Micruroides Erymanthos*), Sonoran Coral Snake. Poisonous; Venom: Neurotoxin; Body Length: thirteen to twenty-four inches; Indicator: Red, black, and yellow (or white) rings; Diet: Sonoran shovelnose snakes, night snakes, ground snakes, Tantilla snakes, and skink lizards.
- Blacktail Rattlesnake (*Crotalus molossus*). Poisonous; Venom: Hemotoxin; Body Length: twenty-eight to forty-eight inches; Color: Pattern of black, brown, and yellow (or white) scales sometimes mistaken for a diamondback; Indicator: Black tail and rattle, but don't expect it to warn you; Diet: Small mammals, reptiles, rodents, small mammals, and birds.
- Coach Whip Snake (*Masticophis flagellum*). Body Length: thirty-six to 102 inches, Color: Varies according to soil color to camouflage itself, brown and tan patterned scales. Indicator: Big-eyed, dark headed, it's not going to sit still for a selfie. Speed: 3.5 to fifteen miles an hour; Diet: Lizards, snakes, insects, small mammals, birds.
- Common Kingsnake (*Lampropeltis getula*). Body Length: thirty to eighty-two inches, Color: Black to dark brown scales and white rings. Indicator: Chain-like ring pattern, Diet: Snakes (including rattlesnakes), lizards, amphibians, turtle eggs, and small mammals.
- Gopher Snake (*Pituophis catenifer*), Bull Snake. Body Length: thirty-six to 110 inches; Color: Dark brown and tan scale pattern, sometimes mistaken for a rattlesnake; Indicator: No tail rattle; Mimics: Coiled rattlesnake; Diet: Rodents, rabbits, and birds.

- Western Diamondback Rattlesnake (*Crotalus atrox*), Coon Tail Rattlesnake, (from the raccoon's tail-like appearance). Poisonous; Venom: Hemotoxin. Body Length: thirty to eighty-four inches; Color: Varies according to soil color, dark brown, and white diamond-patterned scales; Indicator: Size, "coon tail," aggressive, and will stand its ground provoked or not; Diet: Cottontail rabbits, black-tailed jackrabbits, lizards, kangaroo rats, pocket mice, ground squirrels, lizards, mockingbirds, Gambel's quail, burrowing owls, and other birds. **Warning:** Don't even think about getting close with or without a selfie stick. Diamondbacks can strike one-half to two-thirds of their body length in one-tenth of a second and deliver a deep fatal twin-fanged dose of skin, muscle, blood cell, and skeletal destroying venom.

Scorpions and Spiders

- Bark Scorpion (*Centruroides sculpturatus*). Poisonous; Venom: Neurotoxin; Body Length 2.5 to three inches; Color: Straw-colored translucent, (glows with a black light at night), Indicator: Think a tiny long-tailed lobster.
- Black Widow Spider (*Latrodectus*). Poisonous. Venom: Necrotic. Body length: 1.5 to two inches; Color: Dark brown to black; Indicator: Distinct red hourglass marking.
- Brown Recluse Spider (*Loxosceles reclusa*), Fiddleback Spider. Poisonous. Venom: Necrotic. Body Length: .75 to one inch, the size of a quarter or less; Color: Light to dark brown; Indicator: Violin marking on its back.
- Desert Hairy Scorpion (*Hadrurus arizonensis*), Giant Hairy Scorpion. Body Length: 3.5 to 5.5 inches; Color: Straw colored translucent. Indicator: Its size.

- Desert Millipede (*Orthoporus ornatus*). Body Length: three to six inches; Color: Dark brown, Indicator: twenty to one hundred pairs of legs. **Warning:** Don't try to pick one up, or it will curl up and secrete a noxious skin- and eye-irritating toxin.
- Western Desert Tarantula (*Aphonopelma chalcodes*), Mexican Blond Tarantula. Body Length: three to five inches; Color: Male black legs and red and copper penny-colored body; Female light brown legs and body; Indicator: Distinct leg hairs.

Entry Sources: *Desert Survivor* by John Annerino, National Park Service, Tonto National Forest, and Tonto National Monument.

Sixty-eight-year-old Joseph Head, *Coi-a-ma-auk*, "Rattlesnake Head," reviews the recorded history of the Pima on an *Oos:hikbina*, (calendar stick), carved, notched, and polished on a wooden saguaro rib, 1921, Edward H. Davis print. Courtesy: National Museum of the American Indian.

III
Adventures in the Superstitions

Apache Gáán, "Mountain Spirits," have carried the prayers of the Apache dating back long before Spaniards first ventured into their sacred canyon and mountain domain in search of gold. Copyright © John Annerino Photography

7

The Apache Trails: Through Apache Land

"This is called the Apache Trail. Far more justly should it be called the Apache's Country. Trail! One trail! There are scores of trails; trails in every direction, north, south, east and west, for the Apache roamed over every inch of this region and within a radius of two or three hundred Miles. Strike out for any mountain peak, any canyon, any ravine, any cluster of trees, and you will run into a place reeking of memories and stories of the Apaches. These trails are everywhere, crossing and crisscrossing the country like a dozen cobwebs superposed one upon the other."

—George Wharton James, *Arizona: The Wonderland* (1971)

LANDFORM

From Apache Junction, Arizona, the historic Apache Trail skirts the western ramparts of Superstition Mountain through Apache Gap and makes a dogleg turn east over Horse Mesa. Thereafter, it traces the ancestral course of the Salt River Canyon corridor until it reaches the engineering marvel of its day, Theodore Roosevelt Dam and Lake, pooled-up beneath the forested crags and sacred heights of the

Southeastern Yavapai's 7,657-foot Mazatzal Mountains, *Wikejasa*, "Chopped-up Mountains."

HISTORICAL OVERVIEW

One of the first Europeans to make the rugged desert, canyon, and mountain passage that characterizes the Apache Trail may have been Franciscan Friar Marcos de Niza. Under the direction of Spanish Conquistador Francisco Vásquez de Coronado, de Niza went searching for the mythic Seven Cities of Gold along a route that stretched from Mexico City to the Zuni pueblos of New Mexico and beyond to the distant plains of Kansas. A controversial petroglyph on the east end of Phoenix's South Mountains suggests de Niza crossed the Salt River Valley along the foothills of the range before starting up the Apache Trail. The inscription reads: *Fr Marcos de Niza Corona todo el nuebo Mexico a su costa ano de 1539*, and translates to "Fray Marcos de Niza crowned all of New Mexico at his expense in the year of 1539." Assuming the inscription is not authentic, as some profess, the 1939 map by historian Father Bonaventure Oblasser OFM of de Niza's purported route across the Salt River Valley gives credence to his travels. As do historical accounts and maps that authenticate de Niza visited the Salt River's Tonto Basin en route to the Cities of Gold. Archaeologist and ethnographer Adolph F. Bandelier's description of de Niza's route puts him squarely on the Apache Trail: "The portion of the Lower Río Salado ["Salt River"] between the Tempe Delta on the west and the upper Salt River Valley on the east is almost impassable. The mountains on both sides, the Superstition Range and the Mas-a-sar [Mazatzal Mountains], are rugged, forbidding, and very scantily watered." Interestingly, that would make Fray Marcos de Niza the first gold seeker to journey in sight of the Superstition Mountains.

Those who traced the beaver-rich Salt and Gila Rivers through the stony beaches of the Superstition Mountains between 1826 and 1827 were American and French mountain men that included grizzly, bigger-than-life figures such as Thomas L. "Peg Leg" Smith, Milton Sublette, Michel Robidoux, William Wolfskill, Ewing Young, George C. Yount, Maurice LeDuc, and twenty-year-old Kentucky-born frontiersman James Ohio Pattie, and his father Sylvester. Based out of the trade crossroads and outpost of Santa Fe, New Mexico, young Pattie, his father, and their party of dead-eye mountain men traveled up and down the Gila and Salt Rivers trapping North American beavers (*Castor canadensis*), "hairy bank notes," they also trapped along the rugged riverside course of conquistadors along the Apache Trail. In spite of the bounty of beaver pelts they were tallying, it was not long before the fur trappers were caught by surprise and discovered they had ridden into the domain of the Apache.

On March 3, 1826, James Pattie wrote in his diary:

> I had put down my gun, and stepped into the water, to prepare a bed for my [beaver] trap, while the others were busy in preparing theirs. Instantly the Indians raised a yell, and the quick report of guns ensued. This noise was almost drowned in the fierce shouts that followed, succeeded by a shower of arrows falling among us like hail. As we ran for the camp leaving all [of our] the horses in their power, we saw six Indians stealthily following our trail, as though they were tracking a deer.

There was no place to run, and no place to hide. Pattie added:

> One of our number who could speak Spanish, asked them to what nation they belonged? They answered Eiotaro [Coyotero Apache]. In return, they asked us, who we were. We answered Americans.

Hearing this, they stood in apparent surprise and astonishment for some moments. They then replied, that they had thought us too brave and too good marksmen, to be Spaniards; that they were sorry for what they had done, under the mistake of supposing us Spaniards.

The frontiersman had trapped and skirmished up and down the real Apache Trail, brokered peace with the Coyotero Apache, (*Łiinábáha dinéʼi*, "Many Go to War People") long enough to escape down their native trail, and went on to survive the many exploits that created his legendary stature. During that same Salt River Canyon venture, Pattie tracked a bear alone into a dark cave, killed and skinned it, and came out with ten pounds of bear fat for cooking, shot a mountain lion one pounce short of his bedroll, and was chased up a tree by a wild tusked-herd of javelinas. After his party's escape from the Coyotero, they trapped the length of the Gila River all the way to Yuma Crossing, Arizona, paddled dugout canoes down the lower Colorado River to the Gulf of California, almost drowning in its infamous tidal bore, and nearly died of thirst with his entire seven-man party crossing Northern Baja's fearsome *Laguna Salada,* "Salt Lake," trying to reach the refuge at Mission Santa Catalina on the Pacific Coast. Most memorable and romantic, perhaps, was the night Pattie and two other trappers rode into rescue Jacova, the beautiful daughter of Santa Fe Governor Antonio Narbona, who'd been kidnapped by the Comanche.

Long before Spaniards and mountain men used the Apache Trail, the ancient Salado traveled down the Salt River corridor to trade with the Hohokam. It was the same trail the Coyotero Apaches later used to raid the Pima, and General George Crook's mounted troops used to subdue and massacre the Tonto Apache and Southeastern Yavapai in Skeleton Cave. When the wails of men, women, and children fell silent at the end of the Apache Wars, construction began on the Salt

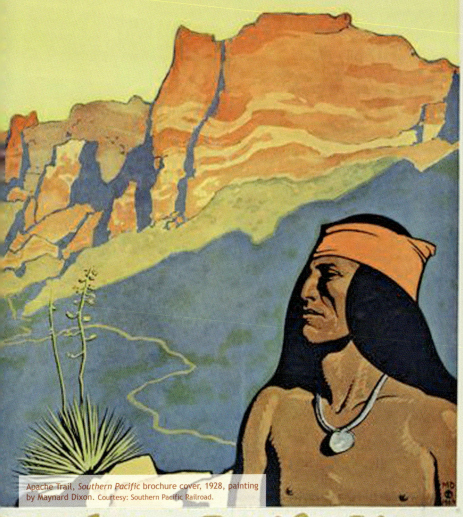

Apache Trail, *Southern Pacific* brochure cover, 1928, painting by Maynard Dixon. Courtesy: Southern Pacific Railroad.

River Project's monumental Roosevelt Dam. Completed in 1911 by Italian stonemasons, and a four-hundred-man workforce of Apaches, Pimas, Anglos, African Americans, and Mexicans, it was the highest masonry dam in the world. The thirty mile-long man-made reservoir had a watershed of 6,000 square miles, and was plugged with a hand cut stone-and-cement, three hundred-foot high and 1,100-foot wide dam that cost $5.46 million. That was a heavy investment at the time, but Phoenix town fathers, bankers, and investors had doubled-down on their bet that the dam would sustain the needs of industrial-scaled irrigation, sprawling development across the Salt River Valley, and Arizona's Five C's that fueled territorial growth: Copper, cattle, cotton, citrus, and climate.

There was one caveat for the vision to become a reality. How to reach the dam site below the confluence of the Salt River and Tonto Creek? Enter the Apache. No one knew the wild trails and country better. They used picks, shovels, and dynamite to construct a steep, winding, and rugged forty-seven-mile long dirt track called the Tonto Road through cliffs and canyons along their indigenous trail for teamsters and twenty-mule teams that hauled workers, food, tools, supplies, equipment, timbers, iron beams, and cables from Mesa to the dam site each day. According to author and photographer George Wharton James, the Apache told US Reclamation Service engineer, Louis C. Hill, how they preferred to work—without supervision: "Tell us what you want us to do; show us how to do it; then leave us alone. We need neither bosses nor spotters. We'll do our work faithfully and well." In a little over one year, hundreds of Apaches had done just that. But not without the help of Al Sieber. He was US Army Chief of Scouts until the end of the Apache Wars when he found himself out of work. The Apache workers called the German-American "iron-man" because it was said he could endure any privation or hardship better than they could.

If you viewed the Walter Hill film, *Geronimo, An American Legend*, (1993), starring Wes Studi as Geronimo, Gene Hackman as Brigadier General George Crook, Jason Patric as Lieutenant Charles Gatewood, and Robert Duvall as Al Sieber, you'll recall that Sieber was killed in a mescal-fueled cantina gunfight protecting the scalp of an Apache Scout named Chato (Steve Reevis) from Redondo (Scott Wilson), a sinister scalp hunter reminiscent of the blue-eyed American scalp hunter James Kirker. Reportedly wounded twenty-eight times during the Apache Wars from bullets, knives, arrows, and spears, and crippled for life when he was accidently shot by the Apache Kid with an 1873 Springfield Trapdoor 45-70 carbine, Sieber died on the Apache Trail on February 19, 1907 when a boulder fell on him while he was working as an Apache crew leader.

Geronimo had reportedly told lawman, cowboy, hired gun, and author Tom Horn what he thought of Al Sieber: "*Sibi* [Al Sieber] was not a good man to be with as he was a man of iron and nothing would turn him and that he did not care to talk, but that his words were all from his heart; that there was no room in his heart for anything that he did not think was right, that his words were as wise as those of any chief, white or red; that he was respected by the Indians, though as iron he was, and that (Tom Horn) being raised by him was of itself a guarantee of faithfulness in war or in council."

When Rough-Rider-turned-conservationist and, later President, Theodore Roosevelt dedicated the namesake dam on March 18, 1911, he proclaimed to his crowd of supporters and well wishers: "I was surprised at the grandeur of the mountains and gorges and at the wonderful beauty of the flowers. I firmly believe that as soon as the East becomes better educated, this will be one of the places to which visitors will come from all parts of the country to make the [Apache Trail] drive I made in the last two days. Moreover, I believe as your irrigation projects are established, we will see 75 to 100 thousand people here."

Come take the drive and see for yourself.

APACHE TRAILS

"This is an exquisite winding mountain drive with sharp and blind curves and hairpin switchbacks leading the traveller over the mountains. Drive with care."
—*Dangerous Roads*

Directions

From Phoenix, drive west to Apache Junction and begin your adventure at the intersection formed by US Highway 60 and Arizona State Route 88. The Apache Trail has been recognized as "one of the first scenic auto tour routes in the world" made in 1905, Apache Trail Historic Road, Arizona's Oldest Highway, Apache Trail National Forest Scenic Byway, and was formerly called the Tonto Road, Mesa-Roosevelt Road, and the Old Highline Road.

Road Log

Mile 0 to Mile 3.5. Apache Junction, Elevation 1,767 feet. Apache Junction was established as Youngberg in 1909 and named after Arizona Territory secretary George U. Young. From Apache Junction, turn left (northeast) on State Route 88 and follow the paved Apache Trail along the spectacular western front of Superstition Mountain. Next to Monument Valley and the Grand Canyon, the Superstitions is one of the American West's iconic backdrops. The picture postcard view is seen by all who venture into the Sonoran Desert wilderness many once called the "Killer Mountains."

Mile 3.5 to Mile 3.6. Road Right: Mountain Vista pullout, Elevation: 1,894-feet. A wonderful view of Siphon Draw can be seen cleaving the crest of the 5,024-foot north summit of Superstition Mountain. (See page 203 Superstition Mountain Skyline Traverse).

Mile 3.6 to Mile 4.1. Road Right: Superstition Mountain-Lost Dutchman Museum, Elevation: 1,980 feet, Weekes Wash. Lost Dutchman Monument erected 1938. Stop in and view artist Ettore "Ted" DeGrazia's original oil on canvas paintings, "Apache Collection." Visit: http://superstitionmountainmuseum.org/

Mile 4.1 to Mile 4.5. Road Right: Historic Mining Camp Restaurant & Trading Post, Elevation: 2,030 feet. Follow the signs .75 Mile east on Mining Camp Street. Visit: www.miningcamprestaurant.com

Mile 4.5 to Mile 5.2. Road Left: Goldfield Ghost Town, Est. 1893, "Gateway to the Legendary Superstition Mountains," Elevation: 2,045 feet. Visit: http://goldfieldghosttown.com/

Ghost Town of Goldfield Historical Marker, Since 1947, Inscription: "During its heyday from 1893 to 1898 when $1,000,000 in gold was mined from this area about 300 people dwelt here with majestic Superstition Mtn. in the background. 300 ft. south of this sign is the old Bluebird Mine found in the gold rush of 1893. A dozen gold mines in the area have produced very rich gold and silver ore. Main Street paralleled the present Apache Trail and was lined with gambling houses, saloons and stores. The old school house stood where the old house is. Sporadic mining operations since 1950 have produced $2,000,000. Population now 8. Elevation 2025 ft." *Source:* Historical Marker Database: "Bite-Size Bits of Local, National, and Global History." Visit: HMdb.org

Goldfield Mining District Marker, Inscription: "This Historical Spot in 1892 to 1898 was part of the Mammoth Mine claims known as the Montezuma in 1893. Then after 1910 became known as Calamity. In 1944 this claim became known as the Bluebird. The Bluebird Mine was found in 1893 and first worked by J. R. Morse and the Merrill Brothers to a depth of 60 feet on a quartz vein up to 3 feet wide. Some of the richest gold in the district. In 1947 to 1952 George (Red) Monagan worked the Bluebird. He dug 140 foot tunnel and used an old Spanish arrista [*arrastra*] to mill the ore. But only low grade ore was found. Historical photo inside. In 1960 Maw and Paw Hamaker and family extended the Bluebird another 85 feet. Then in 1961 the Bluebird claim was patented on an assay of 10 ounces of gold per ton." *Source:* HMdb. The Mammoth Mine reportedly produced $3 million in gold.

    Mile 5.2 to Mile 5.5. Road Right: Lost Dutchman State Park, Elevation: 2,060 feet, prospects. (Hiking trails and camping see page 173).

    Mile 5.5 to Mile 7.7, Road Right: First Water Trailhead Road FS78, Elevation: 2,020 feet. Turn right on FS78, and drive 2.6 miles to the First Water Trailhead. (See page 212).

    Massacre Grounds Trailhead (new), Elevation: 2,140 feet. Turn right on the First Water Road FS78, and drive 0.5 miles to the signed Crosscut Trailhead. From the trailhead the elevated *mesita,* "Little Mesa," is the Massacre Grounds. (See page 221).

    Mile 7.7 to Mile 7.8, Road Left: Government Well, Elevation: 2,107 feet. Dwellings, a corral, and a windmill tank were once fed by pumped ground water, Willow Springs Basin Tank, and Willow Spring. Nestled in the colorful peaks and foothills of andesite and the Geronimo Head Formation in the 3,260-foot Goldfield Mountains, Government Well was a dependable water stop and way station for horses, mules, and for miners and prospectors working the Tomahawk, Golden Hillside, and Black Queen Mines and other prospects in the area. Freighters, teamsters, Concord stagecoaches, horse-drawn carriages, passengers,

Teamsters stop for lunch on the Apache Trail at Grapevine Springs, 1906, William J. Lubken, black and white glass plate negative. Courtesy: US Bureau of Reclamation Collection.

and cowboys also laid over here during the heyday of building the Apache Trail (Tonto Road) from 1902–03 before construction of Roosevelt Dam commenced.

Mile 7.8 to Mile 9.9, Road Right. Weavers Needle Vista, Elevation: 2,100 feet. Poking over the ridge tops nearly seven miles southeast is the 4,653-foot-high landmark. It's the best view you'll see of it from the Apache Trail. But you'll need a 300-mm camera lens or larger to get close enough to take any kind of picture. Or you can follow the route of US Bureau of Reclamation photographer Walter J. Lubkin who struck out from Government Well and photographed Weavers Needle from Parker Pass with a cumbersome wet plate camera during a five-day horse and burro expedition in 1908. (See page 181 for hiking the Peralta Trail and page 189 for climbing Weavers Needle.)

Mile 9.9 to Mile 12.2: Apache Gap, Elevation: 2,304 feet. The Apache Trail climbs and winds like a pit viper to what was reported to be an Apache lookout atop volcanic peaks, dacite domes, basalt lava flows, and lichen-splotched yellow beds and folds of what's called the Geronimo Head Formation that date back to "tuff times" 20.5 million years ago.

Mile 12.2 to Mile 13.2, Canyon Lake Vista, Elevation: 2,009 feet. The Apache Trail winds down off the promontory and makes a dogleg turn east to First Water Creek. After crossing the once fiery lava flows titling down from Apache Gap, it may come as a complete surprise to suddenly view a still river of blue water in the harsh-looking desertscape where plant and animal life exists on its margins. Lost among the declivitous tributary creeks and canyons of the reservoir is Skeleton Cave, or Skull Cave, site of the Salt River Canyon massacre that pitted flimsy bows and arrows against an army of heavy caliber long guns. Beyond 3,068-foot *El Recortado,* "Sawed Off mountain." and 3,567-foot Sheep Mountain, soar above the Painted Cliffs rimming the once virgin course of the Salt River, cut by Blue Tank Canyon and Hells Hip Pocket in the 390-square-mile Mazatzal Wilderness. It remains wild country for those who still cross it on foot.

Skeleton Cave Sacred Site, restricted visitation. Skeleton Cave Massacre Site was surveyed and researched by historians Norm Tessman, Curator, Sharlot Hall Museum, and Alan Ferg, Curator of Special Projects, Arizona State Museum, and submitted to the National Register of Historic Places. The site was listed on February 21, 1991.

Mile 13.2 to Mile 14.4. First Water Creek, Elevation: 1,676 feet. First Water Creek Bridge: Narrow, Camelback through truss bridge, Built: 1924, Span: 159.8 feet, Length: 179.8 feet, Deck Width: 14.8 feet, Height: 14.2 feet above deck. Site: National Register of Historic Places. *Source:* Bridgehunter. Visit: https://bridgehunter.com

Mile 14.4 to Mile 17. Boulder Creek (La Barge Creek), Elevation: 1,669 feet. Boulder Creek Bridge: One lane Parker through truss bridge, Built: 1916, Span: 179.8 feet, Length: 487.9 feet, Deck Width: 14.8 feet, Height: 14.2 feet above deck. *Source:* Bridgehunter. The Boulder Trailhead No. 103 is located on the right (south) side of the Apache Trail.

Mile 17 to Mile 24.1, Road Right: Tortilla Flat, Elevation: 1,752 feet. Population: 6. An early account in the New Deal WPA publication, *Arizona, A State Guide,* attributes the curious name to the locals' description of the area's "giant masses of rocks resembling a platter of tortillas." American novelist John Steinbeck was struck by the townsfolk's name as well, and adopted it for his Nobel Prize-winning 1935 novel, *Tortilla Flat,* set in the Tortilla Flat neighborhood of Monterrey, California, not the territorial way station that offered tent camps, food, water, shade, and redeye for Roosevelt Dam workers, freighters, teamsters, and stagecoach and buck board drivers who laid over or traveled back and forth over the Mesa-Roosevelt Road. Today the lively "ghost-town" is a tourist destination that offers a scenic and colorful detour that pulls back the curtain and offers a romantic view of territorial frontier life. The Superstition Saloon and Restaurant offers leather-saddle bar stools (without the horses), genuine dollar bill wallpaper, the coldest brews and sarsaparilla in town, the biggest burgers, hottest chili and, just in case you didn't see—or get stuck by enough cactus—World Famous Prickly Pear Gelato. Visit: www.tortillaflataz.com

Warning Pavement Ends: The paved Apache Trail ends five miles east of Tortilla Flat, and the rustic, earthy romance of gravel, dirt, sand, and tortilla-sized rocks bordering the narrow road beckon beyond. Watch your speed, steep grades, curves, use lower gears, don't burn your brakes, and don't text and drift into sidewall blowout. Check the radiator and oil, kick the tires, double-check the spare, and stock up on supplies at the General Store and water at the Tortilla Campground. Don't head beyond if you rode the saloon saddle too long, had one too many, and thought you were riding off into the sunset and drive over a cliff.

Tortilla Campground: The historic Tortilla Flat motel is abandoned, but you can camp a stone's throw back down the Apache Trail in the Tonto National Forest Tortilla [bring your own] Campground. It offers: RV Camping, Campground Camping, and Picnicking with Hook-ups (sewage, water, no electricity), seventy-seven camp units with picnic tables and grills. Reservations: First come, first serve, ten reservation sites by phone. Call 1-877-444-6777 or visit www.recreation.gov. *Source:* Tonto National Forest.

(Mile 22. End pavement. Where the fun really begins.)

Mile 24.1 to Mile 25.1, Road Left: Fish Creek Hill Scenic Vista, Elevation: 2,859 feet. Reminiscent but shorter than the Peach Springs canyon road in the western Grand Canyon, and the Batopilas Canyon road in Mexico's Barranca del Cobre region of the Sierra Madre, the Apache Trail's mile-long slalom into Fish Creek Canyon is one of wildest, steepest (15 to 17 percent grade) and exhilarating two-wheel drive descents in the American West. Imagine the Soap Box Derby perched atop Fish Creek Hill. If this is your first run, you may feel dwarfed, white knuckles clutching the steering wheel, fearful to look over the edge, your foot duct-taped to the brake pedal, inching down into the precipice, a caravan of honking vehicles riding your bumper like remoras—not a good place for venting. Relax, take a deep breath, loosen your hands, free your mind, and enjoy one helluva ride! In 1905, teamsters reportedly fired three shots in the air at the top of the hill to warn other wagoneers they were "comin down mountain when they come, 'comin down mountain when they come. . . .'"

Mile 25.1 to Mile 26.1, Road Right: Fish Creek Canyon, Elevation: 2,144 feet, Picnic Area: Downstream on left, Fish Creek Canyon Bridge:

One lane Pony truss bridge, Built: 1923, Span: 73.8 feet, Length: 73.8 feet, Deck width: 14.8 feet. *Source:* Bridgehunter. Spring and sometimes fall seasonal pools of cool water in Fish Creek Canyon refresh hikers and trekkers scrambling up the deep boulder-strewn canyon, one of the most spectacular in the Superstition Mountains. (See Fish Creek Canyon page 229).

Hacksaw Tom. Now imagine, just as you slow your vehicle down to a crawl at the bottom of Fish Creek Canyon, a man suddenly springs out from behind a boulder, startles you, and scares you half to death. He's wearing a white-flour sack mask, dark eyes peering through knife-slit holes, and brandishing a 12-gauge double-barrel sawed-off shotgun. He means business. You offer him your purse or your watch and wallet for your life. He takes the loot, nods, and then dashes up Fish Creek Canyon bounding from rock to rock like a bobcat. According to the display at the Superstition Mountain Museum: "Between the years of 1905 and 1915 a man was reportedly robbing wagons and stagecoaches on the Apache Trail. He was nicknamed "Hacksaw Tom," by the drivers that he held up." The Museum places the site of Hacksaw Tom's friendly armed robberies—no one was ever reported hurt—at Apache Gap. Other historians place the holdups at the bottom of Fish Creek Hill. Hacksaw Tom was never caught, nor was he ever identified. But the "loot" that was first discovered in 1958, and later recovered, was cached in his hidden cave hideout and it didn't amount to much—a military wagon, cartridges, stagecoach tie-down straps, a Mason jar half-filled with pinto beans, matches, horse liniment, locks, a lock pick, and other assorted curiosities. The territorial evidence did substantiate Hacksaw Tom was no more a myth than Jacob Waltz, but he was far poorer. His average take was said to be no more than forty dollars, reportedly the average monthly wage for Arizona Territory cowhands.

Mile 26.1 to Mile 29.6, Old Fish Creek Lodge, Elevation: 2,185 feet, Lewis and Pranty Creek: According to *Arizona Place Names*, the creek was named for "two old timers who settled and prospected on this creek in the early days." Little remains of the once charming streamside tourist lodge that burned down in 1929. When travel writer George Wharton James embarked on his automobile adventure in 1917 to pen the chapter, "Through Apache-Land," for his popular travel book, *Arizona: The Wonderland,* he described the lodge's food: "No! don't expect a description of a banquet. It is a real old-fashioned, pioneer day stage station meal, probably fried ham, boiled beef, cabbage, beans with chili, cold slaw, bread, pie, cheese and coffee, but it is good, for we are hungry, and what the meal lacks in service and elaborate preparation it possesses in staying qualities."

Desert Bighorn Sheep. High above the Old Fish Creek Lodge, 4,349 foot Bronco Butte on the southern escarpment of Horse Mesa is home to agile sure-footed bands of desert bighorn sheep. Between 1983 and 1992 at least 117 wild sheep had been translocated from distant desert ranges like western Arizona's Kofa Mountains National Wildlife Refuge into the Superstition Wilderness atop Horse Mesa, Bronco Butte, Tortilla Mountains, and at Mill Site. If you're quiet and observant you can sometimes view bighorn sheep elsewhere atop Fish Creek Hill, Superstition Mountain, Coffee Flat Mountain, and the Goldfield Mountains.

Mile 29.6 to Mile 30.7, Road Right: Reavis Trailhead Road, Elevation: 2,620 feet. Historic Reavis Ranch can be reached by driving three miles south on USFS Road 212 to Reavis Ranch Trail No. 109. Few knew the eastern Superstition Mountains better, except the Western Apache and Southeastern Yavapai, than Elisha Marcus Reavis, "the Hermit of the Superstitions." Born in Beardstown, Illinois in 1827, what few acquaintances Reavis made in the Superstition Mountains region, never really knew the man behind the scraggly long-beard, dressed in tattered clothes, a rumpled hat, and who was a dead shot with his lever-action Winchester Model 1886 chambered with powerful .45-70 caliber rounds. The clear-eyed, red-haired, college-educated Reavis was not the loner without a backstory most assumed he was by his appearance and rehashed myths. At one time Reavis was married to Mary Y. Sexton who bore their only child, Louisa Maria Reavis, and worked as a teacher in El Monte, California. Like Jacob Waltz, Reavis tried his hand prospecting in the California gold fields and when that didn't pan out headed to Arizona's Bradshaw Mountains Walker Mining District where he also went bust. Moving on to the Salt River Valley, Reavis broke horses and packed horses for the US Army at Fort McDowell, and worked as a US Marshall before cleaving out a niche deep in the Superstition Mountains. On the wooded northwest slopes 6,266-foot Mound Mountain, Reavis built a wooden dugout cabin (with a library) nestled in a cool verdant canyon in 1874. The well-read Reavis cultivated fifteen acres of tillable lands that included an apple orchard, gardens of vegetables and fruit, and plots of potatoes, and raised farm animals. In the course of his life in the Superstition Mountains, Reavis reportedly earned $30,000. In short, Reavis made more money farming a beautiful oasis in his isolated mountain home than most everyone else ever did prospecting the storied range. Vegetables like potatoes fetched him eight cents a pound when he sold them by the mule load to the bustling Silver King Mine and elsewhere. In one season alone, Reavis pocketed $5,000. In 1895 Arizona Territory he was harvesting the Mother Lode in his own field of dreams.

Presumably the lode that Reavis made and salted away in a hidden cache over the course of two decades was too tempting for thieves and dry gulchers to ignore and presumably it proved to be his undoing. When the body of Reavis was found after going over the Reavis Divide on or about April 10, 1896, Superstition explorer and writer Bernice

McGee later wrote: "His dogs and horses remained near his decomposed body. Some say he was partly eaten by wolves and coyotes." Reavis's scattered remains were found four miles from his home and buried near where he fell at an ancient ruin on May 7. His murder remains another Superstition Mountains' unsolved mystery. *Sources:* Author files, and Find A Grave. Visit: www.findagrave.com.

Mile 39.7 to Mile 42.4. Road Left: Apache Lake Scenic Vista, Elevation: 2,580 feet. If you're headed to Apache Lake, turn left and drive 1.3 miles. Towering over a mile above the shimmering waters of Apache Lake are the saw tooth crags of Four Peaks that can be seen to the north crowning the forested flanks of the 7,657-foot Mazatzal Mountains, sacred mountains of the Southeastern Yavapai, who call them *Wikejasa*, "Chopped-up Mountains."

Mile 42.4 to Mile 44.8. Road Left: Theodore Roosevelt Dam, Elevation: 2,200 feet; 0.2 Miles further is Inspiration Point Interpretive Vista, Elevation: 2,200 feet.

President Theodore Roosevelt 1911 Proclamation: "The Apache Trail combines the grandeur of the Alps, the glory of the Rockies, the magnificence of the Grand Canyon and then adds an indefinable something that none of the others have, to me, it is most awe-inspiring and most sublimely beautiful."

Al Sieber Memorial Inscription: "Al Sieber—Veteran of the Civil War and for Twenty Years a leader of scouts for the U.S. Army in Arizona Indian troubles, was killed on this spot February 19th, 1907 by a rolling rock during construction of the Tonto Road. His body is buried in the cemetery in Globe." His pink headstone reads: "In Memoriam, Al Sieber. Erected by the Territory of Arizona to Al Sieber, Born 1844, Died 1907." *Sources:* Gila County Historical Society, Globe Cemetery.

Roosevelt Dam Marker Inscription, 1903–1911: "On September 20, 1906 the first stone was laid in place. Over the next five years,

"Dedication ceremonies of Roosevelt Dam, Col. Roosevelt speaking," March 18, 1911, Walter J. Lubken black-and-white glass plate negative. Courtesy: US Bureau of Reclamation Collection.

350,000 cubic feet of block would be cut, shaped, and fashioned into the Roosevelt Dam.

- The blocks of stone were carved out of the canyon walls. They were lifted by block and tackle and pulled along by cable. It was not uncommon for the hoist to buckle and break. The giant monoliths would be slammed against the canyon wall or dropped into the construction site below.
- On February 6, 1911 the last stone was put in place. When completed, it was the largest stone dam in the world.
- Original Dam Type: Masonry Thick Arch, Structural Height: 280 feet, Top Width: 16 feet, Maximum Base Width: 184 feet,

Crest Length: 723 feet, Crest Elevation (w/o parapets): 2141 feet, Lake Capacity: 1,336,734 acre-feet, Lake Surface: 17,337 Acres." *Source:* Historical Marker Project. Visit: www.historicalmarkerproject.com

Mile 44.8 to Mile 47. Junction of Highway 88 and State Route 188. Turn right onto Route 188 and drive to Tonto National Monument.

Mile 47. Road Right: Tonto National Monument Visitor Center, Elevation: 2,800 feet, Confluence: Cave and Cholla Canyons, drain 5,268 Pinyon Mountain. Visit: www.nps.gov/tont/index.htm

Travel Notes
Returning to Apache Junction

Turn around and retrace your route back down the Apache Trail to Apache Junction. Or turn right and continue on the Apache Trail Circle Route via State Route 188 for 29.5 Miles to Globe, then west on Highway 60 for fifty-eight miles back to Apache Junction.

In Globe you can stop and visit the ancient Salado settlement at Besh Ba Gowah Archaeological Park and Museum. Visit: www.globeaz.gov/visitors/besh-ba-gowah

Apache Trail Circle Route
Sacred Lands of the San Carlos and Western Apache

Going Home: As you drive over Top of the World and wind beyond the sacred ground of Oak Flat (*Chich'il Bildagoteel*) through Devils Canyon and Queen Creek Canyon past Apache Leap, imagine the words of George Wharton James when he wrote about the Apache riding bareback through the spectacular, incomparably rugged scenery that flashes before your windows in an instant: "It is almost impossible for the ordinary mind to conceive that a horse, carrying a human being, can perform such feats as were the every-day experiences of these Bedouins of the American deserts . . . The landscape they rode over, trampled under their horses' feet, was befitting their own nature. It was wild, rugged, desolate, awe-inspiring, weird, mountain-surrounded, different. It was distinctly Arizonan and Apachean. Nothing could tame it, subdue it, bring it under control."

Gila-Pinal Scenic Road/US Highway 60 Road Long

Designated on June 20, 1986, the twenty-six-mile-long Gila-Pinal Scenic Road traverses the Sonoran Desert's mountains, canyons, cliffs, basins, and bajadas between Miami, Arizona and Florence Junction that's every bit as enticing, wildly tortured looking, and beautiful as the Apache Trail. At one time the primeval trail network dating back to Archaic peoples was first trod long before the Western Apache picked up their trails circa AD 1450. As time marched on, the Apache's foot and horse trails became a one-lane wagon road that threaded steep treacherous canyons known as "Stoneman's Grade" in 1878 when Camp Pickett Post was established near the silver mining boomtown of Pinal City. Over the course of decades the rocky foot, bridle, and washboard wagon trail became a stagecoach route for the Arizona Stage Company in 1881. It carried passengers from Florence through Queen Creek and Devils Canyons up the "winding ladder" road to Globe that was developed and variously known as the Apache Trail Bypass, Apache Trail Circle Route, Phoenix-Globe Highway, and Old West Highway before becoming modern US Highway 60.

Mile 0 (Milepost 253). Globe, Arizona, known among the Western Apache, as *Bésh Baa Gowąh,* "place of metal," Elevation 3,509 feet. From the 1875 open pit copper mining town of Globe, drive west on US 60 through Claypool, and Devils Canyon to Big Oak Flat.

Mile 8 (Milepost 245). Claypool, Elevation: 3,334 feet, known to the Western Apache as *Goshtł'ish Tú* (translation not available).

Mile 11 (Milepost 242). Miami, Elevation: 3,436 feet, National Register of Historic Places, also known to the Western Apache as *Goshtł'ish Tú* (translation not available). Notice the gray slopes of the Miami Tailings Pond some call "Miami Beach." Gila-Pinal Scenic Road begins.

Mile 17 (Milepost 337). Pinto Creek Bridge, Elevation: 4,100 feet +/–. Pinto Creek Bridge: Steel arch bridge, Built: 1949, Length: 636.8 feet, Awarded American Institute of Steel Construction's "Most Beautiful Steel Bridge."

Mike 18 (Milepost 236 to 228+/–). **Warning:** Steep Westbound Descent and Dangerous Curves: "two miles of 3 to 4 percent descent, two miles of 6 percent descent, 0.5 mile of 6 percent climb, 1 mile of 5 percent descent, followed by three of 7 percent descent. *Source:* ADOT.

Mile 19 (Milepost 235). Top of the World, Elevation: 4,528 feet. The abandoned military camp was located in what was called Mason's Valley in 1871, and in 1874 became the Pinal Ranch for Colorado cattleman Robert A. Irion who also ran cattle in the Iron Mountain area of the Superstition Mountains. "Top of the World" was reportedly the name of a 1920s era dance hall whose patrons no doubt swilled shot glasses of Whiskey Spring's white lightening ferreted out of the Superstitions on burros.

Mile 24 (Milepost 231). Devils Canyon, Road Straight, Elevation: 3,800 feet. Known by the San Carlos Apache as *Gan Bikoh*, "Crown Dancers Canyon," and Gáán Canyon, the San Carlos Apache considers sacred. Benevolent *Gáán*, "Mountain Spirits," inhabit the canyon and mountains throughout the ancestral homelands of the Western Apache and carry the prayers of the *Ndee*, Apache "People." The US Cavalry Troops reportedly named the canyon, "Devils Canyon," during

"Young San Carlos Apache woman," 1888, A. Frank Randall portrait, Arizona Territory. Courtesy: Library of Congress

the early 1870s because they evidently mistook the Mountain Spirits' sacred headdresses for horns. That could not be further from the truth. Sacred Burial Ground. San Carlos Apache elder Wendsler Nosie Sr. reported: "In the nearby area called Devil's Canyon, we have placed marks, which are symbols of life on Earth, on the steep ledges and canyon walls that rise high above the stream that has carved deep into the Canyon, and we buried our ancestors in the Canyon's heart."

Mile 25 (Milepost 230). Big Oak Flat, Road Left, Elevation 4,076 foot. Also known as *Chich'il Bildagoteel*, "a broad flat of Emory oak trees," to the Western Apache. Few places are more sacrosanct to them than this spiritual, cultural, and traditional area. From Big Oak Flat drive through Queen Creek Canyon to Superior.

Chich'il Bildagoteel

In the words of Wendsler Nosie Sr.: "These are holy, sacred, and consecrated lands which remain central to our identity as Apache People." Archaeological evidence dating back more than two thousand years indicates Oak Flat was the ancestral lands for Archaic peoples and the Hohokam long before the arrival of the Apache circa AD 1450. Ideally situated in a defensive location in an oak woodland basin, surrounded by boulders and inaccessible cliffs, access to deep canyon pools and clear streams of perennial water was critical to the Apache's survival and the wild game they hunted. In their evergreen tablelands and lush riparian streams that were also home to black bear, mountain lion, mule deer, turkey, ocelot, fox, small game, and songbirds, a cornucopia of natural food awaited their seasonal harvests of agave hearts, mesquite beans, piñon nuts, juniper berries, herbs for healing, and perhaps most importantly *Chí'chil*, Emory oak acorns. A crossroads for neighboring peoples including the White Mountain Apache (*Dzil Łigai Si'án Ndee*), Southeastern

Yavapai (*Kwevkepaya*), Pima (*Akimel O'odham*), and other distant people including the Hopi (*Hopitu Shinumu*), Oak Flat offered the San Carlos Apache (*Tiis Zhaazhe Bikoh*and), Tonto Apache (*Dilzhę'é*), and Pinal Apache (*T'iis Tsebán*) a profound place for power, prayer, song, and ceremony that brought them together as a community. Their lives were spiritually linked to the place and the plants, animals, water, sun, moon, stars, lightning, fire, wind, rain, and earth that completed their cycle of life, gave them power to endure, and provided the elements for wisdom, healing, and sharing. This is no more evident, perhaps, than their ceremonial coming of age and healing songs of *Na ih es,* "Getting her ready," drummed and sung by the *diyih,* "one who has power," (medicine man), danced by the masked Mountain Spirits and families. Every year they join together at the sacred consecrated ground of Chich'il Bildagoteel to celebrate the transformation of pubescent girls adorned in beaded buckskins and moccasins to embody the spirit of White Shell Woman, the Mother of the Apache.

    Mile 26 (Milepost 229). Waterfall Canyon Bridge, Elevation: 4,110 feet +/−. Waterfall Canyon Bridge: Concrete Tee beam (4 spans), Built: 1929, Longest Span: twenty-four feet, Length: 96.1 feet. Deck Width: 43.6 feet.

    Mile 26.5 (Milepost 228.5). Queen Creek Tunnel, Elevation: 3,520 feet to 3,480 feet +/−. Queen Creek Tunnel: Built: 1952, Length: 1,217 feet, Height: 22 feet, Width: 42 feet. Replaced: abandoned 1926 Claypool Tunnel drilled and blasted out of solid rock.

    Claypool Tunnel: Use Extreme Care or Don't Go! Named for Senator W. D. Claypool, the 217-foot long tunnel is sometimes used and accessed from Highway 60 at the undeveloped dirt road pullout on left (south) off Highway 60 near the west bound entrance to the Queen Creek Tunnel. It's a two mile hike or bike-and-carry on the rugged dirt side-road through the derelict unsupported tunnel and road to Superior. Remember what happened to prospector Al Morrow when he died from a cave-in at his Needle Canyon mine. (See page 191).

Mile 27 (Milepost 228). Run Away Truck Ramp, Road Right. Watch the signs and your speed!

Mile 27 (Milepost 227). Queen Creek Canyon, Road Right and Left, Elevation: 3,910 feet. Also known as *Gan Diszin,* "Crowndancer Standing," the San Carlos Apache consider sacred. Queen Creek Bridge: Steel arch bridge, Built: 1949, Length: 576.8 feet, Height: n/a, Width: n/a, Replaced: Old Queen Creek Bridge (open-spandrel arch).

~Federal Writers Project Description: An unattributed author writing in the 1940 Federal Writers Project book, *Arizona: A State Guide,* described building the Queen Creek Bridge and digging the 1926-era Claypool Tunnel: "The road chiseled in sheer rock walls winds down through a narrow gorge bordered with spires, balanced rocks, and formations that appear fantastic even in the light of day."

Mile 27 (Milepost 227). Superior, Road Left, Highway 177 junction, Elevation: 2,830 feet. Towering east/southeast of Superior is 4,822-foot Big Picacho and its landmark 600-foot high southwest-facing cliffs of Tertiary dacite capping Paleozoic limestone that produced translucent dollops of obsidian called "Apache Tears."

~Apache Leap Massacre: One of the first known published accounts of the Apache Leap Massacre was written by Stanford University-educated (first graduating class) James Mitchell Barney. His account, "How Apache Leap Got Its Name," was published in the August 1935 issue of *Arizona Highways.* The Superior Chamber of Commerce reportedly printed out the story and gave it away to tourists as handouts. The nuts and bolts of Barney's account provided for that tragic day in 1870 were as follows:

When about two-thirds of the [Apache] band had been killed or maimed by the hail of bullets fired at them [by "the settlers"], the remainder became panic stricken and retreated in the only direction possible—toward the westerly edge of the mountain which on that side, broke off abruptly into sheer cliffs, hundreds of feet high.

Without a moment's hesitation, the fleeing [Apache] . . . threw themselves over the towering cliffs, in the faint hope of escaping fatal injury. But the leap into space was too great . . . The entire Apache band—some 75 in number ["men, woman, and children"]—were wiped out . . . From that time the Big Picacho—grim and forbidding—has been known as Apache Leap—a most appropriate name, perpetuating, as it does, a tragic incident in the early history of Arizona," wrote Barney, then recognized as the "unofficial historian for Arizona."

Historians later scoffed at Barney's story because there were no official military records, as was case for the April 30, 1871 Camp Grant Massacre when Tucson's "Committee of Public Safety" killed, scalped, and burned 144 Apache elders, men, women, and children; and the December 28, 1872 Skeleton Cave Massacre when US Troops under the command of General George Crook cut down seventy-six to ninety-six Yavapai elders, men, women, and children cornered in a Salt River Canyon alcove. Moreover, Barney had also written in his *Arizona Highways* feature: "At daybreak, the settlers made a sudden and determined attack upon the surprised and bewildered Apaches, and wrought terrible havoc among them and their first volleys." Given the record of Camp Grant, Skeleton Cave, and the 1866 planned "exterminate[ion]" of 123 distant Yavapai by the Arizona Volunteers on the Santa Maria

River and Skull Valley, why would unaffiliated "settlers" provide a detailed account of the alleged slaughter of what one San Carlos Apache writer recently wrote was eighty people?

If the barbaric Apache Leap incident wasn't reported by territorial newspapers, witnesses, and historians, it doesn't mean the event did not happen. And, if it had been noted or reported, it does not mean it would have been told in the manner in which the incident unfolded. Based on the massacres at Camp Grant, Skeleton Cave, Skull Valley, and elsewhere throughout the territory where, in 1805, Spanish troops under the command of Lieutenant Antonio Narbona annihilated 115 Navajo elders, women, and children hiding in the Cañon del Muerto tributary of Canyon de Chelly, I'm convinced Apache Leap did occur. In the oral tradition of the San Carlos Apache, the tragic, but noble defeat of the Apache standing their ground against all odds is still passed down from one generation to the next 150 years later.

During San Carlos Apache Tribal Chairman Wendsler Nosie Sr.'s November 1, 2007 testimony before the US House Natural Resources Committee regarding "foreign owned mining giants" to open pit mine on sacred Apache ground, he testified: "The escarpment of Apache Leap, which towers above nearby Superior, is also sacred and consecrated ground for our People . . . You should know, however, that at least seventy-five of our People sacrificed their lives at Apache Leap during the winter of 1870 to protect their land, their principles, and their freedom when faced with overwhelming military force from the US Calvary which would have required them to surrender as prisoners of war."

Mile 29 (Milepost 225). Silver King Mine Road, Road Right, Elevation: 3,668 feet, Silver King Mine. Turn right (north) on FR 229, and the graded dirt road leads up through Silver King Wash to the mine that kept some Lost Dutchman prospectors afloat while they searched the Superstition Mountains for their own mother lode. Located in the basin between 4,916-foot Peachville Mountain (northwest) and 5,541-foot Kings Crown Peak (east), springtime often rewards photographers with hillsides covered in Mexican golden poppies, Coulters purple lupine, and red maids—if they get there before free-ranging cattle eat the colorful wild bouquets.

Mile 31 (Milepost 223). Picket Post Mountain, Road Left, Elevation: 4,375 feet. Also known as Camp Pinal, it was established by General George Stoneman on November 28, 1870. The site later flourished with one thousand residents who called Pinal City home in 1877 until the Silver King Mine went bust in 1888 and became a territorial ghost town almost over night. Copper mining magnate William Boyce Thompson reinvented the spot as the Boyce Thompson Arboretum and Picket Post Mountain Research Natural Area that attracts local visitors, winter snowbirds, and seasoned travelers from across the nation.

Visit: https://arboretum.ag.arizona.edu/

Mile 37 (Milepost 217). González Pass, Elevation: 2,652 feet.

Mile 42.3 (Milepost 212). Florence Junction, Road Left, Highway 79, Elevation: 1,884 feet. Gila-Pinal Scenic Road ends.

Mile 50 (Milepost 204). Peralta Road, Road Right, Elevation: 1,808 feet. (See page 160).

Mile 58 (Milepost 196). Apache Junction, Elevation: 1,767 feet, End. (See page 64).

Hallowed ground for the Apache and Pima, Superstition Mountain's treacherous ramparts challenge hikers on the historic treasure trail to Senner's Lost Gold.
Copyright © John Annerino Photography.

8

Weavers Needle: Locus for the Lost Dutchman's and Peralta's Gold

"Old Weaver's Needle rose against the evening sky, wrinkled with wear, wrapped in shadows, resting on its pedestal of stratified volcanic tuft, surrounded by clusters of goblin rocks—dumbbells, gargoyles, drunken soldiers . . . Easter Island stone faces, petrified tyrannosaurs."
—Edward Abbey, *Cactus Country* (1973)

LANDFORM

Weavers Needle is a stone wraith that defies normal perceptions. It's a compass point that rises out of a fossilized eruption of mountains, ridges, and domes cut by canyons, creeks, and arroyos that proved to be mind-bending "look-alike" terrain in the desert heat and shimmering mirages that brought gold seekers to their knees groveling in the sand for water, where some found their barren deathbed among hot lonely rocks and thorny shade less bushes, and others escaped the stony inferno which sent them ". . . 'packin to get the hell outta here—and I hain't 'goin back, neither. No sir." Named for Tennessee-born mountain man, territorial scout, and prospector Powell "Paulino" Weaver, 4,663-foot Weavers Needle is walled in on the west by battlements of serrated ridges, brush-choked canyons, and twin domes that formed the hoodoo-crowned volcanic massif of 5,057-foot Superstition Mountain. On the east, what vaqueros and cowboys tracking maverick cattle would have also called *mal país*, "bad country," the inhospitable terrain gives way to the rolling thunder of lightening-struck mesas, bluffs, divides, wooded creeks, and 6,056-foot Iron Mountain, a cool forested anomaly that goes against the grain of a landscape created by fire and brimstone shoehorned in between the Salt River to the north and the Gila River to the south.

HISTORICAL OVERVIEW

Who were the first to climb what early storybook writers called the "Finger of God"? Conceivably, they were daring, knee-length, moccasin-clad Western Apache. There may have been six of them, the *Di yih*, "One Who has Power," the medicine man, *Libaiyé*, "The Gray One," the messenger, and the *Gáán*, "Mountain Spirits," who scaled the loose talus, rocky chutes, and rough cut chimney that split the east side of Weavers Needle into twin summits above the depths of Needle Canyon. Gathering century plant stalks which grew in abundance atop their lofty ceremonial touchstone, they painted their faces, lit up the night, and started dancing in a small foot-worn circle beaten into the sloping summit perch, the medicine man beating his buckskin-covered drum and chanting a traditional song: "White lightning flashes in these moccasins, White lightning streaks in angular path, I am the lightning flashing and streaking!" The messenger whirled his bullroarer faster and faster until it hummed like a howling wind, and together with the four masked Mountain Spirits waving sacred wands adorned with eagle feathers, they carried the prayers of the Apache in the four directions to their one God, *Ussen*, "Creator of Life."

The medicine man's drumming and chanting echoed through the canyons far below and the roaring fire cast its flickering light far and wide in the starlit heavens signaling the *Ndee,* Apache "People" who encircle their mountain stronghold:

> Thus speaks the earth's thunder:
> Because of it there is good about you.
> Because of it your body is well:
> Thus speaks the earth's thunder.
>
> —*Apache Earth's Song*

Did the mercurial compass point of Weaver Needle solve the riddle, or did its cardinal points send fevered men and women into ever maddening circles through a labyrinth of stone, discovery, or folly in a confusing and life-long journey of hope and despair they were *this* close to finally locating the **X** on their treasure maps that Weavers Needle promised would be theirs? Many were convinced they had found it or were on the right track piecing together clues to solving mystifying maps that few men could read: Jacob Waltz whispered hints about it from his deathbed in 1891. Writer and treasure hunter Pierpoint C. Bicknell described it for *San Francisco Chronicle* readers in 1895. US Bureau of Reclamation photographer William J. Lubken photographed it from Parker Pass, perhaps taking the first known photograph of the mythic icon in 1908. Treasure hunter Adolph Ruth lost his life riding and limping within sight of the landmark in 1931. And mysterious Spanish, Mexican and Anglo treasure maps, some dating back centuries, some genuine, some forged, others fraudulent, featured it as El Sombrero, Picacho, and Weavers Needle that hypnotized all those who followed the puzzling clues into believing it offered the trove of gold they sought at the end of a monsoon rainbow. As a result, most everyone viewed Weaver's Needle as a prism through which to view or embark upon their quest to find Peralta's Gold, Lost Dutchman's Gold, Cave of the Gold Bars, Lost Jesuit Gold—call it what you will. But the pillar of stone was not something anyone but the Western Apache, Southeastern Yavapai, or Pima may have sought to climb, or those who may have come before, the ancient Mogollon, Salado, or Hohokam, who may have also scaled it as a rite of passage, to seek a vision quest, or to bless their people. In his popular 1970s book, *The Story of Superstition Mountain and the Lost Dutchman Gold Mine,* Robert Joseph Allen wrote: "A strange, phallic finger of smooth, black basalt rock, Weaver's Needle emerges perpendicularly from the plateau and towers hundreds of feet into the air. Incredibly deep crevices, sheer cliffs, and ravines choked with catclaw, prickly pear, palo verde, saguaro, and ocotillo guard its base."

Who would willingly venture into such country? Retired Saint George, Utah, Judge Bob Owens and the "Climbing Kachinas." Hauling coils of 120-foot goldline climbing ropes, ball-peen hammers, hand-forged pitons, water, food, and bedrolls in canvas Army packs, Owens and the original members of Kachina Mountaineering Club reportedly climbed Weavers Needle during a three day expedition November 27–29, 1947. In Joseph Stocker's 1948 *Boy's Life* magazine feature, "Ladders to the Clouds," the veteran magazine writer described the climb, in part: "Last Thanksgiving, the Kachinas staged one of their biggest climbing expeditions so far, scaling Weaver's Needle in the Superstition Mountains . . . The mysterious purple mountains bulging up from the desert . . . The climb itself was dangerous and exhausting, involving one 200-foot traverse, the frequent use of pitons, and almost continuous rope work."

The "Climbing Kachinas," as they nicknamed themselves after Hopi *Katsinas*, "spirit beings," that dwell atop northern Arizona's 12,633-foot San Francisco Mountains, had perfected their rock climbing techniques in the Salt River Valley, scaling new climbing routes in Echo Canyon up the headwall of Camelback Mountain on smooth vertical walls where ". . . it seemed at times they were clinging to nothing but the discolorations in the rock."

In an August 4, 1992 letter, Owens, a pioneer of climbing desert rock, wrote that their ascent ". . . was keyed to a Don's Trek of tourists to Peralta Pass [Fremont Saddle]. Our job was to haul crank case oil and rags to build a smoky fire on top and make the Needle look like a volcano." It was the Superstition Mountains' version of Yosemite National Park's annual "Yosemite Firefall" over El Capitan's 1,520-foot Horsetail Falls. Imagine the fiery Needle erupting with flames and embers, tourists and snowbirds gasping in wonder, chuckwallas, coyotes, and cactus wrens gazing down on the murmuring crowd wondering what all the fuss was about.

A tragedy was brewing on the summit of Weaver Needle sixteen years later that sparked the Wednesday, March 27, 1963 *Arizona Republic* newspaper headlines: "Mountain Tragedy. Photographer Tells of Aiding Rescuers in Hunt for Body. Needle Climber's Plunge to Death." Los Angeles opera singer turned prospector Maria Celeste Jones had hired thirty-year-old Phoenix mining engineer Vance N. Bacon and reportedly paid him $200 for two days' work to climb to the top of Weavers Needle to assay the mineral wealth of one of her mining claims. In a 1960 *Ebony* magazine feature about African American prospectors, "New Search for Lost Gold: Amateur Prospectors Follow Legends in Hunt for Millions in Buried Treasure," the editors wrote: " . . . a year after she began her search the buxom singer declared she had found it, and has since filed 36 claims . . . [in] the labyrinth of tunnels through the volcanic rock of Weaver's Needle." Jones, "her co-workers say she can shoot a fly off a burro's nose at 100 paces," surmised the Lost Dutchman's Gold—some historians profess she was looking for the Lost Jesuit Gold—might be located in a fissure or cave on top of Weavers Needle.

Using Jones's tall wooden "ladders to the clouds" at the base of the climb, Bacon and his twenty-year-old companion Ray Gatewood relied on one-inch steel pipes that Jones and her men had drilled into the porous rock for safety anchors on the first rope length they climbed. Shortly after reaching the summit, Bacon fell off. Gatewood was stranded, struck with terror, and started screaming for help. Amazingly, two prospectors working a mining claim on 4,152-foot Bluff Spring Mountain heard the confusing screams echoing across Needle Canyon from the summit of Weavers Needle, and yelled to Gatewood they were going for help. Chicago native Joseph Roider and Apache Junction local Ted Herrick walked out of the mountains down Barks Canyon, drove to Apache Junction, and reported the emergency to the Pinal County Sheriffs. They called Williams Air Force Base to launch a helicopter rescue. Meanwhile Montana climber Clay Worst climbed up "the sheer face of the Needle" to aid the daring helicopter rescue attempt. Maneuvering the Vietnam-era UH1 Huey in perilous winds above the summit, the pilot hovered the ship and plucked Gatewood, then Worst, off the perch with a sling dangled from a cable.

Pushing forward on the cyclic, the ground dropped 1,500 feet from beneath the chopper carrying frightened Gatewood, and the rotor wash blew across the desert as the pilot landed in the Pinal County Sherriff's basecamp set up near Celeste Jones's camp. During the flight, Worst had spotted Bacon's body at the top of talus and radioed the location to *Arizona Republic* photographer Nyle Leatham who joined the Sheriff's horseback posse to recover the body at the foot of the Needle. Gatewood later told reporters: "Bacon threw a rope over the sheer east face of the Needle, preparing to descend to the camp below. Bacon climbed down the rope and seconds later I saw his body hit the rocky base." Someone reported hearing rifle fire, and suspected foul play that Bacon had been shoved 500 feet over the edge. Who knew? During the early 1960s the Superstition Mountains was still a wild and lawless domain. Three men were murdered in cold blood, one man was shot in the back, another was shot to death in Needle Canyon, and a third was killed near First Water. No one was charged, or brought to justice, cases closed. (See page 187).

Directions: See page 184.
Map: Weavers Needle 7.5-minute Quadrangle

Trail Log: (See Peralta Trail page 181)

Mile 0 to Mile 2.2. Hike from the Peralta Trailhead to Fremont Saddle.

Mile 2.2 to Mile 3. Hike from Fremont Saddle to Piñon Camp staging area. Cache food and water here in East Boulder Canyon for your return.

The Approach

From your cache or camp in East Boulder Canyon, climb approximately 900 vertical feet up the steep talus to the foot of the gully that splits the twin summits of Weavers Needle on the west side, or what some call the West Chimney Route. To enter the gulley climb up the Class 3 or 4 "dog route" which follows the black water streak over a conglomerate bench to reach the foot of this steep gulley. In the early 1970s reports indicated there were still weathered sections of old wooden ladders on these lower rock steps dating back to the days of Celeste Jones and Ed Piper. (See page 187). Continue scrambling up to the bottom of Pitch 1.

Pitch 1, Chockstone Pitch: The pitch is marked by a tubular pipe drilled into the rock twenty feet above the bench at the start of the pitch and climbs up the near-vertical crevice-cut chute to the chockstone wedged above. At one time, two other pipes slung with nylon webbing offered the best protection on the porous rock, but someone has placed bolts and hangers on the route. The Chockstone: You can turn it on the left (5.6), or if you're carrying a pack, remove it, and spelunk (crawl) under it and wiggle out the other side. You can belay from several belay bolts hammered into the chockstone. Leading students, I always backed up these bolts with nylon webbing anchored nearby.

The Notch between Weavers Needles's northwest summit and its 4,080-foot south summit is a wonderful spot. It offers spectacular views of Needle Canyon to the east and the Superstition Mountains to the west. The shaded setting is welcome during warm spring and fall weather—if you're up here during the summer you should know that—and can be cold and windy during monsoon rains, icy and snow-covered during winter weather.

Pitch 2, The Notch Step: From the Notch, scramble up a fifteen-foot-high rock step on your left (north). The depths of Needle Canyon are on your right (east).

Pitch 3, The Gully: Head north up a long, steep gully broken by a series of rock steps. This gully leads to the base of a headwall immediately below the summit. Turn left (west) and continue along the base to the west end.

Pitch 4: The Rockstep: The easiest and most exposed pitch on climb. But it's also the most dangerous, simply because there isn't a good place at the bottom of the pitch to put in a natural bombproof belay anchor—short of drilling a bolt. Climb a short ramp diagonally left, then straight up an obvious crack with jug-sized holds to a horn near the top of the pitch. If this hollow-sounding horn unnerves you for a belay anchor, back up your belay on two rappel bolts fifty feet north.

Weavers Needle Summit

Summit Register: Someone had the audacity to forge Alex Honnold's name in the notebook on February 16, 2016: "More of a hike than a climb.—Alex Honnold." In case you're unfamiliar with his name, Honnold climbed free solo (without ropes) "Freerider" up Yosemite

National Park's 3,000-foot high El Capitan in three hours, fifty-six minutes on June 3, 2017, among other ground breaking rock climbing ascents and alpine traverses that put the climbing world on notice, including the once thought impossible ice-encrusted saw-toothed granite ridgeline traverse of Patagonia's Cerro Fitz Roy massif with Tommy Caldwell, featured in the documentary film, *A Line Across the Sky.*

Summit View: If smog and smelter pollution don't obstruct the 360-degree panoramic summit view, you can spend hours picking out landmarks, near and far, on the horizon. Bring a map! Time your climb for clear skies during fall, winter, and spring. On most any days, you can see, and sometimes hear, how the Killer Mountains earned their foreboding reputation. An 1893 quote from *The Oasis* reads: "When heavy winds blow against the south and east sides of the mountain, the terrified listener hears the most piercing and heart-rending and unearthly shrieks and howlings and . . . soul piercing sounds proceeding from out the caves and caverns, inaccessible crevices of the mountain." If you start hearing these "unearthly shrieks and howlings" emanating from Weavers Needle, you'll know it's time to rappel off.

Descent

From the summit, rappel from two bolts over the headwall. Retrace the Gully back to the Notch, and rappel off the Chockstone all the way down Pitch 1. Atop the Chockstone, you'll need to hit your mark throwing your rappel rope down the narrow chute or it will get hung up.

Travel Notes

- Suggested Gear: A helmet, two 150-foot ropes, nylon slings, small- to medium-sized cams or nuts.
- Warning Advisory: Summertime is the worst and deadliest time of the year to climb Weavers Needle.
- Primary Access: Peralta Canyon Trailhead.

- Elevation: Peralta Trailhead 2,420 feet, Fremont Saddle 3,761 feet, Piñon Camp area 3,000 +/- feet, Weavers Needle 4,663 feet.
- Biotic Communities: Sonoran Desert scrub (Arizona upland subdivision) and interior chaparral.
- Total Elevation Gain and Loss: 5,808 feet (2,964 vertical feet each way).
- Mileage: 7.2 miles roundtrip (3.6 miles one way to the Weavers Needle summit).
- Water: No perennial water en route. Seasonal intermittent creek flow and bedrock tanks in Peralta Canyon and East Boulder Canyon.
- Cache Points: Secluded areas beneath Fremont Saddle, East Boulder canyon, benches beneath Pitch 1.
- Escape Route: Peralta Trail
- Seasons: Late fall through early spring are best. Avoid Weavers Needle on busy spring weekends when the bottleneck above or below Pitch 1 can rival the wait times on Mount Everest's Hilary Step on summit day (before it cleaved off Everest during the May 2017 climbing season).
- Map: Weavers Needle Quadrangle (7.5 minute).
- Camping: Low impact dispersed camping in East Boulder Canyon.
- Nearest Supply Points: Apache Junction, Superior, and Globe.
- Managing Agency: US Forest Service, Tonto National Forest.
- Permits: Not required; firewood scarce.

Gold painted boulders and hoodoos on the West Boulder Trail to Superstition Mountain. Copyright © John Annerino Photography.

9

Superstition Mountain: Where the People Turned to Stone

"Senner called them Superstition pines and marveled at their spires which pierced the sky . . . Just forty feet away, hidden in one of the pocked crevices dotting the moon-like landscape was his cache . . . He had better than a thousand pounds of pure gold . . . So the cache would bring maybe two hundred and twenty thousand dollars . . ."
—Helen Corbin, *Senner's Gold* (1933)

LANDFORM

Three hundred and ten days of sunshine a year bathes and burns the western front of Superstition Mountain's crags, pillars, and ramparts that can take on the specter of jagged nuggets, flakes, and crystals of orange-tinted gold that, in its prospecting heyday, you could walk up to and touch, pick and pry off the mountain side, and lug the stones on your burro back to camp to crush in a crude milling stone. It was yours for the taking. No one asked, and no one would tell—though they'd probably 'gad about you at the local watering holes that you'd been out in the sun too long. Gold that you'd think could be easily plucked from the igneous rock was not gold (AU), nor even Fool's Gold, (FeS_2, iron pyrite), but volcanic sandstone, welded yellow tuffs, basalt, dacite, conglomerate rock, foliated granite, and schist from twin mounds that erupted and eroded into a ten-mile long, northwest-trending, 5,057-

foot high, hoodoo-horned massif that stood more than three thousand two hundred feet above the mouths of Hieroglyphic Canyon, Hog Canyon, Monument Canyon, and Siphon Draw. The real gold was behind you in the western bajadas tunneled into the foothills of the Goldfield Mountains beneath the Goldfield Mine (60,226 ounces gold, 21,402 ounces silver), Mammoth Mine (40,000 ounces gold), Bull Dog Mine (6,700 ounces gold), Black Queen Mine (6,000 ounces gold), Old Wasp Mine (2,500 ounces gold thirty feet from surface in 1983), and Bluebird Mine (gold production unknown). Guarded behind the Hadrian's Wall of Superstition Mountain were hidden caches, caves, and an eighteen-inch wide seam of quartz streaked with a six-inch vein of pure gold that Jacob Waltz whispered on his deathbed would "make twenty men millionaires." Stories abounded beyond the mountain's façade that there was Spanish gold bullion and ore (including aristocrat dental gold); stamped Jesuit *pesetas* (little gold bars), crosses, and statues; placer gold, wire gold, gold dust, high-graded gold, hand-cobbed gold concentrate, floats of gold; and, perhaps the most difficult of all specimens to find was the gold fever-induced, "I found it, but I can't find the mine again" gold. It was all yours for the taking. If you could find it.

HISTORICAL OVERVIEW

Where the Western Apache and Southeastern Yavapai once reigned over the interior and peripheral canyons and mountains, the Pima identified with the lone mountain that could be seen from their traditional settlements at Blackwater and Sacaton. Earliest accounts and songs indicate they first crossed the sweeping bajadas that fanned out from the base of Superstition Mountain to hunt Sonoran pronghorn antelope and scaled its imposing heights above to hunt desert bighorn sheep. Superstition Mountain, *Kakâtak Tamai*, "Crooked Top Mountain," was also at the center of their flood myth when floodwaters surged high above the banks of the Gila River and threatened their very existence. Territorial historian Thomas Farish wrote in his 1918 *History of Arizona* that:

> When Earth Doctor stuck his staff into the ground to cause the flood, and water covered the earth, most of the people perished, but some escaped and followed White Feather, who fled to the top of Superstition Mountain. The water rose, covering all the [Salt River] valley until it was as high as the line of white sandstone which is a conspicuous landmark. White Feather, surrounded by his followers, tried all his magic in vain to prevent the further rise of the flood. When he saw he was powerless to prevent this, he gathered all his people and consulted them, saying, "I have exhausted all magic powers but one, which I will now try." Taking in his left hand a medicine stone from his pouch, he held it at arm's length, at the same time extending his right hand toward the sky. After he had sung four songs he raised his hand and seized the lightning and with it struck the stone which he held. This broke into splinters with a peal of thunder and all his people were transformed into the pinnacles of stone which can now be seen projecting from the summit of one of the peaks of the Superstition Mountains.

Spanish diarist and Franciscan missionary Pedro Font accompanied Mexican Captain Juan Bautista de Anza's expedition along the Gila River to *Alta California*, "Upper California," in 1775–76, and he wrote that the Pima described the flood's high water line across Superstition Mountain that can still be seen with observant eyes today:

> This ridge is called the Ridge of Foam because at its summit, which ends gradually and, accessible after the fashion of the edge of a bastion, may be descried near the very top a white crest like

a cliff, which follows horizontally along the ridge for a good space. The Indians say that this is a mark of the foam of the waters which reached that height.

US Geological Survey

One of the first to see and cross the mythical white crest was a US Geological Surveyor identified as J. S. H., who rode a pack mule to the top of the Superstition Mountain's highest point in 1899. At the time, J. S. H. built the first survey monument atop the 5,057-foot South Summit, and he noted: "Located on eastern end of Superstition Mtn. on high sharp point, probably highest point on Mtn, which is almost inaccessible except from southern face."

When the U. S. G. S. returned in 1910 on what J. S. H. described was a "2 ½-hour pack of rough going," he hand-drilled and cemented a U. S. G. S. disk into what they named Superstition Point. Under the best of conditions, that was no easy task. Riding 3 miles from the Criswell Ranch (Old Barks Ranch) to a saddle (above Carney Springs), J. H. S. noted the "Peak is rugged but with care pack animals can be taken within 50 meters of top."

Perhaps unknown to the U. S. G. S., Superstition Point was holy ground for the Pima. When ethnographer Frank Russell interviewed the Pima and compiled their traditional songs and myths in 1904–05, he described "The Legend of the Stone Ghosts of Crooked Mountain" that emanated from their spiritual landmark. Elder Brother sang: "Powerless! Powerless! Powerless is my magic crystal. Powerless! Powerless! I shall become as stone."

The First Skyline Traverse?

Little more was known about the human history of the summit crest, and the canyons that radiated from it. Awhile back, that got me to thinking: *Why not go see for yourself, and traverse it on foot?* At the time

I was an outdoor educator and wilderness guide, schooled in British climbing literature and their concept of mountain traverses that were much higher and far more rugged and dangerous than Superstition Mountain. My students and I had already successfully traversed the twelve-mile long ridgeline of the 4,067-foot McDowell Mountains near the confluence of the Salt and Verde Rivers on several occasions. Why not give Superstition Mountain a go? We did.

To our delight, apart from what appeared to be an historic grave marker at the head of Hieroglyphic Canyon, we found no trails on our traverse, or remnants, cairns, historic campfire scars, stone rings, rusty tin cans, mining lode claims folded inside weathered red-and-yellow 1918-era Prince Albert Tobacco tins protected by monuments of stone, or any contemporary signs. The first night we camped beneath the 5,057-foot U. S. G. S. Superstition Point benchmark and gazed over the rugged cross-country route we had just traced in the hoof prints of J. H. S. who had somehow ridden a mule to the summit. To the west was the sea of Phoenix lights that would not turn off unless you slept facing east. The following morning, we pushed on past the point of no return, and our diminishing drinking water supply, to a break in the ridgeline where we hand lowered backpacks and one-gallon water jugs, pushed on to the 5,024-foot North Summit past the anvil-shaped Flat Iron, and route-found a safe descent line into the steep canyon of Siphon Draw to our shuttle vehicle parked near the Mining Camp Restaurant. The Superstition Mountain traverse, and grilled steaks, became a favorite trek for my students.

SUPERSTITION MOUNTAIN SKYLINE TRAVERSE

Directions

From US Highway 60, drive eight miles east of Apache Junction, turn north on the signed Peralta Road near Mile Post 204, drive six miles north on the Peralta Road to an unsigned dirt road on your left (northwest) at BM 2206 that leads 0.6 miles to the undeveloped parking lot.

Maps

Goldfield and Weavers Needle 7.5-minute Quadrangles

Trailhead

Carney Springs was a reliable water source at the foot of the 800-foot high Dacite Cliffs, and was reportedly named for Carney Mining Company president Peter G. Carney. According to the listing in the 1918 world mining industry volume, *The Copper Handbook,* a 100-foot deep shaft and 800-foot drift tunnel were dug to exploit a vein of gold-copper. Plans were made to build a cyanide mill, but the mine failed to profit from Arizona's "copper rush" that put the little border town of Bisbee, Arizona, and its rich open-pit Copper Queen Mine, on the map that in a century of mining, yielded $6.1 billion in ore (8,032,352,000 pounds copper, 2,871,786 ounces gold, and 77,162,986 ounces silver) that proved to be the "richest copper camp in the world." Imagine an open pit mine here today. *Source:* Queen Mine Tours. Visit: www.queenminetour.com

Trail Log

Note: All Mileages are approximate and will vary depending on your line of travel.

Mile 0.0 to Mile 1.6. Carney Springs Trailhead, Elevation: 2,300 feet +. From the parking area, walk the old Carney Springs Road to the Superstition Wilderness boundary gate (0.6 miles) and follow the West Boulder Trail north along the left (west) side of the arroyo across brushy flats, rises, and climbs *1,380 vertical feet up the trail and rugged switchbacks past a landmark trail boulder to the West Boulder Saddle.

(*As a gauge for you, Phoenix's Piestewa Peak Trail is 1.2 miles long and has a 1,208-foot elevation gain).

Carney Springs Wall Canyon, Alternate Route: A shorter, more direct and rugged cross-country route I sometimes used climbs the first steep canyon drainage west of the Carney Springs Trailhead beneath the northeast-facing Carney Springs Wall that gains the 3,540-foot saddle west of Peak 3,826. Seasonal water is sometimes found in the upper reaches of this canyon.

The Apache Kid's Cave: From published accounts that nearly pinpoint its exact location, the popular Wave Cave near the foot of the Carney Springs Wall was what pioneers called the "Apache Kid's" cave of *Haskay-bay-nay-ntayl*, "A tall man destined to come to a mysterious end." The "Kid" was a White Mountain Apache and US Army Scout-turned renegade who had been reportedly adopted by Al Sieber, Chief of Scouts, during the US Apache Wars and the Geronimo Campaign. During a *tiswin* (corn beer)-fueled scuffle among Apache Scouts at San Carlos, several men were killed, the Apache Kid escaped, then surrendered, and served hard time in Alactraz and Yuma Territorial Prison where he later escaped and rode into Old West legend and children's comic book fame. In an enlightening historical account on page one of the July 25, 1897 *San Francisco Call*, headlined, "Found the Lair of the Apache Kid. Hidden Cave Discovered in the Superstition Mountains. Arizonans Locate the Hiding-Place of the Notorious Redskin. Almost Inaccessible Cavern In the Side of a Precipitous Incline," it details the Apache Kid's use of the cave during the 1890s:

> PHOENIX, Ariz. July 21.— Two men of reputed veracity, J. M. Burnett and W. H. Bonsall, who have recently returned from a trip in the Superstition Mountains, give a very graphic description of a wonderful mountain rendezvous that they discovered in their journeyings. It is known as "Apache Kid's" cave, and white men are less acquainted with its interior than they have

been with Cochise's famous stronghold in the Dragoon Mountains [133 miles southeast]. For six or seven years the "Kid" is known to have rendezvoused in this retreat, and it afforded him safe shelter.

- Territorial Route and Cave Description: "The 'Kid's' cave is three miles from Bark's ranch (Quarter Circle U), and so situated that the mouth of it overlooks the surrounding country for miles. The opening is approached by a steep incline of not less than fifty degrees, and is about four hundred feet in length . . . The rearwall is covered with a crystalline salt deposit. About the cave were many traces of deer and mountain lions. The deer came to lick the salt and the lions to lick the deer. Many evidences of Indian occupation still remain (eleven excavated beds with boughs, and a location map of the cave), and there is a large quantity of brushwood for fuel. Surrounding the mouth of the cave is a large, level platform, most difficult of access and offering a splendid vantage point for a marksman like the 'Kid,' or any of his band. With ammunition and food in such a stronghold the 'Kid' could and did hold out against the soldiers in that part of the Territory."

From his redoubt, the Apache Kid could see far and wide all the way to Picket Post Mountain used by the Apache to watch troop movement at Camp Pinal and for signal fire messaging. With ready access to water at Carney Springs, Peralta Springs, Willow Springs in West Boulder Canyon, and Apache Springs (Hieroglyphic Springs), the Apache Kid could run or ride like the wind in any direction he needed.

Mile 1.6 to Mile 2. West Boulder Saddle, Elevation: 3,680 feet +. From this saddle veer left (west), and contour the north and west side of unnamed Peak 3,826 into the 3,540-foot saddle that bridges the head of Carney Springs Wall Canyon to the south and West Boulder Canyon to the north. Pot shards and stone alignments I'd once studied in this pass indicate it was used by the Apache, or earlier by the Hohokam, to travel between Carney Springs and Willow Spring. From West Boulder Saddle contour west along the ridgeline through razorbacks of sheer rock that stick out of the southeast ridge like bifurcated dinosaur spines, and climb up to Peak 4391 to gain the southeast summit crest of Superstition Mountain.

Robbers Roost Route. From West Boulder Saddle, an elusive cross-country route through boulders, hoodoos, bear grass, and clothes-tugging brush winds in and around the rugged stone garden in a northeasterly direction atop the Dacite Cliffs to 3,761-foot Freemont Saddle and the Peralta Trail. I haven't traced the route, so I can't provide a first-hand description. I understand the payoff is an enjoyable orienteering adventure that leads to the cave roost and a natural arch.

Backstory: During an overnight exploratory hike from Carney Springs to Willow Spring, a companion and I bivouacked in West Boulder Saddle. We heard two women screaming in the distance. We called out and started walking in the evening light along the head of West Boulder Canyon toward the screams and echoes. Fortunately, we found the two middle-aged women emerging from a thicket of brush below us. They were dressed in torn clothes, and their arms and legs were streaked with bloody scratches from their cat fight with "wait a minute" acacia-thorned bushes. They'd gotten turned around clambering through the maze of stone pillars and jumble of boulders on the Robbers Roost route. I prodded them with water and snack food, then tried my cell phone and reached the Pinal County Sheriff's Search and Rescue. They dispatched three SAR members to care for the women and assist them back down the mountain in the dark. Rescue? No. We just happened to be in the right place at the right time, and to my surprise my cell phone pinged a tower.

Mile 2 to Mile 2.62. Peak 4391, Elevation: 4,391 feet. Follow the airy, rugged, and spectacular southeast summit crest to the South

Summit. Along this section, I'd also discovered odd lithic scatters and stone alignments indicating prehistoric people had visited the area. Imagine the moccasin clad Apache, Pima, or Hohokam hunting and gathering in the lofty reaches along summit crest. In the area, I also discovered mountain lion scat entangled with hair and the tiny hooves of a mule or whitetail deer fawn, and a disarray of cremated human bones and ashes tossed from an airplane that took the romance out of the notion, "When I die, scatter my ashes over . . ."

Mountain Vistas: During one clear crisp skyline traverse, I took copious notes of the views my companion and I could see along the summit crest. From Peak 4391, I noted we could see: 6,663-foot Galiuro Mountains seventy-five miles east/southeast, 9,157-foot Santa Catalina Mountains eighty miles southeast, 4,513-foot Sierra Estrella forty-five miles southwest, and incredibly the one thousand-foot high summit dome of the 7,714 foot Baboquivari Mountains 115 miles south/southwest on the US/Mexico border.

Mile 2.62 to Mile 3.7. South Summit, Elevation: 5,057 feet. The flat ground beneath the Stonehenge cluster of hoodoos that forms the South Summit is a good place to camp if your hiking out-and-back to the summit, or a good water, snack, or lunch stop if you're traversing the crest end-to-end. From the South Summit, contour around the west side of the South Summit and follow the summit crest north to the unnamed Peak 4790, then northwest into the Hieroglyphic Canyon/West Boulder Canyon Saddle.

Sacred Mountain Altar?

A short time after the U. S. G. S. surveyed the South Summit in 1899, they visited with rancher James Bark at his Bark Ranch, what later became the Quarter Circle U Ranch, and showed him some "arrowheads of moss agate" they'd found during their survey. Without

Superstition Mountain: Where the People Turned to Stone

The sacred heights of Superstition Mountain was conceivably an altar for the Apache and Pima who offered, or cached, more than one thousand arrowheads to the "People Who Turned to Stone" hoodoos long before a USGS surveyor rode a mule to the South Summit in 1899. Copyright © John Annerino Photography.

mentioning a word to them, Bark climbed the difficult peak, poked around, and made an unimaginable discovery of a fragile olla wedged in a hidden rocky crevice. In the October 5, 1889 *Arizona Daily Herald*, the small headline read: "Jim Barks Find, Old Olla Found on Superstitions Filled with Aztec Arrowheads." During the second known ascent of Superstition Mountain's South Summit, "Jim Bark," according to the news account, "brought out a sack [the olla broke] and rolled out onto the bread table 887 of as perfect moss-agate Aztec arrow heads as were ever seen in the world." Bark displayed the collection to a group of Mesa arrowhead collectors who'd just returned from Superstition Mountain bragging about the 107 arrowheads they'd picked up after they'd heard of the U. S. G. S.'s find. Not counting the U. S. G. S.'s unknown quantity of arrowheads they'd picked up, how many Native Americans does 994 arrowheads represent? How many Western Apache and Pima climbed the sacred mountain to pay homage at the hoodoo altar of stones? And where is the collection now? With the Western Apache, Southeastern Yavapai, Pima, or in a musem basement?

Living Landscape

When the Indian Claims Commission was established in 1946, Native American elders and medicine men identified the spiritual boundaries of their traditional homelands by identifying mountains, mesas, landmarks, creeks, and springs that were used or associated with sacred songs, myths, and ceremonies. Conversely, pioneers, mountain men, prospectors, surveyors, and artists identified important landmarks they viewed, overcame, utilized, wrote about, painted, or photographed. Landmark memories, imaginings, and myths bring the landscape to life. While you're traversing the crest, try pinpointing the landmarks most memorable to you.

Summit Vista. We could clearly view the snowy crown of the 7,657-foot Mazatzal Mountains twenty miles north, 7,694-foot Sierra Ancha Miles thirty-five miles northeast, and the 7,845-foot Pinal Mountains thirty-five miles east/southeast. To the west we could view all of the Hohokam's peaks and ranges in the Salt River Valley from which we, among many other people, often viewed Superstition Mountain beckoning to the east: 2,608-foot Piestewa Peak, 2,706-foot Camelback Mountain, 2,526-foot South Mountains, and even 1,663-foot Papago Buttes.

Desert Bighorn Sheep. Keep your eyes peeled for desert bighorn sheep browsing or bounding across the crest or the crags and ridges below. Seen from above along this skyline traverse, this is an ideal location to view bighorn sheep that were first translocated on Superstition Mountain, and elsewhere throughout the wilderness, between 1983 and 1992.

Mile 3.7 to Mile 4.35. Hieroglyphic Canyon/West Boulder Canyon Saddle, Elevation: 4,280 feet +. From this saddle follow the summit crest northwest from unnamed Peak 4777 and Peak 4869 to Hog Canyon Saddle/North Fork. When prehistoric and protohistoric indigenous peoples crossed the Great American Desert, they either followed perennial or seasonal rivers and creeks, or they traveled across the open desert from one distant spring or waterhole to the next. The cross-mountain traverse from Apache Spring (Hieroglyphic Spring) up Hieroglyphic Canyon to Willow Spring in West Boulder Canyon, though difficult for many modern hikers, was undoubtedly an "Indian Pass" used to utilize seasonal hunting and gathering grounds on both sides of Superstition Mountain.

Mile 4.35 to Mile 5.28. Hog Canyon Saddle/North Fork, Elevation: 4,517 feet. From this saddle follow the peaks and saddles along the crest from unnamed Peak 4642, Peak 4453, Peak 4613 and Peak 4402 to the Old West Boulder Canyon Saddle. Between Peak 4613 and Peak 4402, we chanced upon a field of "exploding cactus." Clusters of hedgehog cacti had literally blown their tops off, scattering cactus skin and spines up to five feet distant. From what I could surmise at the time, these hedgehogs, swollen fat from late winter rains, blew their tops when rain saturated pulp in their thorn-ribbed trunks and stems froze and expanded.

Mile 5.28 to Mile 6.74. The Notch, Old West Boulder Canyon Saddle, Elevation: 4,240 feet+, beneath Peak 4402 feet. You'll need to scramble down this short rock step into the Notch carrying your daypack, or hand lower your backpack. From this saddle climb up the unexposed rock steps to regain the summit crest at Peak 4662, contour safely above the head of Monument Canyon, and thread the pass between the 5,024-foot North Summit of Superstition Mountain on your right (northeast) and the unnamed Peak 4,861-foot highpoint above the Flat Iron on your left (south). The standard route descends the head of Siphon Draw.

Hiker's Gold

In her compelling 1993 book, *Senner's Gold,* historian Helen Corbin revealed the tale of the mountain's trove of lost gold. One of the most ardent Superstition Mountain hikers, now or back in the gold rush heydays, was cowboy-turned Goldfield miner and invester Al Senner. During the winter of 1893–94, Senner reportedly high-graded over 1,000 pounds of rich ore stolen from the Mammoth Mine he helped develop. There was only one place to hide the heavy bounty from the prying eyes of Goldfield miners: on top of Superstition Mountain. The most direct route from Goldfield was up Siphon Draw, where few could follow and get the drop on Senner. The one-armed Senner reportedly made the difficult three-hour climb many times, carrying fifteen-pound loads of the "richest ore imaginable" to the basin below the North Summit. Senner had reportedly cached four hundred pounds of hidden gold in the vicinity; some profess it was cached over the other side of the mountain somewhere in the depths of Old West Boulder Canyon, where loose gold that may have been Senner's was later found. Al Senner's lost cache remains undiscovered, so the lost treasure Illuminati professes. Greed reportedly caught up with Al Senner in 1894 when his horse, Lady, and pack mule slipped and fell, or were pushed or spooked into Monument Canyon while hauling out his last remaining buckskin pouches of pure gold.

Mile 6.74 to Mile 7.69. Siphon Draw, Elevation: 4,760 feet. The heavily-used route is well marked by footsteps, cairns, and painted route markers. It snakes and zigzags through brush, rock steps, ledges, and outcrops, a twelve-foot step that can be down-climbed or turned and avoided on the right (north), and descends through sometimes slick long ramps, seasonal waterfalls, black water streaks, and exfoliated granite slabs to the Siphon Draw Trail No. 53 that leads to the Lost Dutchman State Park trailhead.

Mile 10.39. Siphon Draw Trailhead, Lost Dutchman State Park, Elevation: 2,060 feet.

Vehicle Shuttle: Plan on a twenty-mile vehicle shuttle one way between the Carney Springs Trailhead and Lost Dutchman State Park.

Travel Notes

- Warning Advisory: Summertime can be brutal hiking up to West Boulder Saddle, or Siphon Draw: Winter can be treacherous with snow and ice.
- Primary Access: West Boulder Trail via Carney Springs Trailhead. Alternate Route, Carney Springs Wall Canyon.
- Elevation: Carney Springs Trailhead 2,300 feet, West Boulder Saddle 3,680 feet, South Summit 5,057 feet, North Summit 5,024 foot, Siphon Draw Trailhead 2,060 feet.
- Biotic Communities: Sonoran Desert scrub (Arizona upland subdivision) and interior chaparral.
- Total Elevation Gain: No less than 4,500 vertical feet.
- Total Elevation Loss: No less than 4,700 vertical feet.
- Mileage: Approximately 10.5 to 11 Miles +/- point-to-point, will vary according to your line of travel.
- Water: No perennial water en route. Seasonal intermittent I've used: Upper Carney Springs Wall Canyon, Siphon Draw, Summit Crest pothole Peak 3,915; and tributary canyon streams seen but not used, Hieroglyphic Canyon, Hog Canyon, and Monument Canyon.

- Cache Points: None for the point-to-point traverse, secluded areas in West Boulder Saddle for an out-and-back South Summit trek.
- Escape Route: South Summit vicinity, southeast summit crest and West Boulder Trail to Carney Springs; North Summit basin, Siphon Draw to Lost Dutchman State Park trailhead. In between the South Summit and the North Summit, you'd be faced with precipitously steep western tributary canyons to try to reach water with no guarantees.
- Seasons: Late fall through early spring are best.
- Map: Weavers Needle Quadrangle (7.5 minute), Goldfield Quadrangle (7.5 minute).
- Camping: Low impact dispersed camping in East Boulder Canyon.
- Nearest Supply Points: Apache Junction, Superior, and Globe.
- Managing Agency: US Forest Service, Tonto National Forest.
- Permits: Not required; Firewood is scarce.

Pinal County Search and Rescue

Phone Numbers
Emergencies: 9-1-1
Non Emergency: 520-866-5111

IV.
Trails and Tales of the Mystery Mountains

Miner's dynamite box, Goldfield, Arizona. Copyright © John Annerino Photography.

10

Trails of the Superstition Mountains

"Gold is Where You Find It."

—Clements Ripley, 1936

LANDFORM

Stretching southeast from the Massacre Grounds, sweeping bajadas fan out from the western foot of Superstition Mountain all the way to Hieroglyphic Spring and beyond to Peralta Canyon. These "plains," as old timers called them, were cut by deep flashflood-swept arroyos that spilled down from the mouths of Siphon Draw, Monument Canyon, Hog Canyon, and Hieroglyphic Canyon. The park's hiking trails cross these wonderful bajadas that flower with yellow, red, and lavender spring wildflowers and cactus blossoms that bud among mesquite and palo verde trees in the foreground of a ten-mile-wide mountain cyclorama that glows with burnt copper-hued colors at sunset. Where better to day hike and camp before venturing into the rugged depths of the Superstition Wilderness.

LOST DUTCHMAN STATE PARK: HISTORICAL OVERVIEW

Named for the trove of gold discovered by German American Jacob Waltz who prospected the Superstition Mountains between 1868 and 1891—who by all accounts was never "lost"—the 320-acre Lost Dutchman State Park was established in 1972. Its Wild West history is associated with the bustling Goldfield boomtown and rich gold strikes of the Blue Bird, Mammoth, and Goldfield Mines located only a fist-sized gold nugget toss west of the park. Prospectors once probed the bajadas at the foot of Superstition Mountain with "gloryholes," as foot, horse, wagon, and freighter traffic traveled back and forth along the Apache Trail.

Directions

From Apache Junction, turn left (northeast) on State Route 88 and drive the paved Apache Trail 5.5 miles to the Lost Dutchman State Park turnoff, on right.

Map

Goldfield 7.5-minute Quadrangle. (Trail map see page 298)

Self Guiding Trails

Note: You can hike all, or sections, of each trail, alone or in combination with other trails. Six of these trails begin in the State Park and pass through the Superstition Wilderness.

- Discovery Trail. Distance: 0.1-mile interpretive trail, Trailhead: Palo Verde Day Use Area or Campground. Features a bench, birdfeeder, and man-made wildlife pond.
- Native Plant Trail. Distance: 0.25-mile paved interpretive trail, Trailhead: Visitor Center.

- Prospector's View Trail No. 57. Distance: 0.7 miles, Access: Reached by hiking one of the trails it intersects, (Treasure Loop Trail, Jacobs Crosscut Trail, or Siphon Draw Trail). Trailhead: Saguaro Day Use Area or Siphon Draw Trailhead.
- Jacob's Crosscut Trail No. 58. Distance: 0.8 miles, Access: Reached by hiking one of the trails it intersects. (Treasure Loop Trail or Prospector's View Trail). Trailhead: Cholla Day Use Area, Saguaro Day Use Area, or Siphon Draw Trailhead. Contouring the base of Superstition Mountain southeast from the Siphon Draw Trail, Jacob's Crosscut Trail can be hiked another 4.5 miles across the Superstition Wilderness to the end of Monument Canyon at the Broadway Road Trailhead. You can hike this stretch out-and-back from the park, and if you have the water and stamina, detour to visit the Broadway Cave. Viewed from the trail, look for the golden eye (at sunset) at the top of a steep saguaro cactus forest 380 vertical feet above the trail. Beyond the fifty-foot-wide mouth of the cave that's been measured twenty feet tall and thirty foot deep is what looks like a pick, pry bar, and shovel excavated tunnel. (Directions: You can car shuttle from Lost Dutchman State Park by leaving a vehicle at the Broadway Trailhead accessed by driving east from Apache Junction on E. Broadway Avenue past the junction of South Mountain View Road to the trailhead).
- Treasure Loop Trail No. 56. Distance: 2.4 miles, Trailhead: Cholla Day Use Area or Saguaro Day Use Area, Elevation Gain and Loss: 500 feet +/-.
- Siphon Draw Trail No. 53. Distance: 2 miles (4 miles out-and-back) to what day hikers call the "Basin," Trailhead: Siphon Draw, Elevation Gain: 1,000 vertical feet +/-. If you're conditioned, acclimated to the desert weather, experienced, and your knees can take it, it's a 2.7 mile, and 2,700 vertical foot trek

(5,400 vertical feet round trip) and hands-and-feet scramble up to the Flat Iron. (See Superstition Mountain page 155).
- Mountain Bike Loop Trail. Distance 4 miles. Trailhead: Visitor Center, or pick your spot anywhere in the park. This new trail encircles the perimeter of the park south of the Superstition Wilderness boundary.

Contact

Lost Dutchman State Park, Open Year Round
Easy Day Hiking, Tent Camping, and RV sites
Phone: (480) 982-4485
Visit: https://azstateparks.com/lost-dutchman

SUPERSTITION WILDERNESS

Hieroglyphic Trail

Distance: 1.2 miles, Elevation Gain: 790 vertical feet, Trailhead: Hieroglyphic Springs/Lost Goldmine Trail. At one time, Hieroglyphic Springs was known as Apache Springs for the Western Apache who frequently used the semi-perennial stream of gurgling water to sustain themselves and their horses.

The Ancient Record

Viewing the ancient Hohokam petroglyphs that adorn the stony gateway into Hieroglyphic Canyon, I'm convinced—viewing the "rock art" through the prism of having traversed Superstition Mountain—that this was the sacred passage the Hohokam, Pima, and Western Apache used to scale the mountain to their hunting grounds. Among the hand-chiseled and hand-pecked symbols called petroglyphs, mistakenly confused with ancient Egyptian symbols called hieroglyphs, are desert bighorn sheep, pronghorn antelope, mule deer, singing birds, serpents, lightning, anthropomorphs, mazes, textile patterns, pipettes, and lightning. What a place of wonder to imagine and behold the stealthy hunts of the Pima and Apache searching for life's real treasure, fresh drinking water, red meat, and plant sustenance that maintained their spirit, strength, families, and clans they found near this artist's oasis where they were inspired to inscribe their written record of survival and ceremony in their harsh ancestral homelands.

Directions

From US Highway 60, drive north on Kings Ranch Road, turn right (east) on Baseline Avenue and drive 1.6 miles, turn left (north) on S. Mohican Road and drive 0.3 miles, turn left (northwest/north) on Valley View Drive and Whitetail Road and drive 0.3 miles, turn right (east) on Cloudview Avenue and drive 0.7 miles to the trailhead. Parking is limited.

Map

Goldfield 7.5 minute Quadrangle

LOST GOLDMINE TRAIL

Distance: 5.7 miles, Trailhead: Hieroglyphic Trail, or Peralta Trail. From Hieroglyphic Canyon, this new serpentine undulating path courses east and skirts the southern boundary of the Superstition Wilderness across the cholla- and saguaro cactus-studded bajadas of the Barkley Basin beneath the foothills, towering cliffs, and ramparts of the South Summit of Superstition Mountain all the way to the Peralta Trailhead. Bring a comb, tweezers, and tape in case you're ambushed by a "jumping" teddy bear cholla bud. The Lost Goldmine Trail was built over a ten-year period in 2002 under the auspices of the

Superstition Area Land Trust, SALT, to protect 16,700 acres of verdant Sonoran Desert lands, open space from future development, and to provide permanent access for hikers, equestrians, mountain bikers, and recreationists. It remains a sanctuary for flora, fauna, reptiles, birds, raptors, and archaeological sites that include ridge top trails and lookouts, springs, bedrock mortars, lithic scatters, petroglyphs, campsites, traditional hunting and gathering areas, and broad washes and arroyos that sustained *ak chin* (floodwater) agriculture.

Directions, East End

From US Highway 60, turn north on the signed Peralta Road near Mile Post 204, and drive 7.2 miles on the paved and graded (6 miles) Lost Goldmine Trail sign parking.

Map

Goldfield 7.5-minute Quadrangle

Contact

Superstition Area Land Trust
PO Box 582
Apache Junction, AZ 85117
Phone: 480-983-3454
Visit: www.azsalt.org/lost-goldmine-trail.html

The hidden symbol of a Jesuit cross is mute testimony that Spanish Jesuit priests may have cached gold bars in the Superstition Mountains, and elsewhere in the region where savvy treasure hunters unearthed eighty-two pounds of Lost Jesuit Gold bars called *pasetas* valued at more than $410,000. Copyright © John Annerino Photography.

11

The Peralta Trails

"Granted they did not find the riches of which they had been told, they found a place in which to search for them . . ."

—Pedro de Casteñada de Nájera, *The Journey of Coronado* (1540)

LANDFORM

Peralta Canyon winds beneath twin hoodoo-spired ridges that emanate from the unnamed 4,160-foot high point of the Dacite Cliffs on the northwest and a 3,800-foot summit on the northeast. During torrential monsoon storms, floodwaters from Peralta Canyon periodically discharge into Queen Creek. More often than not the seasonal runoff evaporates or dissipates in the sand before reaching the Gila River tributary. For early travelers, Peralta Canyon formed a landmark corridor that lead into the heart of the Superstition Mountains to infamous Weavers Needle that beckoned them in search of the Golden Fleece.

HISTORICAL OVERVIEW

Long before Spaniards and prospectors ventured up the ancestral passage of Peralta Canyon, it was used by the Hohokam and perhaps the Mogollon, and later by the Western Apache and Pima. The seasonal flow of water in upper Peralta Canyon and the bedrock tanks in East Boulder Canyon offered reliable drinking water, shaded camps, and hidden lookouts during hunting and gathering forays into their stony domain.

Peralta Trail

Reportedly named for one of the Peralta family patriarchs, perhaps Don Miguel Peralta of Arizpe, Sonora, Mexico, who was reportedly a cattle baron and the owner of the *Minas de Sombrero,* "Sombrero Mines," which operated in the Superstition Mountains in the heyday of gold prospecting during the 1840s. The Peralta genealogy, and the myriad stories associated with the family, lead in many directions and contested conclusions. Coming from Mexico up the Santa Cruz and Gila Rivers, the Peralta mining caravans could follow the course of the Apache Trail around the southwestern front of Superstition Mountains, or they could beeline up Peralta Canyon, or nearby Barks and Needle Canyons, to travel more directly to their mines. Jacob Waltz reportedly used several routes to reach his secret lode, one left the Board House at what later became the Quarter Circle U Ranch in close proximity to both canyon corridors.

Don's Club Trail

Founded in 1934 by a group of local businessmen, the Don's Club adopted their name from Spanish *Don* (a man of honor), such as Don Miguel Peralta, and *Doña* (a woman of honor), and dressed in regal costumes that today resemble Mexican *charros* (horsemen) and *Escarmuzeas* (horsewomen). Every year since their founding, the Don's Club has hosted an annual rendezvous and trek at Don's Camp beneath the headwall of the Dacite Cliffs near the foot of the Peralta Trail. One of their most popular attractions that celebrated the Lost Dutchman Gold Mine's history and lore was their annual search for the hidden mine. As many as 1,200 people attended their colorful festivities that included the long rugged day hike up Peralta Canyon beneath "Eye on the Trail" to Fremont Saddle, where they descended what became the Cave Trail to Geronimos Cave, and continued down the "Devils Slide" back to

Don's Camp. Ever since those popular annual treks, the Peralta Trail has become one of America's most popular hiking trails, luring locals, winter snowbirds, and visitors who travel from across the country and around the globe after they'd heard the siren call or were touched by the irresistible lure of mythical gold symbolized by Weavers Needle that they could almost reach out and touch from Fremont Saddle.

A Literary No-Man's-Land

If Peralta Canyon was located anywhere else in the continental United States that offered a more benevolent environment and reputation, it would attract naturalists like bees to honey. It didn't offer the diverse climates that ornithologist John James Audubon explored in Key West, Dakota Territory, and Labrador to study, paint, and write about avifauna that appeared in his lavish magnum opus, *The Birds of America,* illustrated with remarkable color plates. It didn't offer magnificent granite walls, towering cascades, and cloud piercing snow-covered minarets and sierras of Yosemite that John Muir hiked, studied, and wrote about in *Our National Parks,* and many other travel and conservation books. Nor was it still inhabited by Native Americans that brought the landscape to life in the writings and musings of American author Mary Hunter Austin who explored the vast Mojave Desert from its salt pans up to the heights of the Sierra Nevada for her beautiful book, *The Land of Little Rain.* From the dearth of books on library and bookstore shelves, no other naturalist was enticed by the Sonoran Desert sanctuary that was hidden behind the cloak of unsavory characters and cryptic legends, an inhospitable landscape of cliffs, goblins of stone, and canyons baked by brick oven heat, and guarded by spine-covered cactus, rattlesnakes, Gila monsters, gun-wielding prospectors, and hostile "Apaches." One writer savored what he called, "A Dry Corner of the Continent." Enter author, environmentalist, and literary rabble rouser

Edward Abbey, who gained national prominence with his seminal book of essays, *Desert Solitaire: A Season in the Wilderness* (1968), and popular novel, *The Monkey Wrench Gang* (1975).

Abbey's Road

"One brutally hot day in mid-April," the irascible Abbey wrote, he and a friend hiked up Peralta Canyon and camped below Weavers Needle. In his *Time-Life* book, *Cactus Country* (1973), he later wrote that the Superstitions Mountains attracted ". . . gun happy cranks, touchy old prospectors, truculent treasure hunters from faraway cities . . . coming here to live out their childhood fantasies of the Wild West." Hiking up to Fremont Saddle in the blazing heat, the pair hiked over to Geronimos Cave, backtracked to the hoodoo-marked pass, descended into East Boulder Canyon, cooled off in deep bedrock tanks, and camped at Piñon Camp near the foot of Weavers Needle. Here, only the naturalist that Abbey was could discover the fragile beauty in the hellish landscape that would escape most others, if there'd been anyone else hiking and camping out there that blistering spring day. Evidently there was not, and Abbey wrote: ". . . below Weavers Needle, we came upon the flamboyant little orange blossoms of globe mallow, woolly golden desert marigold, violet placelia, the delicate slender blue flower by the name of bluedick." Someone did find gold in the Superstitions that day, but not the gold most others had come looking for before them.

Directions

From US Highway 60, drive eight miles east of Apache Junction, turn north on the signed Peralta Road near Milepost 204, and drive 7.2 miles on the paved and graded (six miles) to the Peralta Trailhead. During the heyday of the Silver King Mine between 1875 and 1900, a five-square-mile area of mesquite, palo verde, and ironwood trees southeast of the Peralta Road was clear-cut by Cornish miners to fuel the Silver King's smelter operations that produced $42 million in silver from the "Glory Hole" claim.

Maps

Weavers Needle and Goldfield 7.5 Minute Quadrangles

Trail Log

Mile 0 to Mile 2.2. Peralta Trailhead 102, Elevation: 2,420 feet. Hike from the Peralta Trailhead to Fremont Saddle. For those who just want to hike up and look at storied Weavers Needle, there's no better vista than the 4.4 mile roundtrip hike to Fremont Saddle. The steep rugged Peralta Trail climbs 1,346 vertical feet, courses along dusty rocky trails, bedrock "sidewalks," welcome intermittent flows of Peralta Creek (about Mile 1.7) beneath the landmark—look for it!—Eye on the Trail, then switchbacks up through some of the most spectacular rock formations in the Superstition Mountains to "Hoodoo Pass." At one time indigenous desert bighorn sheep bounded across the boulder-choked slopes and ridgelines before the last of the magnificent sure-footed, full-curl quadrupeds ended up in prospectors' skillets.

Mile 2.2 to Mile 3. Fremont Saddle, Elevation: 3,766-feet. Hike from Fremont Saddle to Piñon Camp. When you top out on the saddle named for American explorer and Arizona Territory Governor John C. Frémont, you'll see the iconic vista of Weavers Needle, called *El Sombrero,* "The Hat," that appears on Spanish treasure maps. Catch your breath, drink some water, and take in the view from the postcard perch. From Fremont Saddle, you can hike back down the Peralta Trail to the trailhead, or you can head down from the saddle into East Boulder Canyon to Piñon Camp. (See Weavers Needle page 189).

Geronimos Cave/Cave Trail. Early accounts place the Apache Kid in the deep not-too-distant Carney Springs Canyon cave west of Fremont Saddle that pioneers called the Apache Kid's Cave, but according to the research of Geronimo historian and author Angie Debo, there's no documented record of the namesake cave being used by the legendary warrior of the *Bedonkohe* band of the Chiricahua Apache named *Goyakla*, "One Who Yawns." If you're headed to Geronimos Cave, contour right (east) from Fremont Saddle and follow the route the Don's Club pioneered during their annual search for the Lost Dutchman's Mine along the Cave Trail 233 to the alcove. Return back the way you came to Fremont Saddle. Or you can continue tracing the elusive Don's Club trail down the southeast ridgeline overlooking Peralta Canyon that's marked by cairns, and use trails and your sense of natural direction-finding 2.5 miles back to the Peralta Trailhead.

Mile 3. Piñon Camp, Elevation: 3,200 feet. After coming off crowded Fremont Saddle and breezing down the switchbacks into East Boulder Canyon, the descent to Piñon Camp is leisurely and breathtaking and normally offers the welcome solitude you came for. Fall through spring, I've always found Piñon Camp's seasonal bedrock tanks dependable and suspected they were also fed by underground springs. Named for the evergreen pine and piñon trees that once grew here, Piñon Camp is an undeveloped area that offers a rest, water, and lunch spot and low impact at-large camping above the creek bed. At one time it was a shaded micro oasis and wonderful campsite.

Backstory: This was the trail my dog and I hiked, and the spot we camped in, when the Superstition Mountains beckoned us over the horizon from our lofty bivouac cave in Papago Buttes several years earlier. I rolled out the same wool blanket, drank from felt-covered prospector canteens, carried a new army surplus canvas pack, and cooked canned chili instead of pork and beans over a small fire. Hot beans hissed in the coals, and the fire cast flickering shadows against dark stones that loomed beneath heavens streaked with shooting stars as coyotes howled and yelped running down the Peralta Trail through East Boulder Canyon. We had made it into the Superstitions alone, and discovered, as Henry David Thoreau wrote: "This was that Earth of which we have heard, made out of Chaos and Old Night."

Jones's Camp. "*There's something out in that mountain that drives men mad.*" The area encircling the Weavers Needle has figured prominently in the quest for the Peralta's Gold, Lost Dutchman's Gold, and Lost Jesuit Gold since the landmark appeared on the 1848 Peralta Map as *Negro, El Sombrero,* "Black, The Hat." On November 11, 1959, the long-standing Hatfield and McCoy-type shooting feud between the rival camps of African American opera singer Maria Celeste Jones and sixty-five-year-old Edgar "Ed" Piper came to a head at Jones's Camp below Piñon Camp. Claiming self defense when he was approached by Jones's pistol-brandishing young bodyguard, Robert St. Marie, Piper shot him in the stomach and watched him fall fifty feet from a cliff where, according to an *Ebony* magazine photograph, the newlywed lay dead curled in a fetal position far from his young wife. The Pinal County Sheriff cleared Piper of St. Marie's death. Several weeks later on November 25, 1959, Vernon Rowles was shot and killed by Ralph Thomas at Piper's Camp, situated in the flats below Jones's Camp.

Piñon Camp. Chiricahua Apache Camp. According to the deathbed account, elder Lydian Perrine told her grandson, Walter Perrine, that she was "a full blooded Chiricahua Apache, and was born near the base of Weaver's Needle in 1860," in what was the traditional homelands of the *Dilzhę'é,* Tonto band of Western Apache. The elder also confided to Walter, "she lived at the base of Weaver's Needle with a small band of Apaches, until she was around 10 years old." One day the Apaches reportedly showed the young girl what was later called the Cave of the Gold Bars. According to a treasure map drawn by a man named John Combs it was located on Black Top Mesa.

Mile 3 to Mile 6.2. Peralta Trail 102/Dutchman Trail 104 junction, Elevation: 2,300 feet, Hike from Piñon Camp to the end of the Peralta Trail. The hike from Piñon Camp is largely a downhill cruise through open eye-tugging scenery above East Boulder Creek the Chiricahua Apache may have trod beneath Upper Black Top Mesa Pass through the corridor formed by 2,933-foot Palomino Mountain on your left (west) and Black Top Mesa on your right (east). From this trail junction, you can camp, and return back to the Peralta Trailhead, hike any trail combination that entices you deeper into the mesmerizing terrain, or through-hike the Dutchman's Trail 4.5 miles to the First Water Trailhead. (See Page 212). Look for Aylor Arch below the ridge top. It was named for Chuck and Peg Aylor, who worked the Palomino 1 mining claim on Palomino Mountain and occupied Caballo Camp in East Boulder Canyon during the 1950s.

Cave of the Gold Bars. Think about the possibilities as you hike down the trail from Piñon Camp through East Boulder Canyon toward the Cave of the Gold Bars near the end of the Peralta Trail. It's right there around the east end of 3,354-foot Black Top Mesa beneath the Spanish petroglyph symbol of a rising sunburst over the Spanish word ORO, "gold." The stone symbols are anchored at the foot of a large sharp flint-shaped directional boulder spilt down the middle with a sunburst pecked across the face of it. (See Black Top Mesa page 218).

PERALTA TRAILHEAD HIKES AND TREKS

From the Peralta Trailhead there are many enticing loop hikes, journeys, and adventures that wind through canyons, mountains, pinnacles, and needles to fresh water springs and streams. Following are three of the most enticing treks and adventures that brought me, companion hikers, mountain runners, and client-prospectors back time and again: Needle Canyon/Weavers Needle, Miners Needle, and Coffee Flat Mountain/Reeds Water.

Needle Canyon/Weavers Needle
Landform
The 13.8-mile Barks/Needle Canyons and Peralta/East Boulder Canyons circuit courses through a twin canyon system that parallels Weavers Needle on the east and west and loops around the north side of Black Top Mesa. Since the time of Manuel Alejandro Peralta's 1753 map, *Cuento de Oro del Río Salado del Norte,* Erwin C. Ruth's 1913 Mexican Revolution era González-Peralta Maps, *Perfil Mapa* and *Mapa del Desierto,* Jacob Waltz's 1891 deathbed hints and clues, and treasure hunter Adolph Ruth's 1931 notes up to the present, this confined sector of mystifying needles, pinnacles, passes, canyons, caves, and dead ends has been the most heavily searched, prospected, and perhaps discovered area in the quarter-millennium-long quest to locate Peralta's Gold, Lost Dutchman's Gold, and Lost Jesuit Gold.

Trail Log
Mile 0 to Mile 2.1. Peralta Trailhead, Elevation: 2,420 feet. Hike from the Peralta Trailhead to the Terrapin Trail. From the Peralta Trailhead, hike the Bluff Spring Trail 235 north 2.1 miles through Barks Canyon to the Terrapin Trail 234 junction. Barks Canyon was named for New York born James E. Bark who bought the Quarter Circle U Ranch in 1891 and trekked north through this canyon with author and friend Sims Ely for what he believed was the Peralta's cache of gold hidden in the vicinity of 4,152-foot Bluff Spring Mountain.

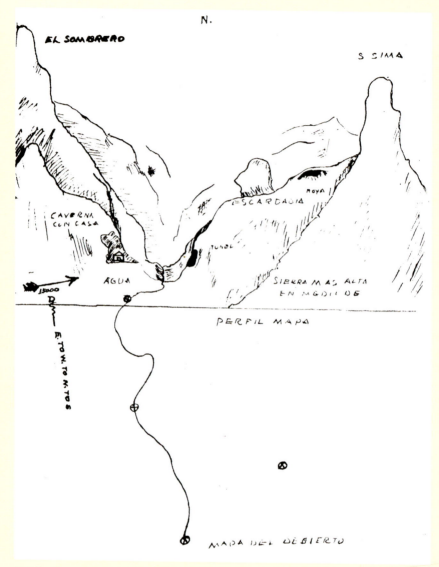

1913 González-Peralta Map, originally known as the Perfil Mapa, "Profile Map," and Mapa del Desierto, or "Map of the Desert." The mysterious Spanish landmarks on the crude map include: El Sombrero (The Hat), Caverna con Casa (Cave with House), Agua (Water), S[ur] Cima (South summit), Hoyo (Hole), Escardada (Hoed), Tunel, (Tunnel), and Sierra Mas Alta en Medio (Highest Range in Between). One of many considerations is the perspective: Is this the view from Bluff Saddle, Fremont Saddle, Black Top Mesa, or distant Red Mountain near the Verde River?

Mile 2.1 to Mile 4.9. Terrapin Trail 234 junction, Elevation: 3,150 feet. Hike from the Terrapin Trail to Dutchman Trail junction. Take the left (northwest) fork, and hike 2.8 miles over 3,420-foot Bluff Saddle into Needle Canyon beneath the eastern talus slopes of Weavers Needle. Hike over 3,189-foot Terrapin Pass through Needle Canyon to Upper Black Top Mesa Pass Trail. You can turn left (west) and hike one mile over the 2,710-foot Upper Black Top Mesa Pass to reach the Peralta Trail in East Boulder Canyon. It is 5.4 miles back to the Peralta Trailhead. Or you can stay on the Terrapin Trail and continue following it to the Dutchman Trail junction.

Between Here and There. This was the approximate location I horse-packed two New Jersey treasure hunters into Needle Canyon three years running. I'd pick them up at the Phoenix Sky Harbor International Airport, drive them to the trailhead, load their gear on stable horses, ride in and help them set up camp, and leave them to their guns and wanderings for three to five days. I suspected they were using a treasure map to survey Needle Canyon for landmarks that corresponded with their guesstimates of where they should look. But I never asked. It was none of my business.

Al Morrow's Camp. Prospector Alfred Erland Morrow was known to those he welcomed into his remote camp as the "Good Samaritan of Superstition Mountains." The lone prospector hand dug a hard rock tunnel unsupported by timber roof beams and searched for Spanish treasure in Needle Canyon. When he was visited by writer Ron Butler during a prospecting trip with artist Ettore "Ted" DeGrazia two weeks before Morrow would die, Butler wrote, "He showed us a Spanish mule shoe with a small clump of gold embedded in the bottom, proving, he said, the accuracy of his claim." Content in his desert camp that was his home for twenty years, the friendly Morrow never hit pay dirt and tragically died broke within view of Weavers Needle on November 9, 1970 when he was crushed by a boulder during a cave-in. It was a similar fate that befell Al Sieber, Chief of Scouts, working as an Apache crew leader on the Apache Trail in 1907.

Mile 4.9 to Mile 5.7. Dutchman Trail 104 junction, Elevation: 2,560 feet. From the Upper Black Top Mesa Pass Trail junction, continue hiking 0.8 miles north on the Terrapin Trail through Needle Canyon along the east slope of Black Top Mesa to Dutchman Trail 104. Along this stretch in Needle Canyon you can scan the steep slopes near the summit of Black Top Mesa and search for Walter Perrine's Cave of the Gold Bars and use Spanish clues I provided to locate your piece of the pie.

Mile 5.7 to Mile 7.2. Peralta Trail 102 junction, Elevation: 2,300 feet. From the Dutchman Trail junction, turn left (west) and hike 1.5 miles out of Needle Canyon over 2,790-foot Bull Pass down to the Peralta Trail 102 junction. It's a 6.2-mile hike through East Boulder and Peralta Canyons back to the Peralta Trailhead.

Miners Needle Trail

Landform

The 8.5-mile Miners Needle circuit courses across Barkley Basin and through Miners, Bluff Spring, and Barks Canyons that loop around Cathedral Rocks, Miners Needle, and Miners Summit. Miners Needle has sometimes been interpreted as the *S. Cima,* "south summit," that's drawn on the 1913 González-Peralta *Perfil Mapa,* "Profile Map."

Trail Log

Mile 0 to Mile 2.6. Peralta Trailhead, Elevation: 2,420 feet, Hike from the Peralta Trailhead to Miners Canyon. From the Peralta Trail hike the Dutchman Trail 104 north/northeast 2.6 miles across the northern bajadas of Barkley Basin beneath the 300-foot-high pinnacles of

Cathedral Rocks towering over the trail on left (north) en route to Miners Canyon and the Coffee Flat Trail junction.

Mile 2.6 to Mile 4.2. Miners Canyon, Elevation: 2,550 feet. Hike from Miners Canyon to Miners Summit Pass. Turn right (east), stay on the Dutchman Trail, and hike 1.6 miles up to Miners Summit Pass and the Whiskey Springs Trail junction.

Miners Needle. The peak that towers over one thousand feet above the trail junction in Miners Canyon is 3,648-foot Miners Needle. Some profess Miners Needle is a keystone, or keyhole, monument that was carved by Spanish miners to mark a trail leading to gold, or the hidden cave that may have held a cache of gold—look closely!—on the southeast side of the Miners Needle beneath the "eye." The trail to gold conceivably led James Bark up this trail to an alcove above Bluff Springs, where according to Sims Ely's popular 1953 book, *The Lost Dutchman Mine: The Fabulous Story of the Seven-Decade Search for the Hidden Treasure*, Bark discovered ". . . were stored several hundred sandals, of the sort worn by Mexicans."

Mile 4.2 to Mile 5.4. Miners Summit Pass, Elevation: 3,270 feet. Hike from Miners Summit to Crystal Spring. Turn left (north), stay on the Dutchman Trail and hike 1.2 miles along the east side of 3,516-foot Miners Summit to Crystal Spring and the Bluff Spring Trail junction.

Mile 5.4 to Mile 6.4. Crystal Spring, Elevation: 3,040 feet. Hike from Crystal Spring to Barks Canyon. Turn left (west), stay on the Bluff Spring Trail and hike one mile to Barks Canyon and the Terrapin Trail junction. About 0.3 miles before the trail junction look to your right (north) and a secondary trail leads to the Williams Camp mine site that operated between 1938 and 1946 and was reportedly worked by a dozen miners sheltered in six cabins on the south end of Bluff Springs Mountain.

~Williams Camp. From the old mine site you can see Weavers Needle 1.5 miles northwest. The camp may or may not have been named after forty-one-year-old World War I veteran and prospector, Charles Williams, who went missing in the Superstition Mountains during the 1930s. After four days, most figured Williams had given up the ghost, but he staggered out to the Apache Trail and the depression-era newspapers were eager to share his story of newfound wealth discovered in a cave of gold nuggets.

The page 1 Extra on the January 4, 1935, *Arizona Republic* headlined: WILLIAMS ESCAPES SUPERSTITIONS, APPEARS, WEAK, HAPPY, WITH GOLD, "Vet Defeats Mystic Curse of Mountain."

And did Williams have a tale to tell the *Arizona Republic*: "I was following the clues of an old map I had in some of the roughest terrain in the Superstition range when I became disoriented and lost my way. I came up over a ridge and in the distance I saw a small cave near the base of a pointed peak [Miners Needle cave?]. Tired and in need of rest I made my way toward the cave. Once inside the cave I cleared a spot to rest and this is when I discovered the floor of the cave was covered with gold nuggets, some of them as big as walnuts."

Mile 6.4 to Mile 8.5. Barks Canyon, Elevation: 3,150 feet. Hike from Barks Canyon to the Peralta Trailhead. Turn left (south) stay on the Bluff Spring Trail and hike 2.1 miles down Barks Canyon to the Peralta Trailhead.

Coffee Flat Mountain Trail
Landform

The 18.4-mile Coffee Flat Mountain circuit courses through Whiskey Springs, Upper La Barge, Red Tanks, and Randolph Canyons that loop around Picacho Butte and Coffee Flat Mountain to Reeds Water and beyond. Apart from the sweltering heat I sometimes encountered while crossing Barkley Basin during late spring, this largely shaded well-watered route was my favorite mountain run through the wilderness that offered beauty, solitude, hanging canyons, and slick rock footing. This precise route was reportedly traveled on foot many times in 1894 by a prospector named Wagoneer who discovered a hidden lode of rose quartz gold that became known by those who tried unsuccessfully to rediscover it as "Wagoner's Lost Ledge."

Trail Log

Mile 0 to Mile 2.6. Peralta Trailhead, Elevation: 2,420 feet. From the Peralta Trailhead hike the Dutchman Trail 104 east 2.6 miles across Barkley Basin to Miners Canyon and the Coffee Flat Trail junction.

Mile 2.6 to Mile 4.2. Miners Canyon, Elevation: 2,550 feet. From Miners Canyon hike the Dutchman Trail 1.6 miles to Miners Summit and the Whiskey Springs Trail junction.

Mile 4.2 to Mile 6.1. Miners Summit Pass, Elevation: 3,270 feet. Hike from Miners summit to La Barge Canyon. Turn right (east) on the Whiskey Springs Trail 238 and hike 1.9 miles through Whiskey Springs Canyon to La Barge Canyon and the Red Tanks Trail junction. According to *Arizona Place Names*, La Barge Canyon was named after Canadian-born prospector John LeBarge who was reported to be a companion of Jacob Waltz in 1890.

Moonshine Springs. Six miles is a long way for most folks to walk for a cool drink of spring water. Evidently not for Prohibition era moonshiners who built a timber, copper, and galvanized iron, one hundred gallon-capacity still at Whiskey Springs and other canyon springs presumably hidden from the long arm of Prohibition Agents. The roaring fire-fed furnace distilled forty gallons of moonshine a day (two hundred gallons a week) from sugar, grain, yeast, and pappy's secret additive. Once the white lightning was packed out on burros, the hooch sold for $10 a gallon at local speakeasies. According to the Sunday, May 25, 1924 *Arizona Republic,* the "Prohis" who made the nighttime Whiskey Springs bust reported, "The seizure was carried on long poles held between the agents for several miles . . . Difficulty of the hauls was demonstrated by the fact that burros were found at the first still and were used by the agents to transport the seizures to the cars of the officers . . . and [the suspects] were locked in the county jail last night." Imagine sneaking six miles across this country in the dark to get the drop on armed moonshiners who'd been "product field testing" for who knew how long. For some time, what remained of the Tennessee hills-style still was packed out and put on display at the Blue Bird Mine Curio Shop on the Apache Trail.

Whiskey Springs Canyon. During a routine training flight from Glendale, Arizona's Thunderbird Field on February 21, 1942, a Royal Canadian Air Force pilot and student crash-landed their Waco-Ryan PT-6 trainer in Whiskey Springs Canyon. How they managed to thread the cliffs, canyon, and saguaro cactus in a twenty-eight-foot span, fixed-wing aircraft is not known. Nor was it disclosed who at the Army Air Force Training Command signed off on their flight plan. Why were the unidentified allied pilots flying over the Superstition Mountains where there were scant strips of level ground to land in case of an emergency? Was it to one-up the American, British, and Chinese pilots who were also training at Thunderbird Field that was built with $1 million ponied-up from Hollywood investors and actors Jimmy Stewart, Cary Grant, Henry Fonda, and Ginger Rogers? Were they itching to become movie stunt pilots? Or was it just plain old gold fever? Incredibly, the pair survived and managed to hike six and a half miles out to the Quarter Circle U Ranch.

Mile 6.1 to Mile 7.5. La Barge Canyon, Elevation: 2,820 feet. Hike from La Barge Canyon to Upper La Barge Box. Turn right (northeast) on the Red Tanks Trail 107 and hike 1.4 miles through Upper La Barge Box Canyon past beautiful pools of seasonal water beneath the flanks of 4,294-foot Picacho Butte on your right (south) and 4,018-foot Herman Mountain on your left (north) and the Red Tanks Trail junction.

    Chuning's Cave. Fifty-four-year-old Silver King miner John Chuning reportedly lived in a cave in Lower La Barge Box Canyon between 1898 and 1904. He spent the rest of his life searching for a lost mine that had yielded to his friend, Joseph Deering, four pounds of rich gold ore that Deering had showed Chuning before he was killed in a cave-in at the Silver King Mine.

    Herman's Cave. Look for Herman's Cave in Upper La Barge Box Canyon on the left (north) high above that's marked by an odd-looking pinnacle. The area was worked by the pioneer German American prospector Herman Petrasch. Herman's brother Rhinehart and Jacob Waltz's friend Julia Thomas were privy to the Dutchman's coveted deathbed clues and directions. Go take a look and see what you can see or find—if you're prepared for the journey.

    Mile 7.5 to Mile 11.7. Upper La Barge Box, Elevation: 3,215 feet. Hike from Upper La Barge Box to Dripping Springs. Turn right (southeast), stay on the Red Tanks Trail and visit or hike past the turnoff on right (west) to La Barge Spring No. 2, located beneath the flanks of 4,621-foot Coffee Flat Mountain. Climb over the 3,690-foot Red Tanks Divide, and continue hiking 4.2 miles through Red Tanks Canyon to Dripping Springs.

    Mile 11.7 to Mile 13.7. Dripping Springs, Elevation: 2,740 feet, located beneath the confluence of Red Tanks, Fraser, and Randolph Canyons. Hike from Dripping Springs to Reeds Water. Turn right (southwest), stay on the Red Tanks Trail and hike 2 two miles through Randolph Canyon to Reeds Water and the Coffee Flat Trail junction. According to *Arizona Place Names*, Randolph Canyon was named after Colonel Epes Randolph, vice president of the Southern Pacific Railroad.

Mile 13.7 to Mile 15.8. Reeds Water Windmill, Elevation: 2,470 feet, located on the north fork of Whitlow Canyon, a stage station run by early cattleman Charles Whitlow who herded thirsty beeves in the canyon. The creaky singing windmill echoing through your camp at night is at times eerie, evoking every haunted legend emanating from the Mystery Mountains. Hike from Reeds Water to Miners Canyon. Turn left (west) on the Coffee Flat Trail 108 and hike 2.1 miles to Miners Canyon and the Dutchman Trail junction.

Wagoner's Lost Ledge. According to author John Dahlmann's 1979 book, *A Tiny Bit of God's Creation,* illustrated by Superstition prospector and artist Ettore "Ted" DeGrazia, freighters and stagecoaches once traveled to Whitlow Ranch, then up rugged storm-swept Randolph and Fraser Canyons. A mysterious stranger stepped off the Pinal-Mescal stagecoach one day in 1894 carrying a bedroll and a suitcase full of grub, hiked the route you've nearly completed, and worked a vein of gold beyond imagination. During an earlier prospecting adventure grubstaked by Pinal miners, Wagoner ran out of food north of the Salt River, hiked south cross country from Tortilla Flat, and walked day and night headed for the trail he knew down Red Tanks Canyon that would take him to the stage stop at Whitlow Ranch. Caught by nightfall, Wagoner bivouacked and at daybreak he made his remarkable discovery. As author Barry Storm wrote in the February 1945 issue of *Desert Magazine:*

> He started down over the broken hills to the east of Miner's Needle [Picacho Butte] and within the hour stumbled upon a rose quartz vein outcropping on a southern slope. Knocking off a few pieces with his prospector's pick, he found the pinkish, glassy rock to be literally studded with bright yellow gold. Here were all his dreams come true—freedom from want and worry, from having to beg strangers for grubstakes, and freedom to pursue his

easy-going, nomadic life . . . And breaking off a few pounds of the bonanza rock to put in his suitcase, he went on into Pinal." Pinal miners tried to follow Wagoner on his repeated cross-country journeys to Picacho Butte. Like a veteran border smuggler, Wagoner waited, watched, and then disappeared, dragging a burlap sack behind him to brush out his tracks. He hand-cobbled so much gold, he needed to carry two new suitcases that stagecoach driver Fred Mullins sometimes had a difficult time hoisting up to the luggage rack. To prove the suitcases' contents, Wagoner said, "Look and see. This is my last trip anyway." And Mullins opened

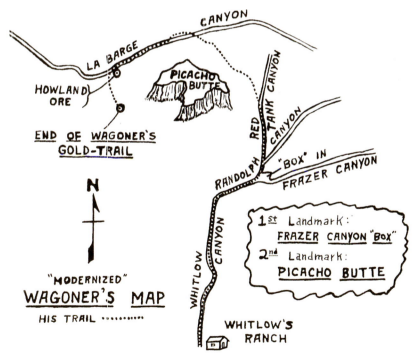

Wagoner's 1894 Lost Ledge Treasure Map." Original map drawn by Barry Storm. *Courtesy: Desert Magazine,* February 24, 1945.

one of the bags to find it stuffed with hand-picked gold ore of the highest grade—bonanza rock!" Then Wagoner vanished, but not before drawing a map for his confidant, Mullins, to pay for the free passages he'd provided when he was broke. Then pffft! Gone. Without a trace. You can search for the Wagoner Map "Modernized," and follow your hunches in and around Picacho Butte for the 'lost ledge'.

Mile 15.8 to Mile 18.4. Miners Canyon, Elevation: 2,550 feet. Hike from Miners Canyon to the Peralta Trailhead. Turn left (southwest) on the Dutchman Trail 104 and hike 2.6 miles across Barkley Basin to the Peralta Trailhead.

A Sonoran Desert sunset promises a new day for adventurers and treasure hunters following their dreams through the Superstition Mountains. Copyright © John Annerino Photography.

12

Superstition Mountains Transect

"There are other treasures than gold in the desert for those with eyes to see and soul to feel, delicate vistas of stark beauty, enchanting scenes ever new. Silent but somehow eloquent, nature's own song stills the noise of man."

—Barry Storm, prospector and adventurer, 1945

LANDFORM

The J. F. Trail follows a panoramic divide that traverses the heart of the Superstition Mountains from south to north. On the east/northeast loom the wilderness' high seldom-traveled wooded mountains that include 5,557-foot Montana Mountain, 6,056-foot Iron Mountain, 6,100-foot White Mountain, and 6,266-foot Mound Mountain. On the west/southwest a seemingly perplex labyrinth of deep canyons drain the divide and the hardscrabble country of 4,621-foot Coffee Flat Mountain, 5,077-foot La Barge Mountain, 4,066-foot Horse Ridge, and 3,765-foot Peters Mesa. Taken alone, this boundary-to-boundary Superstition Mountains transect is one of the shortest—if you limit your crossing to the J. F. Trail. However, if you include the rugged four-wheel drive roads that extend in both directions, it is one of the Superstition Mountains' longest point-to-point through-hikes. In either case, this is a remote, infrequently traveled trail where the consequences of being unprepared or exercising poor judgment can prove serious.

HISTORICAL OVERVIEW

Like much of the Superstition Mountains, the area's cultural history is associated with the ancient Salado and Mogollon peoples, and more recently the Western Apache and Northeastern Yavapai. You may recall that Iron Mountain was the site of a Yavapai encampment who dwelled among its tablelands for five years before they were attacked by the Pima in 1871. At least thirty Yavapai were killed and sixteen children were kidnapped then forced to walk from their mountain redoubt across the brutal Sonoran Desert to Blackwater. Among them was *Wassaja,* Carlos Montezuma, who was adopted by pioneer Italian photographer Carlo Gentile.

Trouble in Paradise

Six-year-old Carlos Montezuma was fortunate to have escaped the depredations of the eastern Superstition Mountains. In 1892, a thirteen-year-old boy named Charlie Dobie was in the wrong place at the wrong time when he was killed at the J. F. Ranch. Established as a line camp by pioneer cattleman John J. "Jack" Fraser, the ranch was ideally located in a shaded grove of cottonwood trees fed by a rare perennial Sonoran Desert stream that flowed through Fraser Canyon. "Who Murdered Charlie Dobie, KILLED BY PERSONS UNKNOWN," read the page 1 Sunday, June 5, 1892 *Arizona Republic* headline. Indeed, who would shoot the likeable young man in the back who was visiting Jack Fraser's ranch to help with the late spring cattle roundup while his father toiled away "making little rocks out of big ones" at the nearby Silver King Mine. Answering their own headline, the *Arizona Republic* report immediately suspected it "Looked Like Indian Work . . . Apache Indians . . . red men . . . the "[Apache] Kid" . . ." Studying the pages of history, it appeared to be another Superstition Mountains unsolved, case-closed murder mystery. When Frazer, Jim Thomas, and P. R. Young reportedly returned to the ranch at 4 the next morning, the ranch house had been pillaged and ransacked, and Dobie's body was found outside the house fifty yards away. The grim details of young Dobie's injuries need no repeating here, except to underscore that he was reportedly shot in the back with a lever action 44-40 Winchester rifle, the "wound was not one that would have proven fatal," and he was hit in the head with a rock. The reporting sounds suspect. Modern hunters report shooting deer with the 44-40 Winchester rifle's 217-grain bullets at "distances from one to two hundred yards and in every instance, the bullet passed clean through the body." Unless the bullet just grazed Dobie, the hemorrhaging would

Eleven-year-old Santiago (Jimmy) McKinn was abducted by Geronimo and raised as a Chiricahua Apache until he reluctantly returned to his parents, March 27, 1886, Camilius Sidney Fly photographic print, Courtesy: Library of Congress.

have proven fatal within the hour, according to frontier surgeons who operated on such wounds.

The crime scene observations raised two other questions. Why would the "Indians" kill the young man? As demonstrated by the Pima's 1871 attack on Iron Mountain, they made considerable effort to march the kidnapped children out of the mountains to sell them as slaves, not kill them. Events also suggest the Apache would not have killed Dobie, either. When the Chiricahua Apache warrior Chato and his party attacked the wagon of Judge H. C. McComas and his wife Juanita in New Mexico and shot and killed them on March 27, 1883, they tracked down their six-year-old son Charlie McComas and raised him as one of their own. Secondly, if the Apache had attacked Charlie Dobie they wouldn't have missed the shot at close range with a Winchester rifle that, throughout the Apache Wars, had proven to be a deadly extension of their honed vision.

Was there another suspect? The *Arizona Republic* news account suggested John M. See, who had proven to be a bad man, was also a suspect in killing Charlie Dobie to "conceal his identity" and to delay the search of the three-mile long getaway tracks after robbing the house and stealing Jack Fraser's horse, saddle and bridle. According to the May 21, 1892 edition of the *Arizona Silverbelt* newspaper, on the evening of May 18, John M. See "shot and killed his wife at William Gann's Ranch on Spring Creek, six miles from Salt River in Gila County." Mrs. Anne See had reportedly left her husband, "owing to his profligate habits, his association with vicious characters, and for abusive treatment and failure to provide for her and her child." Why wasn't See in a perp walk straight to a hanging tree outside the Tunnel Saloon near the new Pinal County Courthouse? The *Arizona Republic* reported: "The verdict arrived at was that Charlie Dobie was killed by persons unknown, but believed to be Apache Indians."

Directions

From US Highway 60, drive twenty miles to the Queen Valley Road turn-off. Turn left (north) and drive the paved road two miles to the Hewitt Station Road 357 junction. Turn right (northeast) and drive the gravel road three miles to the J. F. Road 172 junction. Turn left (northeast) and drive up the four-wheel drive Hewitt Canyon road beneath 3,110-foot Robles Butte on right (east) and continue 9.3 miles through the scenic, frequently flashflood-swept canyon along the east slopes of 4,230-foot Hackberry Butte on left (west) to the trailhead for the J. F. Trail 106 and Woodbury Trail 114. **Warning:** Beware of seasonal flashfloods in Queen Creek and Hewitt Canyon. Use common sense and four-wheel drive.

Map

Iron Mountain and Weavers Needle 7.5 minute Quadrangles

Trail Log

Note: I ran this 21.3-mile Superstition Mountains transect from Queen Creek Station north to the Apache Trail during a month-long journey run from Mexico to Utah. I have not included the 9.3-mile Hewitt Canyon four-wheel drive section to the Woodbury Trailhead in this mileage log.

Mile 0 to Mile 0.6. Woodbury Trailhead, Elevation: 3,480 feet. Hike the J. F. Trail 106 north 0.6 miles to the Woodbury Trail Junction.

Mile 0.6 to Mile 3.1. Woodbury Trail Junction 114, Elevation: 3,475 feet. Hike 2.5 miles from the Woodbury Trail junction to Tortilla Pass. From the Woodbury Trail junction, hike the J. F. Trail 106 through Randolph Canyon before you begin the steep 980-vertical-foot climb beneath 5,077-foot La Barge Mountain on left (west) to Tortilla Pass and the Rogers Canyon Trail junction.

The Mysterious Woodbury Brothers. What little is known about the Woodburys is listed in the "The Mining Summary" in the March 22, 1919 *Mining and Scientific Press:* "The Maverick group of 20 claims in the Superstition mountains, owned by the Woodbury brothers, have been sold to the Pillsbury interests for a consideration said to be $100,000. The property [in Rogers Canyon] is to be churn-drilled." That buys a lot of skillet-grilled pancakes and Dutch oven-cooked bran muffins.

Mile 3.1 to Mile 8.3. Tortilla Pass, Elevation: 4,450 feet. Turn left (northwest), stay on the J. F. Trail and hike 5.2 miles northwest across the panoramic serpentine highline divide that separates the west and east sections of the Superstition Wilderness to the Hoolie Bacon Trail junction.

The Military Trail? Some "Dutch Hunters," as Lost Dutchman Gold seekers often call themselves, profess the J. F. Trail was one of the old military trails that was mapped and noted by Captain John Gregory Bourke during the US Army campaign against the Apache under General George Crook. Using one of Jacob Waltz's deathbed clues with Bourke's maps and notes from his book, *On the Border with Crook,* some Dutch Hunters postulate the Lost Dutchman Gold is located in the eastern Superstition Mountains within riding distance of the J. F. Trail. On March 3, 1873, Bourke and his party conceivably rode horseback on what's also been called the Old Horse Trail through the piñon, juniper, swaying century plant stalks, and high prickly pear cactus grasslands, and camped at Tortilla Ranch: "From my mine," Waltz whispered from his deathbed, "I could see the soldiers on the Old Military Trail, but they could not see me." Others profess the Military Trail passed through First Water within view of Weavers Needle.

Mile 8.1 to Mile 8.9. Hoolie Bacon Trail junction, Elevation: 3,410 feet. Turn right (north), stay on the J. F. Trail and hike 0.8 miles to the remote Tortilla Trailhead.

Mile 8.9 to Mile 12. Tortilla Trailhead, Elevation: 3,130 feet. If you've driven your high clearance four-wheel drive vehicle up the rock steps to reach this Tortilla Trailhead, this is the end of the trail. If not, hike the four-wheel drive Road 213 northwest 3.3 Miles to the two-wheel drive parking lot off the Apache Trail, Highway 88, at Elevation: BM 2882.

Vehicle Shuttle: Plan on a sixty-mile vehicle shuttle one way between the Woodbury Trailhead and the Tortilla Trailhead.

Tortilla Trailhead Directions. From Apache Junction, drive northeast twenty-three to the Tortilla Road 213 junction. Turn right (south) and two-wheel drive parking is available here. If you have a high clearance four-wheel drive, you can crawl up this track 3.3 miles to the Tortilla Trailhead and access the J. F. Trail 106, Peters Trial 105, and Hoolie Bacon Trail 111.

No single image verifies what Jacob Waltz looked like, and many old photos, sketches, and paintings hint at his appearance. This old prospector came closest to my impression of what the Dutchman may have looked like. Copyright © John Annerino Photography.

13

The Dutchman's Trails

"She is the most beautiful mountain in the whole world. The more you see her, the more attractive and magnificent she will become. Soon you will succumb to her, and she will possess you completely. Then she will own you, because your thoughts will always be with her and you will want to be close to her."

—Ettore "Ted" DeGrazia,
His Mountain, The Superstition (1972)

LANDFORM

Named after Jacob Waltz, the Dutchman's trail once linked his Phoenix homestead—and on at least one occasion Fort McDowell—with the stony First Water Creek gateway on the northern end of Superstition Mountain. The rough route-turned-trail traversed scenic passes and wound through captivating stream-fed canyons east, then southeast, beneath 4,041-foot Bluff Springs Mountain. At one point, only the Dutchman could say, his trail meandered around a great stone needle back to his southern passage to the Board House at what later became known as the Bark Ranch (Quarter Circle U Ranch).

HISTORICAL OVERVIEW

The myriad trails that led in many directions through the Superstition Mountains were first used by ancestral Hohokam and Salado peoples, and later by the Pima, Southeastern Yavapai, and Western Apache. Ore-laden caravans of Spanish miners and mules followed the incipient paths that became more defined by pioneers, prospectors and cattlemen who were at times safe-guarded by US Troops from the 1st Arizona Volunteers, California Volunteers, and the US Army under General George Crook.

First Water Ranch Trail

The trailhead was named after First Water Ranch, one of three ranches that included the Three R's and Quarter Circle U Ranches and were used by pioneer cattleman William Augustus "Tex" Barkley. The outpost ranches supported Barkley's outfit, the Barkley Cattle Company, which held grazing rights to run cattle throughout the Superstition Mountains until his death in 1955. The Tennessee-born cowboy, stockman, and gold hunter played a pivotal role in the search along the Dutchman's trails for missing treasure hunter Adolph Ruth in 1931. (See page 24)

El Viejo's Wild Bunch Trail

Locked and loaded, brandishing Winchester lever-action carbines and cartridge-filled bandoliers, artist Etorre "Ted" DeGrazia (right) and Oscar-winning friend Broderick Crawford ride through "the roughest, rockiest, most treacherous terrain in the United States" in search of Lost Jesuit Gold. Courtesy: DeGrazia Gallery in the Sun. © All Rights Reserved

The year was 1988, and the posse in search of adventure and "Spanish gold, Apache gold, and silver artifacts from Spanish missionaries," might have ridden straight out of Sam Peckinpah's *The Wild Bunch,* a blazing, shoot-anything-that-moves, leave-no-man-behind silver screen saga of aging outlaws on the run in Old Mexico during the Mexican Revolution. The epic starred William Holden (Pike Bishop), Ernest Borgnine (Dutch Engstrom), Robert Ryan (Deke Thorton), Edmund O'Brien (Freddie Sykes), Warren Oates (Lyle Gorch), and "That's very smart for you damn gringos," Jaime Sánchez (Angel).

Back in his day, the real life lineup included the salt-and-pepper bearded gun-toting leader and artist Ettore "Ted" DeGrazia, also called "El Viejo," who wore a sweat-stained short-brimmed rumpled white cowboy hat, brandished a lever action Winchester rifle with a bandolier slung across his shoulder, and sipped Chivas Regal when he hosted buddies, Oscar-winning best actors Lee Marvin (*Cat Ballou*) and Broderick Crawford (*All the King's Men*) at his Gallery in the Sun. Riding shotgun for El Viejo and his eight-horse and mule pack outfit was Papago tracker Tom "El Indio" Franco, loaded leather bandoliers crisscrossing his dark bare chest Pancho Villa style, and his weathered lever action Winchester rifle ready to draw down on the first snake or two-legged varmint that rattled in the brush. There was DeGrazia's friend Gene "Shorty" Thorn whose parents aptly named him at birth for the giant saguaro cactus forests and prickly pear thickets that lined the trails El Viejo's outfit rode through, and tough-but-aging, knife-wielding, Spanish-speaking Don Vincente Garzas. Leading the pack string was trail guide Bill Crador and wranglers leather-faced, too-tall Slim Fogel and toothless tobacco-chewing Jeff Beal, followed by native Yaqui flute player, Bernadino Valencia, and New York "New York City!" writer, Ron Butler, nicknamed "City Slicker." The only items missing from *The Wild Bunch's* battlefield bloodbath checklist against tequila-soaked

General Mapache (Emilio "El Indio" Fernández Romo) for El Viejo's party were wooden kegs of dynamite, a water-cooled 30-06 Browning M1917 machine gun, sixteen cases of 30-06 Springfield rifles, a wagon load of ammunition, and sacks of worthless metal washers that had been mistakenly stolen as payroll gold. El Viejo's outfit rode east along a trail that twisted like as Blacktail rattlesnake and braved the hot dusty blood-stained canyons where hundreds of souls had already perished on the trail of the Dutchman's Gold in what Butler later wrote was "one of the roughest, rockiest, most treacherous terrain in the United States." Saddle up, or lace up your boots, and follow El Viejo's 'Wild Bunch Trail' through the labyrinth of cliffs to Charlebois Springs and beyond to wherever your lust for gold or quest for adventure takes you.

Directions

From Apache Junction, drive 5.5 miles northeast on the Apache Trail, Highway 88, to the signed turnoff on right (northeast) to First Water. Turn right on Road FS 78 and drive 2.5 miles to the First Water Trailhead that provides access to the Dutchmans Trail 104 and Second Water Trail 236.

Maps

Goldfield and Weavers Needle 7.5-minute Quadrangles

Note: Shortly after turning off the Apache Trail, you'll pass the new Massacre Grounds Trailhead located at Mile 0.5 on the right (southeast). See Massacre Grounds Hike at the end of this chapter.

Grand Enchantment Trail

"The Grand Enchantment Trail: 770 Miles Across the American Southwest" links Phoenix, Arizona with Albuquerque, New Mexico by crossing the Sonoran and Chihuahua Deserts, the Continental Divide, and all the wild, rugged, and scenic mountains, rivers, and streams in between. Reportedly "much more primitive in character and more challenging to navigate" than the Appalachian Trail, in brief the segments are broken down as follows: 425 miles of foot trails, eighty-five miles of cross-country orienteering, 145 miles of four-wheel drive dirt roads, eighty-five miles of two-wheel drive dirt roads, and thirty miles of paved roads.

Superstition Enchantment Route

Conceived in 2003, the western leg of the Grand Enchantment Trail starts at the First Water Trailhead and traverses 30.3 miles of the Superstition Wilderness, tracing the Lost Dutchman Trail to Charlebois Spring and beyond to Rogers Trough Trailhead. Visit: Grand Enchantment Trail. www.simblissity.net/get-home.shtml

Dutchman Trail Log

Mile 0 to Mile 0.3. First Water Trailhead, Elevation: 2,970 feet. Hike 0.3 miles to the junction of the Dutchman Trail 104 and Second Water Trail 236.

At a Glance: Second Water Trail

Second Water Trail 236 leads 1.5 miles across Garden Valley to the Black Mesa Trail 241: Turn right (southeast) and it's three miles across 2,850-foot Black Mesa to the Dutchman Trail 104 loop back to the First Water Trailhead. Turn left (north) on the Second Water Trail and it's 1.7 miles beneath 2,785 foot Hackberry Mesa on left (northwest) to the junction of the Boulder Canyon Trail 103 near 2,797-foot Battleship Mountain. The Boulder Canyon Trail leads 3.2 miles south through Boulder Canyon to the Dutchman Trail 104 loop back to the First Water Trailhead, or 3.8 Miles north within view of 3,363-foot Geronimos Head on right (east) to the Boulder Canyon (Canyon Lake) Trailhead.

Boulder Canyon Trailhead Directions. From Apache Junction, drive 14.4 miles northeast on the Apache Trail to the signed Boulder Canyon Trailhead 103 located on the right (southeast) side of the road.

Second Water, The Dutchmans Trail?

Second Water was a descriptive name for the next spring Jacob Waltz, miners, and cattlemen used after First Water during their travels through the western Superstitions. It was also a vague milepost the Dutchman whispered about on his Phoenix deathbed on October 25, 1891 to locate his mine: "Go to First Water, then to Second Water—then take the Old Government Trail [Calvary Trail 239 ?] to San Carlos—where the trail turns south—you will see—over the point of the ridge—a rock—standing in the brush—it looks like a man!"

Route Described: Dutchman Trail 104

Mile 0.3 to Mile 2.6. Dutchman Trail/Second Water Trail junction, Elevation: 2,360 feet. From the trail junction The Dutchman Trail traces First Water Creek and crosses and recrosses the desert creek six times and winds through wonderful rock formation 2.3 miles to Parker Pass.

Mile 2.6 to Mile 3.9. Parker Pass, Elevation 2,670 feet. From Parker Pass hike 1.3 miles east to the Black Mesa Trail 241 junction.

~West Boulder Canyon. From Parker Pass, a secondary spur trail leads 0.8 miles right (southeast) into O'Grady Canyon and over Tims Saddle to West Boulder Canyon. You might find it easier and more convenient to hike east off Parker Pass approximately 0.7 miles to the confluence of West Boulder Canyon and Old West Boulder Canyon on the right (south) to start a West Boulder Canyon trek to Willow Spring. Depending on your line of travel it's approximately 3.5 miles, and a 500-vertical-foot hike, scramble, and bushwhack to follow the elusive trail of treasure hunter Adolph Ruth to 2,820-foot Willow Spring. Willow Spring was Ruth's first and last known camp before he was murdered, or perished, during his fateful search for the Lost Dutchman's Gold when he went missing on June 14, 1931. (See Ghost Trail page 24).

O'Grady Canyon and Tims Saddle were reportedly named after an "old white bearded prospector" "Rattlesnake" Tim O'Grady," who prospected the Superstition Mountains between First Water and Charlebois Spring from 1945 until 1980. *Source:* Tom K., DesertUSA.

Mile 3.9 to Mile 4. Black Mesa Trail 241 junction, Elevation feet 2,260. Hike 0.2 miles to the Peralta Trail junction. The Black Mesa Trail is the first of three closely-grouped trail junctions. Turn left (northwest) and the Black Mesa Trail leads three miles northwest over Black Mesa to the Second Water Trail. One tenth of a mile east of the Black Mesa Trail junction, the Boulder Trail leads 3.2 miles north through Boulder Creek beneath 3,061-foot Yellow Peak to the Second Water Trail.

Mile 4.2 to Mile 5.7. Peralta Trail 102 junction, Elevation 2,300 feet. Hike 1.5 miles to the Terrapin Trail junction. Turn right (southeast) and the Peralta Trail leads 6.2 miles southeast through East Boulder and Peralta Canyons to the Peralta Canyon Trailhead.

A mystifying petroglyph on Black Top Mesa bears the same symbol as those etched in stone at Charlebois Spring. Copyright © John Annerino Photography

(See Peralta Trail page 181). From the Peralta Trail Junction, it's a 500 vertical foot climb to 2,790-foot Bull Pass.

Black Top Mesa

From Bull Pass a rough use trail climbs 564 vertical feet and leads cross country through black boulders to the mystifying panorama of 3,354-foot Black Top Mesa that includes legendary landmarks drawn on Spanish, historic, and contemporary treasure maps, hidden tunnels, and the Cave of the Gold Bars. (See page 83).

   Mile 5.7 to Mile 6.1. Terrapin Trail 234 junction, Elevation 2,480 feet. Stay on the Dutchman Trail and hike 0.4 miles to Marsh Valley. Turn right (south) and the Terrapin Trail leads through Needle Canyon beneath landmark Weavers Needle on right (west) and Bluff Springs Mountain on left (east) over Bluff Saddle through Barks Canyon to the Peralta Trailhead. (See page 181).

Lost Jesuit Gold

When El Viejo, Ted DeGrazia, visited Al Morrow in Needle Canyon during their prospecting expedition two weeks before Morrow died from a cave-in at his mine, Morrow was dressed as usual in a ball camp, light jacket, and long trousers that hung from his thin frame. Expedition writer, Ron Butler, wrote: "We visited Al Morrow, an old grubsteak prospector with skin as pale and powdery white as his clothes." It was rumored that Morrow was searching for Lost Jesuit Gold, which many had scoffed at and declared never existed. (See page 50). But sixty-six-year-old assayer Lee Boyer told *Arizona Republic* reporter Mary Leonhard in 1965 of one find that corresponded with the gold nugget in the Spanish mule shoe Morrow had discovered. Boyer said it was "a Bible that the Smithsonian Institution has confirmed is a Jesuit Bible and a pair of conquistador spurs made in Mexico. A Smithsonian curator offered me $150,000 for the spurs and I laughed at him."

Mile 6.1 to Mile 7.5. Marsh Valley, Elevation: 2,360 feet. Stay on the Dutchman's Trail and hike 1.4 miles to Charlebois Spring.

Garzas Gold. El Viejo's expedition pressed on slowly, riding haggard horses that were as sure-footed as desert bighorns two to three miles an hour in the "Arizona heat. The relentless, dry heat of pottery kilns," until they reached the cool cottonwood tree-shaded oasis of White Rock Spring in Marsh Valley at the foot of 3,648-foot Black Mountain. Somewhere in Marsh Valley keen-eyed Vincente Garzas, who'd lost his eye glasses the day before, discovered sixty to seventy pounds of rich ore. El Viejo's outfit hauled the load back to camp, crushed the rocks, and watched Garzas grind them with a mortar and pestle for two days straight until he produced two ounces of gold. In 1988, the spot gold prices hovered around $410.00 an ounce! Not far from Garzas's lode, missing treasure hunter Adolph Ruth's skull was discovered on December 10, 1931. Unsubstantiated accounts tell of Peralta miners racing horses 110 yards across Marsh Valley on what cowboys later called the "Spanish Racetrack." Still popular in the sierras of rural Sonora, Mexico, it's called *carrera de caballos,* "horse racing." Where the story goes off the rails and spirals like campfire smoke into the dark heavens is the account of Joaquin Murrieta joining the racing and mescal-fueled gambling and festivities.

Joaquin Murrieta and the Spanish Racetrack

The inspiration for the 2005 movie, *The Legend of Zorro,* (starring Antonio Banderas, Catherine Zeta Jones, and the best horseback stuntmen seen on film at the time), Joaquin Murrieta Carrillo became, some insist, a Mexican "Robin Hood" after his wife, Rosa Feliz from the silver mining town of Vayoreca, Sonora, Mexico, was brutally murdered and Murrieta was tied to a tree and horsewhipped by Anglo miners in the Mother Lode Country of California's Sierra Nevada Mountains. On the run with his sidekick Manuel "Three Finger Jack" García, avenging dark angel Murrieta hunted down the five miners who violated and killed his wife and became a legendary horse thief, and some profess he was a cold-blooded killer who rode the length of California, sometimes returning to his place of birth in Trincheras, Sonora. In the quiet pueblo, where chicken pull horse racing had deep roots, it's been whispered Murrieta quietly retired after he was "killed" by California Rangers on July 25, 1853.

Mile 7.5 to Mile 8.5. Charlebois Spring, Elevation: 2,510 feet. From the Charlebois Trail junction, the Peters Trail 105 turns left (east, then north), and leads 6.5 miles across Peters Mesa's hidden troves of treasure and courses through the pass between 4,916-foot Tortilla Mountain on left (northwest) and 4,023-foot Horse Ridge on right (southeast) to the Tortilla Well and Trailhead. Turn right (south) and hike one mile through La Barge Canyon past Music and Oak Springs on left (east) to La Barge Spring and the Red Tanks Trail junction.

Charlebois Spring

A color photograph by "City Slicker" Ron Butler shows Papago tracker Tom Franco examining the ancient Salado petroglyphs that were also believed be to the Peralta Master Map, with Ted DeGrazia, before they headed home back down the trail with their outfit to the horse trailer "and a hamper full of iced beer" waiting for them at the First Water Trailhead. Adolph Ruth may have studied the same petroglyphs and compared them to the González-Peralta Map before he was reportedly shot point-blank on 3,669-foot Peters Mesa towering above the site and nearby Pistol Canyon. Spanish miners worked the tablelands, where prospectors later searched among the glory holes and detritus and removed 11.45 pounds of gold ore assayed at 996 fine. (See page 19, 23).

Mile 8.5 to Mile 8.3. La Barge Spring, Elevation: 2,640 feet. The Red Tank Trail leads left (southeast) 2.1 miles and connects with the Coffee Flat Mountain and Miners Needle loop trails (see pages 192–194).

Turn right (south), stay on the Dutchman Trail and hike 2.3 miles past Holmes Spring on left (east) and the Giant Saguaro side trail on right (west) and hike through Bluffs Springs Canyon to the Crystal Spring Trail junction.

Mile 10.8 to Mile 16.2. Crystal Spring Trail junction, Elevation: 3,040 feet. Turn left (southeast), stay on the Dutchman Trail and hike 5.4 miles to the end of the Dutchman Trail at the Peralta Trailhead. If you want to shorten your hike, you can turn right (west) at Crystal Spring and follow the Bluff Springs Trail 235 and hike 3.3 miles to the Peralta Trailhead. (See page 181). End Dutchman Trail 104.

The Massacre Grounds Trail

From the Massacre Grounds Trailhead, the rough, rocky, often brushy foot trail climbs over 1,000 vertical feet in 2.65 miles to the 360-degree panorama seen from the unnamed 3,130-foot summit knob. Massacre Falls beyond is often seen during winter rains, winter snowmelt, and July-August monsoons. There are few better places to contemplate the wild history of the area than from this breathtaking point looking south toward Old Mexico.

Directions

Shortly after turning off the Apache Trail on Forest Road 78, the new Massacre Grounds Trailhead is is located at Mile 0.5 on the right (southeast).

Map Goldfield 7.5 minute Quadrangle

Massacre Grounds Trail and the Peralta Mine

The oft-repeated legend, difficult-to-prove tale has been recounted with an assorted cast of characters, "filmed in Mexico" yellow-filter-tinted shading, and suspect death tolls. As I understand the as-told-to story, Don Miguel Peralta of Arizpe, Sonora, Mexico was a cattle baron, patriarch of the Peralta family, and heir to a 1783 Spanish Land Grant from King Charles III of Spain signed over to a Peralta family claimant that included mining rights to the Superstition Mountains. The late Stanford-educated lawyer and author, Sims Ely, provided a glimpse of Peralta's Mine in his popular 1953 book, *The Lost Dutchman Mine:*

> The Peralta family carried on mining operations in the Superstitions for at least three generations, leading large expeditions of peons into Arizona from their base in the town of Arispe, in the State of Sonora. Independent accounts agree that the Peraltas ultimately developed a funnel-shaped pit, some 75 feet across. Peons would carry the ore in sacks slung over their backs, climbing from one terrace to another, using notched poles for ladders. The ore contained heavy concentrations of gold nuggets, which were easily shaken out.

The Peralta Mine was located on the northern periphery of *Alta Sonora,* "Upper Sonora," Mexico during the heyday of gold prospecting in the 1840s. The 1848 Treaty of Guadalupe Hidalgo, and the $15 million 1854 Gadsden Purchase, however, ceded a large tract of northwest Sonora, Mexico to the United States, moved the international border almost two hundred miles south of Peralta's Mine, and rejected a reputedly fraudulent Peralta-Reavis Spanish Land Grant claim. While making a run for the new border with their last horse caravan of gold—"more than three hundred saddle horses for the men to ride"—according to a warrior named Apache Jack who fought against the Peraltas during a three-day running battle before they fled across the desert toward Mexico—those who didn't manage to escape were reportedly massacred by "Apaches" on the western flanks of Superstition Mountain. Peralta's gold was said to be hidden by Apaches.

Trail of Bones

During December 1866, Cavalry Sergeant William Edwards and Private Joseph M. Green were looking for two 1st Arizona Volunteers Apache Scouts who were presumed to be missing in the area when Edwards discovered twenty-five sun-bleached skeletons stripped of their clothing. Sifting through the arrow-riddled bones, "Edwards noticed," according to his diary, "one of the [crushed] skulls bore a tarnished silver tooth." It suggested Spanish aristocracy. When Edwards returned to the Massacre Grounds after he finished his enlistment, he wrote in his diary: "In another skeleton, only this one is whole, got the clothes and all with it. Pick on through the bones and find a knife, rusty and stained, a little medal too rusty to read, and a small poke bag under the mess. In the bag is about a pound of gold quill [concentrated gold ore]. It sure looks rich, and I know for sure they were working a mine around here somewhere about." Edwards never found another nugget anywhere he tracked the "grisly" trail of bones five miles east to White Rock Spring in Marsh Valley where he discovered what appeared to be evidence of Mexican mining. That led to Edwards making a reconnaissance of nearby Peters Mesa where he "made his most significant discovery yet. There in a rocky clearing surrounded by Mesquite, Ironwood, and Laurel trees was the Mexican work camp where they broke up the ore before their trip back to Mexico . . . Edwards picked up several pieces of quartz with free gold attached, identical to the gold found in the dead Mexican's poke sack." The expert tracker Edwards proved to be had connected the Peralta miners trail from Peters Mesa to the Massacre Grounds. But Edwards never came back. His horse was stolen by a lone "Apache" that night. Edwards escaped with his life time and again, every time he tried to reach the Peralta's mine site the "Apaches" were waiting. What are you waiting for?

It wasn't until 1918 that prospectors Carl A. "Silverlock" Silverlocke and Carl "Goldlock" Malm discovered $18,000 of high-grade "float" gold ore in the Massacre Grounds which caused a local gold rush of starry-eyed prospectors. Their discovery did not confirm a gold caravan massacre of four hundred men, or peons. But Ely's account suggests a large group of miners worked the Peralta Mine in the Superstition Mountains, as does Apache Jack's "eyewitness" account of "three hundred saddle horses for the men to ride," and rancher James E. Bark's discovery at Bluff Springs of "several hundred sandals, of the sort worn by Mexicans." Turkey vultures and javelinas, I learned from what I've witnessed working as a photojournalist in the US/Mexico borderlands, will eat, scatter, and carry away human remains. But three hundred fleeing miners aren't going to vanish without a trace in the open desert—unless they drowned crossing a flood-swollen Gila River, walked back to Mexico, or found a new home in southern Arizona—what once was Sonora, Mexico.

Angels Spring ancient Salado cliff dwelling. Copyright © John Annerino Photography.

14

Adventure Challenge Discovery Traverse

"[We] picked our way over a rough and pathless country, lighted only by the stars above. Arriving at the edge of the ravine, what a scene was before us! We looked down into a natural amphitheatre, in which blazed great fires; hordes of wild [Tł'ohk'adigain] Apaches darted about, while others sat on logs beating their tomtoms . . . They were entirely naked, except for the loin-cloth . . . Their feathers waved, their jingles shook, and their painted bodies twisted and turned in the light of the great fire, which roared and leaped on high."

—Martha Summerhayes, *Vanished Arizona* (1874)

LANDFORM

This roundabout route traces the length of the thousand-foot deep Fish Creek Canyon, courses south through Rodgers Canyon to Angels Spring, follows the high ground of the J. F. Trail to Tortilla Well, crosses the hardscrabble tablelands of Peters Mesa, follows the historic Dutchman's Trail west to East Boulder and Peralta Canyons, and terminates at the Peralta Trailhead.

HISTORICAL OVERVIEW

The interconnecting maze of trails that threaded canyons, passes, mesas, and mountains leads to springs, streams, and hunting, gathering, and ceremonial grounds that were first used long ages ago by the Salado and perhaps the Mogollon peoples, and later by the Western and White Mountain Apache, Southeastern Yavapai, and Pima whose songs, stories, and marks on the land are recounted throughout the pages of this book. They still touch the hearts and souls of those travelers who attempt to follow in their footsteps.

Directions

From Apache Junction, drive twenty-five northeast on the Apache Trail, Highway 88, to the Fish Creek Bridge and the small car park on right (southeast). Additional parking is available one mile east down the Apache Trail at the picnic area pullout on left (north).

Maps

Horse Mesa Dam, Weavers Needle, and Iron Mountain 7.5-minute Quadrangles.

Warning

This canyon adventure is for experienced hikers only. Don't hike Fish Creek Canyon immediately before, during, or after summer flash flood season, or during rainy weather at any time of the year. If you're backpacking work in unison to help one another lifting and lowering packs.

Note: I first embarked on this boundary-to-boundary Superstition Wilderness traverse while leading a group of junior high school students who backpacked their own food, water, gear, helmets, ropes, and climbing gear during a ten day journey of "adventure, challenge, and discovery."

Fish Creek Canyoneering Description

Mile 0 to Mile 4.25. Fish Creek Canyon, Elevation: 2,235 feet. Hike, scramble, and trek 4.25 miles and climb over one thousand vertical feet to the upper Tortilla Trailhead. (**Note:** Mileage varies depending on your line of travel.) Deep, rugged, and at times seemingly impassable, Fish Creek Canyon is an immeasurably beautiful riparian corridor half the scale of Zion National Park. Cool perennial stream flows, small charming falls, and deep pools of refreshing water sustain cottonwood and sycamore trees, delightful songbirds, sunbathing turtles, and darting lizards that mock hikers' tediously-slow progress along a fractured fault line through lava and tuff as the canyon winds southeast beneath neck-craningly steep saguaro cactus-covered slopes, puzzling stone barnacles, fossilized benches, and sheer cliffs and caves that soar high above. Colorful lichen-splotched rocks and house-sized boulders impede your progress and limit your traveling speed to a half-mile an hour that requires rock- and boulder hopping, stream crossings, bushwhacking, and patient but keen route finding through the challenging maze to reach the exit out of Fish Creek Canyon south/southwest up Lost Dutch Canyon near Millers Mine.

If you're doing a one-day loop hike, you can hike 1.7 miles out the steep southwest fork of Lost Dutch Canyon from its confluence with Fish Creek Canyon past Lost Dutch Spring (often dry) beneath unnamed Peak 3,537—or hike cross-country up the steep slopes that parallel the canyon on the right (northwest)—pick up the J. F. Trail, and walk north to the upper Tortilla Trailhead near Tortilla Well. You can return the way you came down Fish Creek Canyon, or return to the Apache Trail by hiking four-wheel-drive Road 213 north 3.3 miles to your shuttle vehicle at the two-wheel-drive parking lot. (The Fish Creek Bridge is located 2.2 miles east on the Apache Trail.)

Miller's Mine

Lost Dutch Canyon was named after prospector George Miller's 1920s era mine he claimed was the Lost Dutchman Mine. It was located on the south end of an old burro trail that once led from Tortilla Well. On July 11, 1920, newspaper writer Lewis A. Weise and two companions, Dr. Robert A. Aiton and James G. Simpson, went to investigate Miller's mine that had been tunneled into the steep slopes near the southwest fork of Lost Dutch Canyon. With some trepidation, Weise and Aiton climbed down into the ravine to the mine and probed its twin shafts and narrow 200-foot-long tunnel that Miller was working. They saw the results for themselves; Weise later wrote, "a heavy ore bearing ledge which had been struck at a depth of 95 feet in the main shaft." The gold ore was assayed at $40 a ton.

When Weis asked Miller how he had discovered the site, Weis wrote an investigative account which appeared in the July 24, 1920 *Miami Daily Arizona Silver Belt*: "According to George Miller's story, he started prospecting for the famous "Lost Dutchman" mine away back in 1913. In 1915 he had about decided to abandon his prospecting and had started for Superior when he met an old Apache Indian whom he befriended. This old Indian told Miller that he could direct him to a rich mine; and it was upon the Indian's directions that the mine now under operation was located." In spite of Miller's belief he was working the Lost Dutchman Mine, he went bust, and then toes-up on April 6, 1936. He was reportedly buried alongside two partners next to a half-century-old stone cabin above the mine near where Weis wrote, "trees and rocks have been blazed."

Mile 3.5 to Mile 7.5. Fish Creek Canyon and Lost Dutch Canyon confluence, Elevation: 2,710 feet. Turn left (east) and trek east/southeast through the stream bottom of upper Fish Creek Canyon across river cobble, boulders, and periodic glimpses of the use trail through sycamore trees, Manzanita, and cave-pocked walls past the mouths of Goat and Little Goat Canyons approximately 3.5 miles until the canyon narrows, pinches to a slot, and forms a slick rock plunge pool that must be waded through or scurried around via the safest path of least resistance. After paying your dues climbing past the spring, trash-spewing raucous crowds at the mouth of Fisk Creek Canyon this is a quiet, remote, and welcome upper canyon respite along a seldom-traveled wilderness corridor where, in Martha Summerhayes's days, you'd expect to see the silhouette of an Apache scout and hear the howl of a grey wolf.

Mile 7.5 to Mile 9.2. Fish Creek Canyon and Rogers Canyon Trail 110 Trail junction, Elevation. 2,720 feet. Turn right (south) and hike the Rogers Canyon Trail 1.7 miles through boulders, brush, and sycamore trees and skeletons past Hole Spring to Angels Basin. It may come as a surprise after clawing through Rogers Canyon to emerge in an open meadow surrounded by piñon and juniper trees. And it begs the question: Did the Salado hand-till the Southwest indigenous people's triumvirate of corn, beans, and squash here, surrounded by easy seasonal pickings of piñon nuts and junipers berries, and wooded hills where they could hunt mule deer?

Angel Spring Cliff Dwelling

The unique two-tiered lattice-roofed mud cliff dwelling was built in a sheltered cave and inhabited by the Salado people who lived along the *Salado*, "Salt River" and the northern periphery of the Superstition Mountains between 1250 AD and 1450 AD. For that reason, archaeologist Harold Sterling Gladwin, who was noted for his excavations at Casa Grande and Snaketown, ascribed the name "Salado" to the diverse culture in the 1920s. The former New York City stockbroker-turned-Southwest archaeologist theorized the Salado were comprised of Ancestral Puebloans who migrated from the mesas of northern Arizona, the Hohokam who migrated from the Salt River Valley of central Arizona, and the Mogollon who migrated from the forested mountains of eastern Arizona.

One of the first non-Indians to visit the hidden cliff dwellings was prospector and writer Pierpont Constable Bicknell who wrote a page one feature for the January 13, 1895 *San Francisco Chronicle,* "One of Arizona's Lost El Dorados," that brought national attention to the Lost Dutchman Mine. In the riveting feature that later drew the attention of treasure hunter Adolph Ruth, Bicknell wrote about one of Jacob Watlz's clues that lead him to the ancient Salado cliff dwelling:

> The great clew [sic] for which all the search is now being made is a rock cabin in a cave, which, according to "Old Yoccup's" story [Jacob Waltz], is directly across the canyon from the mine, and not more than 200 feet from it. It was here that the two Germans [Waltz and Jacob Weiser] lived while they worked the mine. It is a coincidence that the writer [Bicknell] succeeded in finding a cabin in a cave, very near the region referred to; but it was the work of cliff dwellers, and, besides, there was no mine on the opposite side of the canyon.

$1.5 Million Up in Smoke

For more than a century after Bicknell's vague description of his visit to the "cabin in a cave," many people would ride horseback, or make the backcountry trek, to visit what amounted to a cliff shrine of the Salado peoples and their culture: Turn of the last century horseback hunters riding north from the J. F. Ranch, Southern Pacific Railroad developers eager to offer a tourist destination for a proposed Fish Creek Lodge, National Geographic photographers, Arizona Highways writers, and the 1949 Merrick Lewis expedition that came looking for the Dutchman's gold but returned from the cliff dwelling with a trove

Artist, treasure hunter, and friend to Native peoples, Etorre "Ted" DeGrazia, found home, inspiration, and adventure in his beloved Superstition Mountains.
Colorized photo courtesy: DeGrazia Gallery in the Sun © All Rights Reserved.

of Salado artifacts they got slapped on the wrist for excavating when they turned over the antiquities to authorities. No one could imagine remote Angel Basin would be the location to protest Inheritance Tax laws imposed on unsold oil paintings. No one, that is, except renowned artist Ettore "Ted" DeGrazia who painted the Superstition Mountains' many moods, as well as the indigenous people he befriended, the Apache, Pima, Papago, Yaqui, and Seri. In an act of civil disobedience and theater in the wilderness, DeGrazia made headlines in 1976 when he used two bottles of Chivas Regal to set fire to a pyre of $1.5 million in paintings and wept at the sight: "Ettore DeGrazia, 73, Burned Paintings to Protest Taxes," read the Saturday, September 18, 1982 edition of the *New York Times*'s "Arts" section. Those paintings that did not go up in flames were bundled and hidden by DeGrazia somewhere in the vicinity that treasure hunters are still reportedly searching for. To paraphrase the words of Georgia Gold Rush prospectors called the Twenty-Niners, "Thar's paintings in them thar hills."

Mile 9.2 to Mile 11.5. Angels Basin, Elevation: 3,670 feet, Angels Spring is located 100 yards due south. From Angels Basin, turn west, stay on the Rogers Canyon Trail and hike 2.3 miles to Tortilla Pass.

Mile 11.5 to Mile 17.5. Tortilla Pass, Elevation: 4,450 feet. Turn left (northwest) on the J. F. Trail and hike six miles northwest past the Hoolie Bacon Trail junction to the Tortilla Trailhead.

Earthquake

On May 3, 1887, the 7.6 magnitude Sonoran Earthquake killed forty-two people in Bavispe, Sonora, Mexico near its epicenter along the thirty-mile-long Pitaycachi Fault. Geologists reported the historical quake "released twice as much energy as any of the other earthquakes recognized in this region," and reverberated throughout the Southwest as far north as Albuquerque and Phoenix. Rock fall closed the Apache Trail Circle Route of "Stoneman's Grade" cavalry and wagon road through upper Queen Creek to Superior and Devils Canyon, impeded or stopped spring flows in Garden Valley and La Barge Canyon, and caved-in or covered up who knew how many Superstition Mountains' mines, tunnels, caves, and glory holes, including, perhaps, Peralta's Gold, Lost Dutchman's Gold, Lost Jesuit Gold, and Cave of the Gold Bars, whichever trails you're hiking in search of them.

Mile 17.5 to Mile 24. Tortilla Trailhead, Elevation: 3,130 feet. From Tortilla Well 200 yards west of the Tortilla Trailhead, hike the Peters Trail 103 southwest 6.5 miles through the pass between 4,918-foot Tortilla Mountain on right (northwest) and 3,916-foot Music Mountain on left (southwest), turn right (northwest) through Peters Canyon, and doubleback south over Peters Mesa and drop into Charlebois Spring.

Dr. Thorne's Gold

Of the many clues that appear in the pages of this book, I think the most intriguing are those reports of the "Apache" showing gold seekers, reportedly their sworn enemies, the location of gold caches, including Chiricahua elder Lydian Perrine's "Cave of the gold bars" atop Blacktop Mesa, and George Miller's "Lost Dutchman's Mine" in Lost Dutch Canyon. Neither of these accounts compare to the description of Dr. Abraham D. Thorne's blind-folded horseback trip to Apache's hidden trove of gold.

According to rancher and prospector James E. Bark's notes, in late 1865 or early 1866, Dr. Thorne was being escorted by fourteen Calvary Troops, when his mule-drawn wagon party of three was attacked by "Apaches" at Maricopa Wells, Arizona. Dr. Thorn was among the four who survived the deadly ambush, but his bag of surgical instruments drew the attention of the warriors' chief. From that moment forward, Dr. Thorne was conscripted to become the Apache's doctor who tended to their bloody wounds and medical needs at their camp on the confluence of the Salt and Verde Rivers that would later become Fort

McDowell. The Apache understood the care Dr. Thorne showed them to the point they consented to take the doctor to their hidden cache of gold they periodically visited to pay for guns and ammunition, Thorne witnessed, they brokered with two white arms dealers. Covering Dr. Thorne's head with a black hood to ward off evil spirits, they road horseback throughout the night to the mine that, from Dr. Thorne's descriptions, conceivably was Peters Mesa. When they removed his black hood, Thorne said: "Gold could be seen lying around in the quartz that had been brought out of the pit and evidently discarded for not being rich enough . . . I was the only one who seemed at all excited. I asked the chief if I could take some, and he said, "Take all you want, as you will never be coming back here again." Thereafter, the Apache abandoned their riverside camp at the approach of mounted US Troops, and Dr. Thorne, left alone with his cache of gold buried under a tree at the abandoned camp, repeatedly tried to relocate the mine over the years with nothing to show for it but another tale of lost gold.

Those who have not discovered Dr. Thorne's Gold by any method, including a divining rod, or dowsing rod, may adamantly profess Dr. Thorne didn't exist, or his mine is not located anywhere near the mine diggings and smelter pots on Peters Mesa that Cavalry Sergeant William Edwards also described during his 1866 reconnaissance when he wrote there was a "Mexican work camp where they broke up the ore before their trip back to Mexico." That is, unless they're among the treasure-hunting Illuminati who may have already found the **X** right there. It could have been dozens of other caves within reach of a day and night roundtrip horseback ride to the mine within view of what Dr. Thorne caught sight of when he was unmasked and called the "Mexican Sombrero" (Weavers Needle) en route back to Apache Camp at the confluence of the Salt and Verde Rivers: Apache Kid Cave, Dead Womans Cave, Skull Cave, *Caverna Tiburon*, "Shark Cave," Geronimos Cave,

Browns Cave, Chunings Cave, Hermans Cave, Millers Cave, Peters Cave, Lydian Perrine's Cave of Gold Bars, or . . . .

Mile 24 to Mile 27.3. Charlebois Spring, Elevation: 2,510 feet. From Charlebois Spring hike the Dutchmans Trail 104 west 3.3 miles to East Boulder Canyon and the Peralta Trail Junction.

Mile 27.3 to Mile 33.5. Peralta Trail 102 junction, East Boulder Canyon, Elevation: 2,300 feet. From the trail junction, turn left (south) on the Peralta Trail and hike 6.2 miles through East Boulder Canyon past Piñon Camp over Fremont Saddle, and down Peralta Canyon to the trailhead.

Weavers Needle Climb (See page 189).
Piñon Camp, Rescue Camp.

As a wilderness guide and outdoor education instructor I always tried to instill safety first, self-sufficiency, and camaraderie. From the start of our ten-day adventure, challenge, and discovery journey we'd embarked upon from Fish Creek Canyon, our escape route was continually evolving in my thinking and planning as we journeyed from one camp and water source to the next camp and water source. What was the safest and quickest route out of the mountains and canyons, and how do we carry one of our own through a stone-rugged wilderness that prohibited aerial rescues in the event of an emergency such a broken ankle or rattlesnake bite? Fortunately, we never needed to use an escape route. But after we spent the last two days climbing, summit sight-seeing, and rappelling down Weavers Needle, I wanted to impart a final lesson with my hardy co-ed adventurers: A three-mile makeshift litter carry over Fremont Saddle down Peralta Canyon. Stripping two nylon backpacks from their aluminum frames, the group improvised, shortened their boot laces, and lashed the pack frames to two stout century plant stalks, tested it with the volunteer victim, and together hoisted the litter over Fremont Saddle and down the rugged trail in lockstep cadence until they tired, when the next six-person carriers relayed the litter, and so on. In the end, the leaner sun-weathered smiling young adventurers proved to themselves they had what it took to traverse these fabled mountains, climb its legendary landmark, and carry an injured climber from the foot of Weaver Needle to the trailhead. They also proved to their parents and teachers they weren't the troubled teens they were made out to be. That was the gold I had come looking for and discovered.

Vehicle Shuttle

Plan on a 40.2-mile vehicle shuttle one way between the Fish Creek Canyon Bridge and the Peralta Trailhead.

Appendix

Death Stalks the Superstitions

Researched and Compiled by John Annerino, Copyright © 2018

"I like to think that, somewhere, old man Reavis, Jacob Waltzer, Saltback Morris, Jake Lemon, and a score of others are lifting their glasses and having a good hearty laugh at us puny mortals scrambling over their land trying to unravel the snarl of mysteries they left behind, and thanking their God they lived in an age where legends were *made* not *told*."

—Bernice McGee, "The Other World of the Superstitions," 1964

IN THE HISTORICAL CONTEXT OF THE OLD WEST, MANY fans of western movies, television series, novels, and nonfiction books view death as part of the "color" or "romance" of the people, the time, and the place. In the boots-and-moccasins-on-the-ground reality of traveling through the Superstition Mountains, death by any means—massacres, battles, gun fights, murders, assassinations, mine cave-ins and explosions, dehydration, heat stroke, snow storms, cliff falls, accidents, jet and airplane crashes, inexperience, poor judgment, old age and poor health, mysterious circumstances, and vanishing without a trace—was terrible for both the victims and their loved ones. Many people, real people—many good, too many bad—died searching for, or protecting, the Superstition Mountains' real and imagined mines, lodes, and caches of gold. Having journeyed down the historic and modern paths of southwestern Arizona's and northwestern Sonora, Mexico's merciless *El Camino del Diablo*, "The Road of the Devil,"

Gold is where you find it—if you live long enough to spend it. Copyright © John Annerino Photography/LIFE magazine.

researching my borderlands book, *Dead in Their Tracks*, this journey has also been unpleasant, at times sad, heart-wrenching, grim, and unconscionable—some cases just too brutal to detail—but it's nearly always been enlightening and thought provoking. In their memory of the region, many victims of Native American, Euroamerican, Latin American, and American lineage, this appendix has been researched and compiled from primary sources—or the only sources available— to contribute to the human legacy and broader understanding of the Superstition Mountains within the scope of the Great Southwest, US/ Mexico borderlands, and ancestral homelands once under siege that many principals traveled through and fought to the death to protect. Unpleasant to imagine, difficult to see and comprehend in terms of "recreation" that a conservative estimate of 654 people likely perished or disappeared in America's most storied wilderness area. Many sources are verifiable only from grim body recoveries, skeletal discoveries, first-hand eye-witness reports, and historical papers. Some are as told-to stories. Those not relied upon are vague or speculative accounts, campfire tales, cantina rants, mumblings, hearsay, and rumors that have been woven into the fabric of the myth. Each of the following entries includes, when known: Date, Victim's Name/s, Location, Cause of Death, Number of Victims, and Sources.

Rest in Peace/ *Que en paz descanse*

- 1843–44: "The Pima went on a war campaign and one Pima was wounded near Superstition M'ts. The Pima known as ragged G String." *Source:* TJPCS, Pima Calendar Stick.
- 1848: Peralta Massacre and Battle, Massacre Grounds, Superstition Mountains, thirty to 400 men. Cavalry Sergeant William Edwards reported discovering twenty-five skeletons in 1866, and another five skeletons when he returned to the same area after his enlistment. A man named Apache Jack who reportedly witnessed the three-day running gun battle provided the following account of the Peralta Massacre, in part:

Apache Jack

In a conversation between an aging warrior nicknamed "Apache Jack" and miner George Scholey, James E. Bark reported: "George asked Jack how many [Peralta miners] there were, and he said he did not know, but there were lots of them and quite a number had been killed further back." Apache Jack had reportedly fought against the Peraltas. "He [George] asked how many horses and mules they had, and Jack replied that there were more than three hundred saddle horses for the men to ride. The rest were packed with some ollas and blankets, but most of the packs were stones [of gold ore]." This is the only eyewitness as-told-to account I'm aware of that supports that upwards of 400 men may have been killed during the Peralta Massacre. *Sources:* CHB, 2002; BJE, 1892 to 1928. (See page 221, Massacre Grounds.)

- 1848–49: "Pima went on a war campaign and killed several Apaches on top of Silver King M'ts." *Source:* TJPCS, Pima Calendar Stick.
- 1852–53: "Pimas killed several Apache where the Roosevelt Dam is now. After the battle was over Pima roasted corn belonging to Apache." *Source:* TJPCS, Pima Calendar Stick.
- 1857–58: "About thirty miles north of Florence Apache were hunting wood rats when the Pima and one white man jumped on them and killed one Apache man and a boy." *Source:* TJPCS, Pima Calendar Stick.
- 1863–64: "East from Silver King M'ts some Apaches were killed by Pimas. Among the Pimas who killed Apaches were Juan Thomas, Sh-Cha Earth and Ca-sha-pa-cha. This happened at a place called gourd piles. [Big Oak Flat?] One Apache tried to hide in the water but was soon discovered." *Source:* TJPCS, Pima Calendar Stick.
- 1864–65: "An Apache was killed in one [of] the battles who has long feet, near Roosevelt. He was killed by Pima Scouts." *Source:* TJPCS, Pima Calendar Stick.
- 1865–66: "In the fall the Pimas went on a war campaign, killed one old Apache and boy, this happened on the Globe Mts, [Big Oak Flat?] while they were gathering some plant seeds." *Source:* TJPCS, Pima Calendar Stick.
- 1866: Thirty Apache and Yavapai at First Water and Garden Valley were killed during an intertribal fight. *Source:* SMM, map, 2016.
- May 11, 1866: Fifteen Apache and Yavapai warriors were reportedly killed by soldiers under the command of Brevet Lt. John D. Walker of the 1st Arizona Volunteers at Hell's Hole in Tortilla Creek, 15. *Source:* KTC, 2007.
- May 11, 1866: Fifty-seven Apache and Yavapai warriors, women, and children were reportedly killed by soldiers under

the command of Brevet Lt. John D. Walker at Dismal Valley, Tortilla Creek. *Source:* KTC, September 7, 2007.
- November 1866: A fully-dressed skeleton of a Mexican miner was discovered atop Peters Mesa by 1st Arizona Volunteer Cavalry Sergeant William Edwards. *Source:* CHB, 2002.
- Summer 1868–69: "Pimas went on a war campaign in the Superstition M'ts. One Pima was killed, one Apache was taken captive. He was known as 'Red Eyes.'" *Source:* PCS, Pima Calendar Stick.
- 1869–1870: "Some other Pimas were on a war campaign to the Globe M'ts. They killed one Apache woman. The man who killed her was "Ni-se-pa." *Source:* TJPCS, Pima Calendar Stick.
- Winter 1870: Seventy-five to eighty Western Apache men, women, and children were reportedly killed, or leapt to their deaths, during an ambush by "settlers" and the US Calvary at Apache Leap. *Sources:* BJM, 1935; NWS, 2007.
- 1870–71: "Their [Pima] expedition to the Superstition M'ts was successful. They killed two Apaches who fought them with guns. One Pima was wounded named "Ni-se-pa." *Source:* TJPCS, Pima Calendar Stick.
- 1871: Wounded after he was attacked by "Apaches," Jacob Weiser, Jacob Waltz's partner, struggled south out of the Superstition Mountains and followed the Gila River to the Pima settlements where two Pima women led him to the home of a Dr. Walker who treated his arrow wounds. Weisser later died, but not before giving Dr. Walker his rawhide map that he and his partner, Jacob Waltz, received in Sonora, Mexico from Don Miguel Peralta. *Source:* CHB, 2002.
- April 1871: An Apache was reportedly killed in the Superstition Mountains. *Source:* SKRT, 1981.

- October 1871: During a midnight raid on Iron Mountain, the Pima killed thirty or more Yavapai and kidnapped sixteen to eighteen children, including a six-year-old boy named *Wassaja,* who later became Dr. Carlos Montezuma. *Source:* MCCG, 1998.
- 1871–72: "In the fall the Pima went on a war campaign in Globe M'ts. They came to an Apache camp where they fought the Apaches at night. The Pima killed many Apaches and take many captives. Among the captives was a boy, now Dr. Montezuma." *Source:* TJPCS, Pima Calendar Stick.
- December 28, 1872: Skeleton Cave Massacre, Salt River Canyon. Under the command of General George Crook, thirty Apache Scouts, ninety Pima, and 120 5th Cavalry Troops killed seventy-six to ninety-six Kwevkepaya Yavapai elders, men, women, and children. *Sources:* BJG, 1872; TNSC, 2006.
- 1872–73: "At the same time US Soldiers and Pimas slaughter Apache at big cave (Big Rock)." [Skeleton Cave]. *Source:* TJPCS, Pima Calendar Stick, 1872–1873.
- 1872–73: "Some time US Soldiers with some Pima scouts and Apache captives went to the Roosevelt Mountains to fight Apaches . . . They killed their leader and many of his followers." *Source:* TJPCS, Pima Calendar Stick.
- Early Spring 1873–74: "Pima killed Apaches south of present Roosevelt Dam." *Source:* TJPCS, Pima Calendar Stick.
- 1877: Three Mexican miners who may have been associated with the Peraltas were shot to death by Jacob Waltz after he befriended them and claim jumped their mine in the Superstition Mountains. If the Holmes Manuscript is verifiable unaltered Gospel truth, Jacob Waltz later killed four other men: two soldiers, his nephew, and a prospector. *Sources:* HGB, 1944; CHB, 2002.

- 1879: December 5: Manuel Peralta was reportedly killed by the "Apache" at what later became the Bulldog Mine. His wounded brother Ramón managed to escape. *Source:* KTC, 2016.
- 1880: The remains of two unnamed soldiers were found north of the Quarter Circle U Ranch after they were reportedly shot in the head. They'd made the mistake of showing $700 in gold they had discovered to locals at Camp Pinal. *Source:* CES, 1972.
- 1881: Joe Dearing who reportedly discovered five pounds of rich gold ore in the Superstition Mountains died after a cave-in at the Silver King Mine when both of his legs were crushed. *Source:* BJE, 1892 to 1928.
- June 18, 1884: Pedro Ortega was reportedly murdered "30 feet" outside the front door of Jacob Waltz's Phoenix adobe by Selso Grijalva. Señor Grijalva used Waltz's double-barrel shotgun without his knowledge and escaped. *Source:* AGZ, 1884.
- October 25, 1891: Jacob Waltz's Phoenix deathbed confession. (See 1877). *Source:* HGB, 1944; CHB, 2002.
- May 31, 1892: Thirteen-year-old Charles M. Dobie was murdered at the J. F. Ranch by "Apaches," or by suspect John M. See. *Source:* AZREP, *Arizona Republic,* 1892.
- 1894: Prospector Al Senner was killed when his horse, Lady, and pack mule fell, or were pushed or spooked off the Flat Iron near the North Summit of Superstition Mountain. *Source:* CHSG, 1993.
- April 10, 1896: Sixty-nine-year-old Elisha Marcus Reavis died in Rogers Canyon four miles from his Reavis Ranch. Some believe the aging hermit died of ill health. Others suspected he was murdered and "beheaded." As discussed elsewhere in the pages of this book javelina and turkey vultures conceivably dragged his skull away from his body. *Source:* CES, 1972.

- 1896: Vague accounts report "2 Easterners" vanished in the Superstition Mountains.
- 1900: Vague accounts report a nine year old boy died from a rattlesnake bite at the Silver King Mine.
- February 19, 1907: Al Sieber, wounded twenty-eight times while serving as US Army Chief of Scouts during the Apache Wars, was killed when a boulder fell on him while leading an Apache work crew during the construction of the Apache Trail to Roosevelt Dam. The Apache called Sieber "Man of Iron." *Source:* ASG, 1907.
- November 11, 1910: Prospector John Chuning died of old age and poor health at Tortilla Flat. *Sources:* various.
- 1910: Vague accounts report the remains of a woman with gold nuggets were found in a cave on Superstition Mountain.
- 1912: Apache Jack was reportedly poisoned with arsenic after leaving First Water for talking about an "Apache" lode with miner George Scholey. *Source:* ESLD, 1953.
- 1914: Vague accounts report that mine foreman Eli Koreavitch was shot and killed at the Carney Springs Mine about a claim dispute.
- June 14 or 15, 1931: Treasure hunter Adolph Ruth was shot to death, or died of thirst, between West Boulder Canyon and the confluence of La Barge and Needle Canyons. *Source:* AU, Author, 2018.
- November 30, 1934: Handlebar-mustached old Scotsman Adam Stewart died near Fish Creek Mountain after two decades of searching for the Lost Dutchman's Gold. *Source:* KTC, 2014.
- April 6, 1936: Miner George Drakulich (Miller) died of a heart attack at Tortilla Well. *Source:* SKRT, 1981.
- December 12, 1936: New York City stockbroker Roman O'Hal fell to his death while searching for the Lost Dutchman's Gold in the Superstition Mountains. *Source:* TRN, 2015.

- April 25, 1947: seventy-nine-year-old Swedish-born Carl J. Malm died at Coffelt's Rest Home in Phoenix, Arizona on April 25, 1947. Malm and his uncle Carl A. Silverlocke became famous after finding $18,000 in smelted gold in the Massacre Grounds in 1912. *Source:* MCJ, 1947.
- November 1937: Guy "Hematite" Frink was found shot to death in LaBarge Canyon with a pouch of gold. *Source:* TRN, 2015.
- 1938: Vague accounts report that a man named Jenkins died of a heart attack in the Superstition Mountains after finding a rock with gold ore while picnicking with his wife and two girls. *Source:* TRN, 2015.
- June 21, 1947: James A. Cravey died of unknown causes sometime after he was dropped off in La Barge Canyon by a Bell Helicopter with a week's worth of food, water, and gear. *Source:* AZREP, 1947.

Warning All Treasure Hunters!

Phoenix Sky Harbor International Airport's weather average temperature for the sixty-two-year-old retired photographer James A. Cravey's doomed adventure averaged 105 degrees Fahrenheit. Plagued by poor health and physical condition that may have kept Cravey home, the Superstition Mountains was the last place on earth he should have tread. His fate was sealed sometime after June 21 when he was dropped off in La Barge Canyon by a single-rotor 1947 Bell soap-bubble canopied helicopter south of Weavers Needle not far from where Adolph Ruth's remains were discovered in 1932. Like Ruth, searchers pulled out all the stops to locate Cravey—"There was no indication that any of his supplies had been used," the *Arizona Republic* reported. Cravey's remains were not discovered until February 24, 1948. Like Ruth, Cravey's skull was disarticulated from his skeleton, probably from javelinas, but peccaries don't make great headlines even on the slowest news days.

The February 23, 1948, the *Arizona Republic* reported: "Superstition Mountains today yielded the bones of [Cravey] yet another who sought and tried to solve the mystery of the Lost Dutchman's gold. But the mountains' fastness still obscured the secret of his death, just as it hides the fate of countless others who thirsted and died in a vain search for the legendary treasure trove."

- December 17, 1947: Thirty-eight-year-old Phoenix miner Ernesto Jacobs died during a premature, missignaled dynamite explosion in a 225-foot deep copper mine shaft at the Palmer Mine near the foot of Superstition Mountain. *Source:* AZREP, *Arizona Republic*, 1947.
- December 29, 1949. Prospector, hermit, and "eastern speaking," penny-pinching stock investor James Kidd disappeared from his Phoenix motel room and vanished without a trace, some profess in the Haunted Canyon area of Pinto Creek in the Superstition Mountains. After his disappearance, the State of Arizona discovered Kidd had accumulated $174,065.69 in assets in a bank vault that, with interest, was worth approximately $297,036.10—later held by First National Bank of Arizona—and wanted the money for the state's general account. It was going to be a slam dunk for the state when they learned they couldn't locate any heirs, until they saw Kidd's short hand-written will. Kidd's will read: "this is my first and only will and is dated the second of January, 1946. I have no heirs and have not been married in my life and after all my funeral expenses have been paid and 100 one hundred dollars to some preacher of the gospitel to say fare well at my grave sell all my property which is all in cash and stocks with E. F. Hutton Co Phoenix some in safety deposit box, and have this balance money to go in a research or some scientific proof of a soul of the human body which leaves at death I think in time their can be Photograph of

soul leaving the human at death, James Kidd." The will sparked a gold rush of 103 claimants at the Arizona Superior Court in Phoenix who queued up during the "Ghost Trial of the Century" to get their share of Kidd's trove of gold, cash, or stock certificates. Kidd was reportedly laid to rest at his hidden mine by his occasional driver who periodically resupplied him during his prospecting forays in the eastern Superstition Mountains. Source: LIFE, 1967.

- 1950: Vague accounts report three Texas boys vanished in the Superstitions Mountains.
- 1951, February: Vague accounts report that Oregon physician, Dr. John "Doc" Burns, accidentally shot himself in the Superstition Mountains.
- 1952: Vague accounts report that Dayton, Ohio native Joseph N. Kelley went missing and his body wasn't discovered until May, 1954. He'd been shot in the head from above, ruled an "accident," while searching for the Lost Dutchman's Gold near Weavers Needle.
- 1952: Vague accounts report two California boys, Ross Bley and Charles Harshbarger, vanished in the Superstition Mountains.
- May 27, 1954: Vague accounts report that "prospectors discover an unidentified human skull in Superstition Mountains."
- 1955: Vague accounts report Charles Massey was hunting in the Superstition Mountains with a .22 rifle and was found shot between the eyes with a high caliber rifle.
- January 1956: Vague accounts report Brooklyn, New Yorker, Martin Zywotho, was found shot in the head in the Superstition Mountains.
- June 12, 1959: Stanley Fernandez was shot in the head by his prospecting partner Benjamin Ferreira in a dispute over "Fools Gold," iron pyrite, they'd discovered in La Barge Canyon near White Rock Spring. Source: AZREP, *Arizona Republic*, 1959.

- November 11, 1959: Robert St. Marie was shot and killed by Ed Piper in a Hatfield and McCoy-style feud near Maria Celeste Jones Camp in East Boulder Canyon. *Sources:* AZREP: *Arizona Republic*, 1959; EBNY, *Ebony* magazine, 1960.
- November 25, 1959: Lavern Rowlee was shot to death near Weavers Needle by Ralph Thomas after Rowlee had an altercation with his wife Donna Thomas. *Source:* AZREP: *Arizona Republic*, 1959.
- October 1960: Reminiscent of Adolph Ruth's death, the skeleton of Austrian student, Franz Harrier, was found at the foot of Superstition Mountain. Several days later his skull was found with two bullet holes in it. *Source:* AU, Author, 2018.
- October 23, 1960: An unidentified body was discovered by two dentists in the Superstition Mountains that was thought to be a missing San Francisco man named William R. Harvey. After comparing dental records, the deceased's identity remains unknown. *Source:* AZREP, *Arizona Republic*, 1960.
- January 10, 1961: The body of fifty-year-old Salt Lake City prospector, Hilmer C. Bohen, was discovered by the children of three families picnicking in the Superstition Mountains. He was buried in a shallow grave of sand with a bullet hole in his back that was officially ruled a "suicide." *Source:* AZREP, *Arizona Republic*, 1961.
- March 21, 1961: The body of fifty-seven-year-old Denver machinist, Walter J. Mowry, was found in Needle Canyon near Weavers Needle. Though the body was "bullet-riddled," the death was ruled a suicide. *Source:* AZREP, *Arizona Republic*, 1961.
- September 6, 1961: Lost Dutchman Gold prospector John A. Swenson "Jabez" Clapp was last seen in Apache Junction on July 6. He stayed missing for three years when his "headless skeleton" was finally discovered. The Swedish born prospector and hermit reportedly lived in a Superstition Mountain mine tunnel, wore a

tie whenever he went to town, and he was well known and liked by locals who called him "Jabez." His death remains a mystery. *Source:* AZREP, *Arizona Republic*, 1961.

- July 24, 1962: Ed Piper died of ulcer complications in Florence, Arizona after he was medivaced by helicopter from his last camp at Piper Springs. *Source:* AZREP: *Arizona Republic*, 1962.

- March 27, 1963: Young Phoenix geologist Vance Bacon died when he fell, or was pushed, 500 feet off Weavers Needle while working for prospector Maria Celeste Jones. *Sources:* AZREP: *Arizona Republic*, 1963; *Ebony* magazine, 1960; AU, Author, 2018.

- April 19, 1963: Before his death at the age of seventy-six, life-long Superstition Mountain cowboy, author, and rancher Wayne Ellsworth Barnard wrote a gem of a little book under his preferred sobriquet Barney Barnard: *The Story of Jacob Walzer: Superstition Mountain and Its Famed Dutchman's Lost Mine.* The old time cowman who established the B bar B Rancho del Superstitions was a World War I veteran, and he gave an engrossing interview about the deaths of strangers who often crossed his rangelands, recorded in part: "I have lived in the shadow of this famous Superstition Mountain for more than fifty years. During that time it has been my misfortune to accompany the posse and help to bring out the bodies of fifty prospectors who had been killed in their search for this fabulous wealthy lost Dutchman mine. Who the killers are, we do not know." *Sources:* Interview, n/a; AZREP, *Arizona Republic*, 1963.

- March 22, 1964: Husband and wife John and Mildred Bertella of Sherrill, New York were murdered on the First Water Road near Superstition Mountain. The suspect was quickly snared by Maricopa County Sherriff Deputies, Indian trackers from the state prison, and bloodhounds while driving the couple's stolen pickup truck across the Sage, Nevada desert. The effort grabbed page 1 headlines: "Killer Suspect Caught." *Source:* AZREP, *Arizona Republic*, 1964.

- November 11, 1964: Brothers Richard and Robert Kermis froze to death in Siphon Draw after one of the brothers got injured in a fall. They stuck together when they were trapped by an unexpected snow storm over Superstition Mountain. *Source:* KTC, 2016.
- 1970s: Vague accounts report that Bob Ward, a thirty-year veteran of piecing together the Spanish clues and marks to lost gold, discovered a cave in West Boulder Canyon that housed two mummies.
- Septmber 10, 1970: Al Morrow, "The Good Samaritan of the Superstitions," died when he was crushed by a boulder during a cave-in inside his Needle Canyon mine tunnel. *Source:* AU, Author, 2018.
- July 26, 1971: 2nd Lt. William J. Stone, Williams Air Force Base, Arizona, died when his T-38 Talon crashed "in a huge fireball which lit up the west face of [Superstition] mountain at the 4,300 foot level [4,570 foot per flight diagram] just 700 feet below the [north] summit of the Superstitions." Twenty-three-year-old Lt. Stone of the 3525 Pilot Training Squadron was on a routine solo training mission and was expected to graduate September 11. *Source:* AAIR, 1971.
- May 12, 1973: Charles Lewing, thirty-two, of Houston, Texas was shot and killed at his mining camp near Weavers Needle [some indicate it was Squaw Box Canyon] by Ladislao Sánchez Guerrero, thirty-five, a Mexican national, in what an East Mesa Justice of the Peace ruled was a justifiable homicide over an employment dispute. *Source:* TDC, 1973.
- September 9, 1976: Prospector Harold Lewis Polling, fifty-five, of St. Johns, Ohio, was shot with a 30-30 rifle (some indicate a 44 Magnum revolver) when it accidentally discharged at his

Charlebois Spring camp. His partner, Ronald Cook, hiked out to First Water and summoned help from the Department of Public Safety. They launched SAR (Search and Rescue) in a Bell Long Ranger helicopter and medevaced Polling to Mesa Lutheran Hospital were he was pronounced DOA. *Source:* AZREP, *Arizona Republic*, 1976.

- February 1977: Vague accounts report a man named Dennis Brown died from a gunshot wound at the Quarter Circle U Ranch.
- April 22, 1978: Mexican vaquero Manuel Váldez was assassinated at the J. F. Ranch where he worked by suspects using high powered rifles. The pair was later captured in a manhunt and convicted of murder. Thirteen-year-old Charlie Dobie was murdered at the J. F. Ranch on May 31, 1892, *Sources:* AZREP, *Arizona Republic*, 1892; SKRT, 1981; AU, Author, 2018.
- December 9, 1978: Sixty-five-year-old retired Red Cross exective, Lee Daniel Krebs, died in a 500-foot fall while hiking up Siphon Draw. Krebs's body wasn't recovered for six days. *Source:* AZREP, *Arizona Republic*, 1978.
- February 11, 1980: Twenty-year-old hiker Ricky Penning died in a sixty-foot fall while hunting in Trap Canyon below Music Mountain. Penning went missing from his March 1979 hunting party, but his remains weren't discovered until January 13, 1981. After many heart wrenching searches for his only son, his father, Frank, spotted his remains below the cliff where Ricky last stood. Pinal County Range Deputies helped recover the remains. Mr. Fenning later returned to pay his last respects at the site, accompanied by a US Forest Service Ranger and reporter. *Source:* AZREP, *Arizona Republic*, 1980.
- January 28, 1981: A Phoenix woman, not named here out of deference to next of kin, was kidnapped in Phoenix, thrown off a cliff, and buried alive beneath Fish Creek Hill by two

suspects. Both men were convicted, one was executed. *Source:* ABC News, 2017.

- June 7, 1982: Hiker Adam Scott was reported missing in the Roosevelt Lake area and vanished without a trace for the next fourteen years. On March 25, 1996, Robert Schoose and Barry Wiegle saw what they thought were human skeletal remains during a helicopter reconnaissance of the Bronco Butte area and called Superstition Mountains' historian Tom Kolleborn to verify who was still missing. Kollenborn called it right on the money, and wrote: "Finally there was closure for Scott's family." *Source:* KTC, 2016.

- May 2, 1984: Chef and legendary Lost Dutchman Gold hunter Walter Gassler did exhaustive research at California's Bancroft Library, spent years tracing the threads, seeking new clues, interviewing locals, and pounding down rugged trails in search of the mythic trove when he mysteriously died of a "heart attack" at Charlebois Spring. It was later discovered Gassler had a backpack full of gold experts said matched the Jacob Waltz's death bed lode, a "candle box stored under his bed that held 48½ pounds of gold ore that was 33 percent pure and was assayed at 5,500 ounces to a ton!" We'll never know, though the lost treasure Illuminati certainly does. *Sources:* AU, Author, 2018; CHB, 2002.

- December 3, 1999: The skeletal remains of convicted bank robber Richard Pietras were discovered by horseback riders near Cholla Tank on Hackberry Mesa. *Source:* KTC, 2015.

- December 4, 2009: Denver Sheraton Hotel bell hop and adventurer, thirty-five-year-old Jesse Capen, disappeared on the first day of his planned one-month search for the Lost Dutchman Gold Mine. His backpack, tent, a boot, and skeletal remains weren't discovered by hikers until late November 2012 at the foot of 4,918-foot Tortilla Mountain. The summit register

included a note from Capen: "Jesse Capen was here. Dec. 4, 2009." Capen's parents kept an urn of their son's remains; his mother, Cynthia Burnett, said: "Those bones were formed in me." Source: DPOST: *Denver Post*, 2013.
- September 10, 2009: Fifty-three-year-old veteran hiker, Kelly Tate, died of a sudden cardiac arrest near the Discovery Trailhead in Lost Dutchman State Park where his body lay for five days before it was discovered. Source: AZREP, *Arizona Republic*, 2009.
- July 11, 2010: Three Salt Lake City, Utah treasure hunters disappeared like campfire smoke after they parked their car at a Lost Dutchman State Park trailhead and went searching for the Dutchman's trove of gold in the brick oven 110-degree summer heat: Curtis Merworth, sixty-seven, Ardean Charles, sixty-six, and Malcolm Meeks, fifty-five. Their remains were not discovered until January 5, 2011 when veteran hiker Rick Gwynn made the first grim discovery of two skeletons on the slopes of 3,061-foot Yellow Peak above the Black Mesa Trail. That led to the discovery of the third victim by SSAR (Superstition Search and Rescue) on January 15, 2011. Sources: ABC News; DSRT, *Deseret News*; AZREP, *Arizona Republic*, 2011.
- November 24, 2011: During a fiery Thanksgiving Day plane crash, a twin-engine Rockwell AC69 disintegrated when it hit the North Summit of Superstition Mountain, killing all six people on board. Now honored with a marble bench facing Superstition Mountain, the memorial is etched with the names of pilot, father and husband, Shawn Perry, the "Angels Three," Luke, six, Logan, eight, Morgan, nine, owner Russell Hardy, thirty-one, and mechanic Joseph Hardwick, twenty-two. Source: ABC News.
- July 6, 2012: Avid hiker Kenneth Paul Clark died of dehydration and heatstroke in the Garden Area 1.5 miles from the First Water Trailhead. Sources: Various.

- April 15, 2013: Thirty-four-year-old veteran Siphon Draw hiker, Christopher Hensley, died in a fall while on an evening hike up to the Flat Iron beneath the North Summit of Superstition Mountain. In spite of his wife Tonya's repeated phone calls for help, Hensley's body was not recovered until four days later. *Sources:* Various.
- August 12, 2015: An unidentified sixty-five-year-old California woman died of heat stroke three-quarters of a mile from the Peralta Trailhead. *Source:* ADI, *Arizona Daily*, 2015.
- February 26, 2016: Twenty-five-year-old Grand Prairie, Texas BASE jumper Brian Head died while carrying his parachute to his remote base jump site above Siphon Draw. Head was a veteran BASE (Building, Antenna, Structure and Earth) jumper with more than 200 jumps. His harness was not strapped on while hiking when he slipped on the loose rocks and fell approximately 100 feet into a crevice. Pinal Country Search and Rescue members later rappelled down to extricate and recover Head's body. *Sources:* Various.
- June 20, 2016: Twenty-five-year-old Anthony Quatela III, ran out of water while hiking the Peralta Trail with a companion and died of heatstroke. *Sources:* Various.

SOURCES

Refer to Select Bibliography Citations, Library Collections, and Online Sources

* * *

AAIR: July 26, 1971
ABC: News Report, 2011, 2017
ADI: *Arizona Daily*, 2015
AGZ: *Arizona Gazette*, 1884
ARJ: Robert J. Allen, 1971
AZREP: *Arizona Republic,* 1892; 1947; 1947; 1959; 1960; 1961; 1962; 1963; 1964; 1976; 1978; 1980; 2009
ASG: *Arizona: A State Guide,* 1907
AU: Author, 2018
BJE: James E. Bark, 1892 to 1928
BJM: James M. Barney, 1935
BB: Barney Barnard, 1964
BJG: John G. Bourke, 1872
BRT: Ron Butler, 1988
CES: Estee Conaster, 1972
CHSG: Helen Corbin, 1993
CHB: Helen Corbin, 2002
CS: Carlson and Stewart, 1995
DSRT: *Deseret News*, 2011
DPOST: *Denver Post*, 2013
EBNY, *Ebony Magazine*, 1960
ESLD: Sims Ely, 1953
GCKM: Curt Gentry, 1968
HGB: George "Brownie" Holmes, 1944
KTC: Tom Kollenborn, 2016
LNVB: Nyle Leatham, 1965

LIFE: Dora J. Hamblin, 1967
MCCG: Montezuma, 1998
MCJ: Medical Certificate, 1947
MGB: Bernice McGee, 1964
NWS: Wendsler Nosie, Sr., 2007
OBO: Oroblanco, 2010
PGD: Prairie Ghosts, 2017
SKRT: Swanson and Kollenborn, 1981
SMM: Superstition Mountain Museum, 2016
SRM: Robert Sikorsky, 1984
TDC: *Tucson Daily Citizen*, 1973
TJPCS: Juan Thomas, 1839-1913
TNSC: Norm Tessman, 2006
TRN: Treasure Net, 2015
WGSM: Gus Walker, 1991
YBLT: Bill Yenne, 1999

Selected Bibliography

AAIR, July 26, 1971. Aviation Archeological Investigation & Research: Northrop T-38 Talon T-38A s/n 61-0921 26 JUL 71 Superstition Mountains AZ HDJ.

Abbey, Edward. "The Mountains of Superstitions," in *Cactus Country*. New York: Time-Life Books, 1973.

Allen, Robert J. *The Story of Superstition Mountain and the Lost Dutchman Gold Mine: The Violent, Tragic, True Account of the Gold-Hungry Men Who Challenged the Treacherous Peak Sacred to the Apaches.* New York: Pocket Books, 1971.

Annerino, John. *Vanishing Borderlands: The Fragile Landscape of the U.S-Mexico Border,* (photography by the author). New York: W.W. Norton, 2008.

___. *Indian Country: Sacred Ground, Native Peoples,* (photography and Native American glossary by the author). New York: W.W. Norton, 2007.

___. *Apache: The Sacred Path to Womanhood,* (photography by the author). New York: Marlowe & Company, 1998.

___. "Dead Man's Tale. A Treasure Hunter, a Skull and Bones and the Lost Dutchman Mine Lead a Writer Along the Hot Trail to a Cold Case," (photography, historical photos and map research by the author). *Arizona Highways Magazine*, Vol. 83, No. 4 (April 2007): 20-25.

___. *Dead in Their Tracks: Crossing America's Desert Borderlands in the New Era,* (photography, maps, and appendices by the author). Tucson: University of Arizona Press, 2009.

Anyon, Roger, T. J. Ferguson, and Chip Colwell-Chanthaphonh. "Natural Setting as Cultural Landscapes: The Power of Place and Tradition." USDA Forest Service Proceedings RMRS-P-36. 2005.

Arizona: A State Guide, Compiled by Workers of the Writers Program of the Work Projects Administration in the State of Arizona, American Guide Series. New York: Hastings House, 1940.

Austin, Mary Hunter. *The Land of Little Rain.* New York: Houghton Mifflin, 1903.

Avey, Gary, Editor. "The Triumph of an Individual," and "DeGrazia: A Retrospective," (etchings and paintings by Ettore "Ted" DeGrazia): "Artist of the People," Maggie Wilson; "Ted DeGrazia: A Personal View," Dick Frontain; "DeGrazia: A Permanent Personality," Joseph Stacey. *Arizona Highways Magazine,* Vol. 59, No. 3 (March 1983): 1, 2-15.

Bahr, Donald M. "Pima and Papago Medicine and Philosophy," in *Handbook of North American Indians, Southwest,* Vol. 10:193-200. Washington, DC: Smithsonian Institution, 1983.

Bark, James E. *The Bark Notes: 1860 to 1938,* [years 1892 to 1928], edited and annotated by Thomas Probert. Published by T. Probert, 19__? Available at the Phoenix Public Library, AZ. Search: https://catalog.phoenixpubliclibrary.org/

Barnard, Barney. *The Story of Jacob Walzer: Superstition Mountain and Its Famed Dutchman's Lost Mine.* Apache Junction, AZ: Barney Barnard, 1964.

Barnes, William C. *Arizona Place Names.* Tucson: University of Arizona Press, 1988.

Barney, James M. "How Apache Leap Got Its Name." *Arizona Highways,* (August 1935): na

Barrett, S. M. *Geronimo, His Own Story, The Autobiography of a Great Patriot Warrior, As Told to S. M. Barrett,* (introduction and notes by Frederick W. Turner). New York: A Meridian Book, 1996. Originally published: *Geronimo's Story of His Life.* New York: Duffield, 1906.

Basso, Keith H., ed. *Western Apache Raiding and Warfare: From the Notes of Grenville Goodwin.* Tucson: University of Arizona Press, 1971.

___. "Western Apache," in *Handbook of North American Indians, Southwest,* Vol. 10: 462-488. Washington, DC: Smithsonian Institution, 1983.

___. *Wisdom Sits in Places: Landscape and Language Among the Western Apache.* Albuquerque: University of New Mexico Press, 1996.

Beezley, William H. *Insurgent Governor: Abraham González and the Mexican Revolution in Chihuahua.* Lincoln: University of Nebraska Press, 1973.

Bicknell, Pierpont C. "One of Arizona's Lost El Dorados, A Mine in the Superstition Mountains. A Half-told Tale of an Old Miser, Afraid to Return to the Source of His Mysterious Wealth." *San Francisco Chronicle* (January 13, 1895): 1.

Blair, Robert. *Tales of the Superstitions: The Origin of the Lost Dutchman Legend,* (introduction Barry M. Goldwater, photos Wink Blair, and maps by Don Bufkin). Tempe, AZ: Arizona Historical Foundation, 1975.

Bourke, John G. *On the Border with Crook,* illustrated. New York: Charles Scribner's Sons, 1891.

Bowden, Charles. *Killing the Hidden Waters.* Austin: University of Texas Press, 2003.

Burbridge, Jonathan S. *Arizona's Monuments to Lost Mines, 1940: Trail Signs, Symbols and Maps.* Reno, NV: Jonathan S. Burbridge, 1969.

Butler, Ron. "Travels with Ted: Artist led Treks to Superstitions in Search of Gold," (photographs by the writer). *Arizona Daily Star,* Sunday (October 2, 1988): 1g, 3g.

Clark, C. M. *History of the Lost Dutchman Mine,* (commentary by Otis M. Blackmer). Los Angeles: Blackmer Company, 1926.

Consaster, Estee. *The Sterling Legend: The Facts Behind the Lost Dutchman Mine.* Baldwin Park, CA: Gem Guides Book Co., 1972.

Conrad, Joseph. *Nostromo: A Tale of the Seaboard.* United Kingdom: Harper & Brothers, 1904.

Geronimo, cradling a 45-70 caliber 1873 trapdoor Springfield rifle, May 16, 1884, A. Frank Randall portrait, Wilcox, Arizona Territory. Courtesy: Library of Congress

Corbin, Helen M. *The Bible on the Lost Dutchman Gold Mine and Jacob Waltz.* Prescott, AZ: Wolfe Publishing, 2002.

___. *Senner's Gold: Over 1000 pounds of Stolen Goldfield Ore Hidden in the Superstitions.* Phoenix: Foxwest Publishing, 1993.

de Nájera, Pedro de Casteñada, Francsico Vásquez de Coronado, Antonio de Mendoza, and Juan Camilo Jaramillo. *The Journey of Coronado 1540-1542, From the City of Mexico to the Grand Cañon of the Colorado and the Buffalo Plains of Texas, Kansas and Nebraska,* (Translated and Edited with an Introduction by George Parker Winship). New York: Allerton Book Company, 1904.

Debo, Angie. *Geronimo: The Man, His Time, His Place.* Norman: University of Oklahoma Press, 1976.

DeGrazia, Ettore "Ted." *DeGrazia and His Mountain, The Superstition.* Tucson, AZ: DeGrazia Gallery in the Sun, 1972.

"Ettore DeGrazia, 73, Burned Paintings to Protest Taxes." *The New York Times, Arts,* (Saturday, September 18, 1982): online.

Dobie, Frank J. *Apache Gold and Yaqui Silver.* London: Hammond, Hammond & Company, 1956.

___. *Coronado's Children; Tales of Lost Mines and Buried Treasures of the Southwest.* New York: Garden City Publishing, 1930, p. viii.

Ely, Sims. *The Lost Dutchman Mine; The Fabulous Story of the Seven-decade Search for the Hidden Treasure in the Superstition Mountains of Arizona.* New York: William Morrow and Co., 1953.

Ezell, Paul H. "History of the Pima," in *Handbook of North American Indians, Southwest,* Vol. 10: 149-160. Washington, DC: Smithsonian Institution, 1983.

Farish, Thomas Edwin, Arizona Historian. *History of Arizona,* Vol. V. Phoenix, AZ: 1918.

Felger, Richard Stephen, and Mary Beck Moser. *People of the Desert and Sea: Ethnobotany of the Seri Indians.* Tucson: University of Arizona Press, 1985.

"Foul Murder: A Mexican is Killed by a Supposed Friend." *Arizona Gazette*, [Phoenix], (June 18, 1884): online

"Found the Lair of the Apache Kid. Hidden Cave Discovered in the Superstition Mountains. Arizonans Locate the Hiding-Place of the Notorious Redskin. Almost Inaccessible Cavern In the Side of a Precipitous Incline." *San Francisco Call*, Vol. 82, No. 55, (July 25, 1897): 1

Gentry, Kurt. *The Killer Mountains: A Search for the Legendary Lost Dutchman Mine*. New York: New American Library, 1968.

Germick, Stephen. "Legend of Apache Leap: A Reevaluation." Tonto National Forest Supervisor's Office. Phoenix, AZ: April 18, 2012

"A Ghostly Inspiration—An Uncanny Spot in Arizona." *The Winslow Mail*, Navajo County, Arizona, Saturday (August 15, 1896): 1

Glover, Thomas E. *The Lost Dutchman Mine of Jacob Waltz: The Golden Dream*. Phoenix, AZ: Cowboy-Miner Productions, 1998.

Goddard, Pliny Earle. "Myths and Tales From the San Carlos Apache." *Anthropological Papers of the American Museum of Natural History*, Vol. 24, Part 1. (August 1918): 3-86.

Goodwin, Grenville, and Keith H. Basso, ed. *The Social Organization of the Western Apache*. Tucson, AZ: University of Arizona Press, 1941.

Hamblin, Dora Jane. "The Strange Quest of James Kidd," (photographs not attributed). *LIFE*, Vol. 62, No. 9 (March 3, 1967): 76-78, 79-80, 83, 85.

Hayden, Julian D. "Hohokam Petroglyphs of the Sierra Pinacate, Sonora and the Hohokam Shell Expeditions." *Kiva*, Vol. 37, No. 2 (Winter, 1972): 74-83.

Harwell, Henry O., and Marsha C. S. Kelly. "Maricopa," in *Handbook of North American Indians, Southwest*, Vol. 10: 71-85. Washington, DC: Smithsonian Institution, 1983.

Hill, J. Brett, Jeffery J. Clark, William H. Doelle and Patrick D. Lyons. "Prehistoric Demography in the Southwest: Migration, Coalescence, and Hohokam Population Decline." *American Antiquity*, Vol. 69, No. 4 (October 2004): 689-716

Holmes, George "Brownie." *Story of the Lost Dutchman.* [S.l.: s.n.], 1944, 41 pages. *****Note:** "s.n." *sine nomine* (without name [of publisher]). Available at the Phoenix Public Library, AZ. Search: https://catalog.phoenixpubliclibrary.org/

Holmes, George "Brownie," compiled by Thomas E. Glover. *The Holmes Manuscript: The Lost Dutchman Mine of Jacob Waltz, Part 2.* Phoenix, AZ: Cowboy-Miner Productions, 2000.

Howell, Georgina. *Gertrude Bell: Queen of the Desert, Shaper of Nations.* New York: Farrar, Straus and Giroux, 2006.

James, George Wharton. "Through Apache-Land Over the Apache Trail" in *Arizona, The Wonderland: The History of its Ancient Cliff and Cave Dwellings . . .* Boston: The Page Company, 1917.

Johnson, David M. "*Chi'chil Biłdagoteel* / Oak Flat." National Register of Historic Places, U. S. Department of the Interior, National Park Service, December 2, 2015.

Johnson, James W., and Marilyn D. Johnson. *De Grazia: The Man and the Myth,* illustrated. Tucson: University of Arizona Press, 2014.

Kearney, James R. "A Death in the Superstitions: The Fate of Adolph Ruth," (map by Don Bufkin). *The Journal of Arizona History*, Vol. 33, No. 2 (Summer 1992): 117-152.

Kehoe, Thomas F. "Paleo Indian Bison Drives: Feasibility Studies." *Plains Anthropologist* Vol. 23, No. 82, Part 2: Memoir 14: Bison Procurement and Utilization: A Symposium. (November 1978): 79-83.

Kenworthy, Charles A. *Treasure Secrets of the Lost Dutchman.* Encino, CA: 1997.

Khera, Sigrid, and Patricia S. Mariella. "Yavapai," in *Handbook of North American Indians, Southwest*, Vol. 10: 38-54. Washington, DC: Smithsonian Institution, 1983.

Kitei, Lynne D., and Gary E. Schwartz. *The Phoenix Lights: A Skeptics Discovery That We Are Not Alone.* Cardiff, CA: Waterfront Digital Press, 2017.

Klauber, Laurence M. *Rattlesnakes: Their Habits, Life Histories, and Influence on Mankind, 2 Volumes.* Berkeley: University of California Press, 1956, 2nd edition 1997, (foreword by Harry W. Greene).

Kollenborn, Thomas J. "Secrets of the Missing," The Tom Kollenborn Chronicles (Friday, September 16, 2016): online.

Krutch, Joseph Wood. *The Voice of the Desert: A Naturalist's Interpretation.* New York: William Sloane Associates, 1954.

Leatham, Nyle. "Photographer Tells of Aiding Rescuers in Hunt for Body. Mountain Tragedy. Needle Climber's Plunge to Death." *Arizona Republic*, Wednesday, (March 27, 1963): 7.

Lutch, Debbie. Tonto National Forest Threatened, Endangered and Sensitive (TES) Species 2000 Draft Abstracts.

Malm, Carl J. Arizona State Department of Health, State File No, 314, Registrar No. 864, Medical Certificate: April, 25, 1947.

Marino, Cesare. *The Remarkable Carlo Gentile: Pioneer Italian Photographer of the American Frontier* (photographs by Carlo Gentile). Nevada City, CA: Carl Mautz Publishing, 1998.

McClintock, James H. "Fighting Apaches, A Narrative of the Fifth Cavalry's Deadly Conflict in the Superstition Mountains of Arizona." *Sunset Magazine*, Vol. 18, No. 4 (February 1907): 340-343.

McGaroin, Thomas G, "The 1887 Sonoran Earthquake: It Wasn't Our Fault." Fieldnotes, Arizona Bureau of Geology and Mineral Technology, Vol. 17, No. 2 (Summer 1987): 1-2.

McGee, Bernice. "The Other World of the Superstitions," (photographs by Don Barnett). *Old West Magazine*, Vol. 1, No. 2 (Winter 1964): 2-60.

McGee, Bernice, and Jack. "Invitation to a Ghost Walk Through the Superstitions," (photos by the writers). *True West*, Vol. 13, No. 4 (March-April 1966): 5-17, 49-50.

Mead, Douglas V. *They Never Surrendered: Bronco Apaches of the Sierra Madres, 1890-1935*. Tucson, AZ: Westernlore Press, 1993.

Minnigerode, Fitzhugh L. "Lost Mines Exert Lure: In the Southwest Tales Persist of Vast Treasures Hidden in the Mountains Lands of Treasure Gold in That Thar Pen The Dutchman's Toll." *New York Times*, Sunday Travel, June 11, 1939.

"New Search for Lost Gold: Amateur Prospectors Follow Legends in Hunt for Millions in Buried Treasure." *Ebony*, Vol. XV, No. 6 (April 1960): 53-54, 57-59.

Nosie, Sr. Wendsler, Testimony of Chairman of the San Carlos Apache Tribe Before the U.S. House Natural Resources Committee, Subcommittee on National Parks, Forests and Public Lands, Concerning the Southeast Arizona Land Exchange and Conservation Act of 2007 H.R. 3301, November 1, 2007: "The Holy and Sacred Sites of Oak Flat, Apache Leap and Devil's Canyon."

O'Keeffe, Georgia. "About Myself" in *Georgia O'Keeffe: Exhibition of Oils and Pastels*, January 22–March 17, 1939, An American Place, 509 Madison Avenue, New York City.

Opler, Morris E. "Chiricahua Apache," in *Handbook of North American Indians, Southwest*, Vol. 10: 401-418. Washington, DC: Smithsonian Institution, 1983.

___. *An Apache Life-Way: The Economic, Social, and Religious Institutions of the Chiricahua Apache*. Chicago: University of Chicago Press, 1941.

Ramses, John Victor. *Quest for Peralta Gold: A Hidden History of Red Mountain*. Sandy, Utah: Oneta Vera Enterprises, 1997-2000, revised ebook, 2005.

Record, Ian W. *Big Sycamore Stands Alone: The Western Apaches, Aravaipa, and the Struggle for Place*. Norman: University of Oklahoma Press, 2008.

Reed, Allen C. "Trek for Gold," (photographs by the writer). *Arizona Highways*, Vol. 27, No. 3 (March 1951): 2-3, 26-27.

Reisner, Marc. *Cadillac Desert: The American West and Its Disappearing Water*. New York: Penguin Books, 1986.

Robinson, Richard A. "Review of Adolph Ruth's California Mine information." 12/28/2013; Upd 3/8/2016, www.lost-dutchman.com/dutchman/angelinaSpringUpdate.pdf

Russell, Frank. *The Pima Indians*, "The Legend of the Stone Ghosts of Crooked Mountain," from the *Twenty-Sixth Annual Report of the Bureau of American Ethnology, 1905-1905*. Washington: Government Printing Office, 1908.

Ruth, Erwin C. "The Fervent Romances in Seething Mexico." Apache Junction, AZ: Superstition Mountain Historical Society, ms. 1931.

___. "The Story of the Mexican Gold Mine." Apache Junction, AZ: Superstition Mountain Historical Society, ms. 1931.

Schaefer, Lake Erie. *Dead Men Do Tell Tales: Stories from the Diary of Frank L. Fish*. Chino, CA: Amador Publishing, 2010.

Scott, G. S., ed. "The Story of Apache Leap: A Region of Romance and Reminiscence transformed by Modern Industry." *Arizona: The State Magazine*, Vol. 5, No. 2, (December 1914): 1.

"The [Apache] Kid's Cave." *Arizona Republican Newspaper*, Thursday, (June 10, 1897): 4.

Shaw, Anna Moore. *Pima Indian Legends*. Tempe: Arizona State University, Indian Education Center, 1963.

Sikorsky, Robert. "Murder in the Superstitions." *The Arizona Republic*, Sunday, (January 8, 1984): 232.

"Skull believed that of missing prospector," *The Arizona Republic*, Sunday Morning, (December 13, 1931): 1.

Steinbeck, John. *Tortilla Flat*. New York: Covici Friede, 1935.

___. *The Log from the Sea of Cortez*. New York: The Viking Press, 1951.

Stocker, Joseph S. "Ladders to the Clouds." *Boy's Life, For All Boys*. (December 1948): 14, 30-31.

Stolley, Richard B. "Mysterious Maps to Lost Gold Mines," (photographs by Bill Ray). LIFE Magazine, Vol. 56, No. 24 (June 12, 1964): 90-94, 96.

Storm, Barry. "Storm Deciphers Peralta Maps, Historical Treasure Troves." *The Treasure Hunter*, Vol. 3, No. 1, (1967): Cover, 4-8, 16-22, 24.

___. *Thunder God's Gold: The Amazing True Story of America's Famed Lost Gold Mines, Epitome of Western Traditions*. Tortilla Flat, AZ: Southwest Publishing Company, 1945.

___. "Wagoner's Lost Ledge." *The Desert Magazine*, Vol. 8, No. 4 (February 1945): 23-24.

___. "Bonanza of the Lost Dutchman." *The Desert Magazine*, Vol. 8, No. 7 (May 1945): 16-18.

Summerhayes, Martha. *Vanished Arizona: Recollections of My Army Life*. Philadelphia: J. B. Lippincott and Co, 1908.

Swanson, James, and Tom Kollenborn. *Superstition Mountain: A Ride through Time*. Phoenix, AZ: Arrowhead Press, 1981.

Tackenberg, David. "Walter J. Lubken: U. S. Reclamation Service Photographer at Roosevelt Dam: A Photo Essay." *The Journal of Arizona History*, Vol. 50, No. 4 (Winter, 2009): 365-392.

Tessman, Norm. "Skeleton Cave through the Haze of 133 Years." *Verde Independent*, (January 11, 2006): online.

Thomas, Juan. "From the Pima Calendar Stick 1839-1913, The Calendar of Juan Thomas of Blackwater," (including Juan Thomas Calendar Markings). From Interviews Recorded by C. H. Southworth, 1914, Transcribed From the Original Notes by James H. Jones, 1961, ms. 32 pages.

Thompson, Richard H. "A Mexican Revolutionary from Notre Dame: A Note." *Indiana Magazine of History*, Vol. 85, Issue 3, (September 1989): 261-264.

Thrapp, Dan L. *Conquest of Apacheria*. Norman: University of Oklahoma Press, 1967.

Turney, Omar A. "Prehistoric Irrigation," *Arizona State Historian*, Vol. 2, No. 1 (April 1929); No. 2 (July 1929); No. 3 (October 1929; No. 4 (January 1930).

Van Dyke, John C. *The Desert: Further Studies in Natural Appearances*. New York: Charles Scribner's Sons, 1901.

Walker, Gus, and Editors. "Superstition Wilderness Mystique," (full-page color map, timeline, and trails). *The Arizona Republic*, Sunday, (October 20, 1991):12.

Walker, Henry P., and Don Bufkin. *Historical Atlas of Arizona*. Norman: University of Oklahoma Press, 1979.

Walton, Travis. *Fire in the Sky: The Walton Experience*. Boston, MA: Da Capo Press, 1997.

Ward, Bob. "Ripples of the Past," in *True Story of Superstition Mountains*: Apache Junction, AZ: Tract Evangelistic Crusade, 1990.

Wasley, William W., and Alfred Johnson. "Salvage Archaeology in Painted Rocks Reservoir, Western Arizona." Anthropological Papers of the University of Arizona, No. 9. Tucson: University of Arizona, 1965.

Webb, George. *A Pima Remembers*. Tucson: University of Arizona Press, 1959.

Weis, Lewis A. "Has Lost Dutchman Mine Now Been Found?" *Miami Daily Arizona Silver Belt*, Saturday, (July 24, 1920): 2.

"Who Murdered Charlie Dobie?" *Arizona Republic,* Sunday, (June 5, 1892): 1.

Wild, Peter, and Neil Carmony. "The Trip Not Taken: John C. Van Dyke, Heroic Doer or Armchair Seer?" *The Journal of Arizona History,* Vol. 34, No. 1 (Spring, 1993):65-80.

Woodward, Arthur. "A Shell Bracelet Manufactory." *American Antiquity*. Vol. 2, No. 2 (October 1936): 117-125.

Worst, Clay. "The Salazar Survey." *Superstition Mountain Journal*, Vol. 4 (February 25, 1984): 24-35. Apache Junction, AZ.

___. "Dutchman Lecture, 2006." Superstition Mountain Museum, Apache Junction, AZ.

Wright, Aaron M., and Pat H. Stein, Barnaby V. Lewis, William H. Doelle. "The Great Bend of the Gila [River]: A Nationally Significant Cultural Landscape," *Archaeology Southwest*, prepared for National Trust for Historic Preservation, (December 2015): 102 pages.

Yenne, Bill. *Lost Treasure*. New York: Berkley Books, 1999.

Maps

TREASURE MAPS

Peralta, Manuel Alejandro. *Cuento de Oro del Río Salado del Norte mapa,* 1753, "Legend of Gold of the Salt River of the North" map, 1753. The map was acquired from the "Chicago group" who discovered it glued inside the back cover of a book and became known as the Burbridge Map for John Burbridge who studied and published the map that was drawn in Spanish and Latin.

Ruth, Erwin C. *Perfil Mapa,* "Profile Map," and *Mapa del Desierto,* "Profile Map," 1913, acquired in Nuevo León, Mexico from Sr. Juan J. González. The maps became known as the González-Peralta Maps.

US GEOLOGICAL SURVEY TOPOGRAPHICAL MAPS/SUPERSTITION WILDERNESS

Weavers Needle 7.5 Minute Quadrangle, USGS: 2004, ID: o33111d3, Maricopa County, Arizona, Scale: 1:24000, Size: 24" × 36." Visit: www.usgs.gov

Goldfield 7.5 Minute Quadrangle, USGS: 2004, ID: o33111d4, Maricopa County, Arizona, Scale: 1:24000, Size: 24" × 36".

Iron Mountain 7.5 Minute Quadrangle, USGS: 2004, ID: o33111d2, Maricopa County, Arizona, Scale: 1:24000, Size: 24" × 36".

Horse Mesa Dam 7.5 Minute Quadrangle, USGS: 2004, ID: o33111e3, Gila County, Arizona, Scale: 1:24000, Size: 24" × 36".

Mormon Flat Dam, 7.5 Minute Quadrangle, USGS: 2004, ID: o33111e4, Maricopa County, Arizona, Scale: 1:24000, Size: 24" × 36".

Filmography

Movies

1996: *Jerry Maguire*, directed by Cameron Crowe, starring Tom Cruise, Cuba Gooding Jr. and Renée Zellweger.

1994: *Blind Justice*, directed by Richard Spence, starring Armand Assante, Elisabeth Shue, and Jack Black, HBO.

1987: *Raising Arizona*, directed by the Coen Brothers, starring Nicholas Cage, Holly Hunter, John Goodman, and William Forsythe.

1970: *The Ballad of Cable Hogue,* directed by Sam Peckinpah, starring Jason Robards, Stella Stevens, David Warner, Strother Martin, and Slim Pickens.

1969: *Charro*, directed by Charles Marquis Warren, starring Elvis Presley, Ina Balin, and Victor French.

1965: *Arizona Raiders*, directed by William Witney, starring Audie Murphy, Michael Dante.

1961: *The Purple Hills*, directed by Maury Dexter, starring Gene Nelson, Kent Taylor, Danny Zapien.

1957: *Gunfight at the O.K. Corral,* directed by John Sturges, starring Kirk Douglas, Burt Lancaster, script by novelist Leon Uris.

1955: *Pardners,* directed by Norman Taurog, starring Dean Martin, Jerry Lewis.

1949: *Lust for Gold,* directed by S. Sylvan Simon, starring Ida Lupino, Glenn Ford, and Gig Young, adapted from treasure hunter Barry Storm's 1945 book, *Thunder God's Gold.*

1948: *Guns of Hate*, directed by Lesley Selander, starring Tim Holt, Richard, Martin, RKO Pictures.

Television

2015: *Legend of the Superstition Mountains,* History Channel series.

1989: *The Lost Dutchman Mine,* "Unsolved Mysteries" episode.

1977: *In Search of—"The Lost Dutchman Mine,"* narrated by Leonard Nimoy, Sci-Fi Channel, Season 2, Episode 1.

1975 from 1952: *Death Valley Days,* guest starring Ronald Reagan, Rosemary DeCamp, Robert Taylor, et al, television and radio anthology produced by Gene Autry.

1963 from 1958: *The Rifleman,* starring Chuck Conners, Johnny Crawford, ABC series.

1963 from 1957: *Have Gun Will Travel,* starring Richard Boone, Kam Tong, CBS series.

1961 from 1958: *Wanted: Dead or Alive,* starring Steve McQueen, CBS series.

1961: *Laramie, "The Lost Dutchman,"* starring John Smith and Robert Fuller, NBC episode.

Pima school girl, Czele Marie, 1907, Edward S. Curtis photographic print. Courtesy: Library of Congress

Glossary

Researched and Compiled by John Annerino, Copyright © 2018

* * *

"My heart belongs to no one now, but the desert." —Gertrude Bell, *Queen of the Desert*, 1907

* * *

Spanish, Mexican, and Native American names of the Great Southwest: Superstition Mountains region, Peraltas Gold, and the US/Mexico Borderlands. All entries without a Native American affiliation are Spanish with English translations.

Acequia. Canal.
Abeja. Bee, as in honey bee (*Apis mellifera*).
Adios. "Goodbye."
Aeropista. Dirt airstrip.
Agua. Water, used on the González-Peralta Map.
Agua Dulce. "Sweet water."
Agua Fria. "Cold water," as in the Agua Fria River in Arizona's Sonoran Desert.
Aguila. Eagle, as in golden eagle (*Aguila chrysaetos*).
Ak chin. Floodwater farming, Pima lexicon.
Ákímel Ó'odham. "People of the River," Pima lexicon.
Alacrán. Scorpion, as in bark scorpion, (*Centruroides sculptumtus*), also *escorpión*.
Alta California. "Upper California," now the state of California.
Alta Sonora. "Upper Sonora," Mexico.
Apachería. "Land of the Apache."
Araña. Spider, as in black widow spider (*Latrodectus mactans*), also *viuda negra*, and brown recluse spider, (*Loxosceles arizonica*).
Arcoíris. Rainbow.

Arena. Sand.
Arete. Horn of rock
Árido. Arid or barren.
Arrastra. Mill used for crushing ore, often pulled by a burro or mule.
Arroyo. Dry wash or river bed thay may offer seasonal water.
Avispa. Wasp, as in umbrella wasp (*Polities flavus*).
Aya. Desert tortoise, (*Gopherus agassizii* and *Gopherus morafkai*), Chemehuevi lexicon.
Bacanora. Moonshine liquor made in remote mountain pueblos of Sonora, Mexico. "Badges? We don't need no stinking badges!" The infamous quote from B. Traven's novel, *The Treasure of the Sierra Madre*.
Bahía. Bay.
Baja California. "Lower California," the 800-mile-long Baja peninsula, now formed by the Mexican states *of Baja California Norte,* (Northern Baja), and *Baja California Sur,* (Southern Baja).
Bajada. Desert lowland, formed by an alluvial fan.
Bandanna. Colorful handkerchief or scarf worn around the neck or head, also *paliacate* or *pañuelo*.
Bandolera. Leather cartridge belt used in the Mexican Revolution
Bandolero. Bandit, also *Bandido*.
Barranca. Canyon.
Baston. Walking stick, or cane.
Bastón del Diablo, El. "The Devil's Walking Stick," referring to the spindly limbs of the ocotillo plant (Fouquieria splendens).
Biznaga. Barrel cactus (*Ferocactus wislizenit*).
Bedonkohe. "In Front of the End People," Chiricahua Band, Western Apache band.
Borrego Cimarrón. Wild sheep, referring to the desert bighorn (*Ovis Canadensis*), native to the Superstition Mountains, extirpated, and reintroduced.

Bosque. Grove of trees along a river or *arroyo*.
Brujería. Witchcraft.
Brujo/a. Male, or female, witch.
Burro. Beast of burden, or a meal of beans or meat wrapped in a flour tortilla.
Caballero. Horseman, also gentleman.
Cabeza de Vaca. "Cow's Head," as in Spanish explorer Álvar Nuñez Cabeza de Vaca.
Caldera. Caldron of liquefied or solidified lava.
Caliente. Hot.
Camino. Road.
Camino del Diablo, El. "The Road of the Devil," in southwest Arizona and northwest Sonora, Mexico, became infamous in 1849 through the 1950s when hundreds of forty-niners and *gambusinos* perished en route to the California gold fields.
Camino Real de Tierra Adentro, El. Named after the Spanish silver coin *real* (worth twelve cents), the 1,600-mile Royal Road linked Santa Fe, New Mexico and colonial silver mines with Mexico City.
Cañón. Canyon.
Cantina. Bar, tavern, or canteen.
Carne. Meat.
Carne seca. Dried meat, or jerky, eaten on the trail.
Carrancistas. Soldiers and followers who fought in the Mexican Revolution under José Venustiano Carranza.
Carrizales. Stand of carrizo cane which usually meant drinking water for Spanish explorers and grass for livestock.
Carrizo Apache. *Tł'ohk'adigain* or *Tł'ohk'adigain Bikoh Indee*, "Canyon of the Row of White Canes People," Western Apache lexicon.
Casa Grande. "Great House," archaeological site, see also *Siwañ Wa'a Ki*.
Cascabel. Rattlesnake, as in Western diamondback rattlesnake (*Crotalus atrox*).
Cascada. Waterfall, as in Reavis Falls.

Caverna. Cave.
Caverna con Casa. Cave with House, used on González-Peralta Map
Cerro. Hill or peak.
Cerveza, Beer, Carta Blanca, Chihuahua, Corona, Dos Equis, Indio, Modelo, Noche Buena, Pacifico, San Miguel, Sol, Superior, Tecate, Toña, Tres Equis, Victoria.
Cew S-wegiom. "Long red," (2,706-foot Camelback Mountain), Pima lexicon.
Charcos. Mud holes that offer emergency potable water if strained, settled, and treated.
Chí. Hematite, San Carlos Apache lexicon.
Chí'chil. Emory oak acorns, San Carlos Apache lexicon.
Chich'il Bildagoteel. Oak Flat, San Carlos Apache lexicon.
Chiricahua Apache. From *Chiguicagui*, "Mount of the Wild Turkeys," Ópata lexicon.
Chubasco. Squall, sometimes used to describe violent summer monsoon storms than emenate from the Pacfic Coast of mainland Mexico and the Baja Penicnusla that pummel the Sonoran Desert with wind, rain, and lightening.
Cielo. Sky.
Cima. Top, or summit, used on the González-Peralta Map.
Colorado. Red, as in Colorado River.
Comcáac, "The People," Seri lexicon.
Contrabandista. Smuggler.
Cordillera. Mountain range.
Corona de Cristo. "Crown of Christ," Crucifixion thorn bush.
Corrido. Mexican folk song.
Coyote. Coyote, as in the four-legged animal (*Cams latrans*), or two-legged smuggler.
Coyotero Apache. *Łiinábáha diné'i*, "Many Go to War People," White Mountain Apache lexicon.
Cruz. Cross.

Cuchillo. Knife, or knife-edged ridge.
Cueva. Cave.
Curandero/a. A medicine man, or medicine woman.
Desierto. Desert.
Desperado. A desperate man, from *desesperar.*
Despoblado. Unihabited land.
Dilzhę́'é. "People with High Pitched Voices," Tonto Apache band, a disparaging Spanish term.
Dios. God.
Dí yin. "One Who Has Power," (Medicine Man), Western Apache lexicon.
Dotł'izhi. Turquoise, San Carlos Apache lexicon.
Dził Łigai. "White Mountains," Western Apache lexicon.
El Dorado. Spanish conquistador's mythic lost city gold.
El último tiro de gracía. Final blow, or execution.
Entradas. "Entries," referring to sixteenth and seventeenth century Spanish explorations in New Spain.
Escardada. Hoed, used on González-Peralta Map.
Escorpión. Scorpion, as in bark scorpion (*Centruroides sculpturatus*), and Gila monster (*Heloderma suspectum suspectum* and *Heloderma suspectum cinctum*), and the Mexican beaded lizard (*Heloderma horridum*).
Espejismo. Mirage.
Extraña. Strange.
Federales. Federal army troops who fought in the Mexican Revolution under Mexican President José Victoriano Huerta.
Frijoles. Beans, usually pinto; also *flor de mayo, ojo de venado,* or *frijoes negros.*
Frontera, La. The Frontier, usually referring to the border region of northern Mexico.
Ga-gautke. "Slanting Mountain," Superstition Mountains, Pima lexicon.
Gambusinos. Prospectors.

Gáán. "Mountain Spirit/s," Western Apache lexicon.
Gan Bikoh. "Crown Dancers Canyon," Devils Canyon, near Big Oak Flat, Western Apache lexicon.
Gan Diszin. "Crowndancer Standing," Queen Creek Canyon (formerly Picket Post Creek), near Big Oak Flat, Western Apache lexicon.
Gran Desierto, El. "The Grand Desert" in northwest Sonora, Mexico.
Golfo. Gulf.
Golfo de California. Gulf of California, also known as the Sea of Cortés, and once called the Vermilion Sea.
Goyaałé. "One who yawns," Geronimo, Western Apache lexicon.
Guarache. Sandals, once made of leather, or yucca fiber, now made of leather and tire tread.
Hâ-âk Teia Hâk. The mythical cave of Hâ-âk Vâ-âk, Hâ-âk Lying, O'odham lexicon.
Hâ-âk Vâ-âk, Hâ-âk Lying. Intaglio-sized human earth figure, O'odham lexicon.
Haskay-bay-nay-ntayl. Apache kid, "The tall man destined to come to a mysterious end," or *Hashkee Binaa Nteel,* "He has angry eyes," San Carlos or White Mountain Apache lexicon.
Ha:san. Saguaro cactus and fruit, O'odham lexicon.
Hechicero. Sorcerer.
Hohokam, or Huhugam. "Those who have gone before," or "Those who have disappeared," Pima lexicon.
Hoya, [Hoyo]. Hole, used on González-Peralta Map.
Incienso. "Incense," Brittle bush.
Jacal. A dwelling made from adobe, ocotillo, or saguaro ribs.
Jarron de Agua. Water jar.
Jornada. That part of a desert journey without water.
Jornada de las Estrellas. "Day's Journey of the Stars," Forty-niner and immigrant trail in Arizona also known as the Forty Mile Desert.
Kakâtak Tamai. "Crooked Top Mountain," (5,057 foot Superstition Mountain), Pima.

Köcha-Hon-Mana (or Qotsa-hon-mana). "White Bear Girl," Lori Anne Piestewa, Hopi lexicon.
Kwevkepaya. "People of the East," also *Kewevkapay*, Southeastern Yavapai band.
Laguna Salada. "Salt Lake," Northern Baja, Mexico's dry lake or salt pan.
Las Aguas. Summer rains.
Las Equipatas. Winter rains.
Legua. League, a measure of distance used by Spanish explorers, variously measured, approximately 2.6 miles.
León. Lion, as in mountain lion (*Felts concolor*)
Lluvia. Rain.
Lluvia de Oro. "Rain of Gold," used to decribe Palo Verde tree's vibrant yellow flowers when they found to the ground.
Lobo. Wolf, as in one of five sub-species of gray wolf (*Canis lupus*).
Loma. Hill.
Los Muertos. "The Dead," archaeological site.
Luna. Moon.
Machete. Long, broad-bladed knife used for harvests, dispatching an enemy or victim during a *machetazo*, or machete blow.
Maguey. Century plant.
Maiz. Corn.
Mal País. "Bad country," or badlands.
Mano. Hand, also the hand held stone used with a *metate* for grinding corn, mesquite beans, etc.
Mapa. Map.
Mapa, *Cuento de Oro del Río Salado del Norte*. "Legend of Gold of the Salt River of the North," Manuel Alejandro Peralta's 1753 map,
Mapa del Desierto. "Map of the Desert," one of the Spanish names for the González-Peralta Map, also *Perfil Mapa*. "Profile Map."
Medano. Sand dunes.
Metate. A mealing stone used for grinding corn, mesquite beans, etc.

Mesa. A table, table-topped mountain or land mass, ie. Black Top Mesa, Peters Mesa.
Mesita. Little Mesa.
Mescal. Agave hearts gathered and baked in stone hearths by indigenous desert dwellers; also a fermented liquor distilled from the sap of agave.
Mezquital. Stand of mesquite trees, shade and water.
Milagro. Miracle.
Mina. Mine.
Misión. Mission.
Montaña. Mountain.
Mordida. "The bite," a bribe.
Muhaagi Do'ag. (2,526-foot South Mountains), Pima lexicon.
Nogales. Walnuts, Arizona black walnuts.
Náhuatl. Aztec, "That which is clearly audible. To be near or close by," Uto-Aztecan language.
Nantan Lupan. "Grey Wolf," Apache nickname for General George Crook.
Ndé. Apache "people," also *Ndee,* Western Apache lexicon.
Neblina. Fog.
Ni para mí, ni para el Diablo. "If I can't have it, the devil can't have it either."
Nina, La. "The girl," the global weather system.
Nino, El. "The boy," the global weather system.
Norte. Cold north wind that blows south.
Nube. Cloud.
Nuestra Señora de Guadalupe. "Our Lady of the Guadalupe."
Nueva España. "New Spain," the territory that once included Mexico, Florida, and much of the United States west of the Mississippi River.
Nüwüwü. "The People,' Chemehuevi lexicon.
Ojo. Eye.
Ojo de Agua. "Eye of Water," a water hole.

Olla. Clay pot used for carrying water, cooking, or food storage.
O'odham, Akimel. "People of the River," also known as Pima.
O'odham, Hia Ced. "People of the Sand," also known as Sand Papago.
O'odham, Tohono. "People of the Desert," also known as Papago.
Oro. Gold.
Oos:hikbina. "Stick cuts upon," calendar stick, Pima Lexicon.
Palma de la Mano de Dios, La. "The Hollow of God's Hand" in California's Colorado Desert.
Palo Fierro. "Iron Wood," referring to the Desert Ironwood tree (*Olneya tesota*), the second heaviest wood in North America used by the Hohokam for digging sticks.
Palo Verde. "Green Stick," referring to one of several variants of Palo Verde trees: Blue Palo Verde (*Cercidiumfloridum*), Mexican Palo Verde (*Parkinsonia aculeata*) and the
Foothill "Yellow" Palo Verde (*Cerdium microphyllum*).
Pantera. Panther, or mountain lion (*Felis concolor*).
Papaguería. Land of the Papago.
Perfil Mapa. "Profile Map," one of the Spanish names for the González-Peralta Map.
Pesos. Mexican hard currency; 100 pesos equals one US dollar.
Picacho. Peak, used to described several geological landmarks in the Superstitions.
Pico. Peak.
Piedra. Stone.
Pimería Alta. "Upper Pima Lands."
Pistola. Pistol.
Plata. Silver.
"Plata o plomo?" "Silver or lead?" as in "Do you want to take the payoff or a bullet?"
Planchas de la Plata. "Ledges of Silver," the legendary Spanish lode of silver discovered on the US/Mexico border.
Playa. A beach, dry lake, or ephemeral water source.

Poncho. Poncho, a cape usually made from a blanket or *sarape*.
Pozo. Well.
Pueblito. Little town.
Pueblo. Town, or indigenous village.
Pueblo Grande. "Big Village," archaeological site.
Puerto. Mountain pass, or a seaport.
Pulque. Fermented liquor made from maguey.
Punta. Point of land.
Quebrada. Broken country.
Ramos. Branches used for making ramadas and jacals.
Recortado, El. Cut, "Sawed Off mountain," above Canyon Lake.
Rancho. Ranch.
Ranchería. Small rural Mexican or indigenous settlement.
Rayo. Lightning.
Remolino. Whirlwind, also called a *tornillo*.
Rillito. Little river.
Río. River.
Río Colorado. "Red River," referring to the Colorado River.
Río Salado. "Salt River."
Rurales. Rural government forces who fought in the Mexican Revolution under Mexican President José Victoriano Huerta.
Saguaro. Tall columnar cactus (*Cereus giganteus*).
Salado. People of the Salt River.
Salvaje. Wild.
Santo. Saint.
Sarape. Blanket.
Sed. Thirsty, as in *Tengo sed*, "I'm thirsty."
Se:he. "Elder Brother," Creator of the Tohono O'odham people.
Seco. Dry.
Séquia. Drought.
Sendero. Trail.
Serrano. Mountaineer, also a small green chile.

Sierra. Mountain range.
Sierra de la Espuma. "Mountain of Foam," 5,057-foot Superstition Mountains.
Sierra Estrella. 4,512-foot "Mountains of the Stars" in Arizona.
Sierra Mas Alta en Medio. Highest Range in Between, used on González-Peralta Map.
Sierrita. Little mountain.
Siesta. Afternoon nap.
Siwañ Wa'a Ki, or Sivan Vahki. (Casa Grande Ruins National Monument), O'odham lexicon.
Ska-kaik. "Many rattlesnakes," (Snaketown) archaeological site, Pima lexicon.
Sol. Sun.
Soldaderas. Women soldiers, and camp followers, who fought alongside and supported troops in the Mexican Revolution.
Sombra. Shade.
Sombrero. Hat.
Sombrero, El. The Hat, (4,653-foot Weavers Needle), used on González-Peralta Map.
S[ur] Cima. South Top, or summit, used on González-Peralta Map.
S-wegi Do'ag. (2,832-foot Red Mountain), Pima lexicon.
Ta-atûkam. 3,010-foot San Tan Mountains.
Temporales. Temporary agricultural plots used by the Pima and Papago for *ak chin* (floodwater) farming at the mouths of desert arroyos.
Tequila. Distilled liquor made from the heart of the blue maguey, containing at least 87 percent blue maguey juice.
Tierra. Earth, or land.
Terra Incógnita. Unknown land.
T'iis Tsebán. "Cottonwoods Gray in the Rocks People," Pinal band, Western Apache.
Tiis Zhaazhe Bikoh. "Small Cottonwood Canyon People," also *Sà'hndè dò t'àn*, San Carlos Apache.

Tinaja. Natural rock tank which collects rainwater.

Tormenta. Storm.

Tormenta Seca. "Dry storm," usually associated with summer monsoon dust storms.

Tornillo. Dust devil (from "screw"), also *remolino*.

Tortilla. A thin cake traditionally made by hand from corn meal throughout Mexico and the Great Southwest.

Trinchera. Prehistoric Indian defense wall or fortification.

Tséé Zhinnéé. "People of the Dark Rocks," also *Tséjìné,* Aravaipa band, Western Apache.

Tséya Gogeschin. Ancestral Apache place of prayer near Big Oak Flat, Western Apache.

Tú Nahikaadi. Ancestral Apache place of prayer near Big Oak Flat, Western Apache.

Tuna. Cactus fruit, most commonly refers to prickly pear (*Opuntia phaeacantha*).

Tunel. Tunnel, used on González-Peralta Map.

Uña de Gato. "Cat claw," Acacia bush.

Vainom Do'og, "Iron Mountain," (Piestewa Peak), Pima lexicon.

Valle de Sol. "Valley of the Sun."

Vaquero. Cowboy.

Vara. Spanish land measurement that approximates 33 1/3 inches.

Vatto. Ramada, man-made shelter for sun and rain, also used by indigenous desert peoples for ceremonies, cooking, and story-telling, Pima lexicon.

Vialxa. "Berdache Mountain," (4,512-foot Sierra Estrella), Pima lexicon.

Vibora. Snake, often referring to a rattlesnake, which are more specifically known as *cascabel* for their "rattles."

Viejo/a. Old man or woman.

Viento. Wind.

Viento Negro. Black Wind.

Villistas. Soldiers who fought in the Mexican Revolution under General Francisco "Pancho" Villa.
Víshúk. Hawk, Pima lexicon.
Viuda Negra. Black Widow Spider.
Wee-kit-sour-ah. "The rocks standing up," Superstition Mountains, Western Apache lexicon.
Wikedjasa. "Chopped-up Mountains," (7,667-foot Mazatzal Mountains), also *Wi:kchsawa,* Southeastern Yavapai sacred mountain.
Wikwaxa. "Greasy Mountains," (Superstition Mountains), O'odham lexicon.

Photography & Illustration Credits

Cover, interior, back cover Copyright © 2018 John Annerino

Page 17: "Portrait of Pima man, Panhop, 1902, Sacaton, Arizona. Frank A. Russell, black and white glass plate negative. Courtesy: National Anthropological Archives, Smithsonian Institution

Page 82. White Mountain Apache Scout, Sergeant William Alchesay, Medal of Honor Recipient. 1888, Globe, Arizona Territory, Andrew Miller cabinet card photograph.

Page 108: Sixty-eight-year-old Joseph Head, *Coi-a-ma-auk,* "Rattlesnake Head," views a calander stick . . . Edward H. Davis print. [U.S. Copyright Office Educational Fair Use]. Courtesy: National Museum of the American Indian.

Page 113: "San Carlos Apache belle," 1888, A. Frank Randall portrait, Arizona Territory. Courtesy: Library of Congress

Page 115: Apache Trail, Southern Pacific brochure cover, 1928, painting by Maynard Dixon." Courtesy: Southern Pacific Railroad online

Page 121: Teamsters lunch at Grapevine Springs, 1906, William J. Lubken, black and white glass plate negative. Courtesy: US Bureau of Reclamation Collection

Page 129: "Dedication ceremonies of Roosevelt Dam, Col. Roosevelt speaking," March 18, 1911, Walter J. Lubken, black and white glass plate negative. Courtesy: US Bureau of Reclamation Collection

Page 199: "Wagoner's 1894 Lost Ledge Treasure Map." Original map drawn by Barry Storm. Courtesy: *Desert* Magazine, February 24 1945

Page 205: Eleven-year-old Santiago (Jimmy) McKinn was abducted by Geronimo and raised as a Chiricahua Apache until he reluctantly returned to his parents, March 27, 1886, Arizona Territory, Camilius Sidney Fly photographic print, Courtesy: Library of Congress

Page 212: Locked and loaded, brandishing Winchester lever-action carbines and cartridge-filled bandoliers, artist Etorre "Ted" DeGrazia (right) and Oscar-winning friend Broderick Crawford ride through "the roughest, rockiest, most treacherous terrain in the United States" in search of Lost Jesuit Gold. Courtesy: DeGrazia Gallery in the Sun. © All Rights Reserved

Page 223: Etorre "Ted" DeGrazia Colorized photo courtesy: DeGrazia Gallery in the Sun © All Rights Reserved.

Page 240: "Gold is where you find it" color image, John Annerino/ *LIFE* magazine photo assignment

Page 262: Geronimo, May 16, 1884, A. Frank Randall portrait, Wilcox, Arizona Territory. Courtesy: Library of Congress

Page 276: "Pima school girl, Czele Marie, 1907, Edward S. Curtis photographic print. Courtesy: Library of Congress

Page 290 : "Lost Dutchman Peralta Locality Map." Drawn by Norton Allen, Courtesy: The Desert Magazine

Page 297: Map 19. Superstition Mountain Traverse Map, Drawn: From the original notes and topographical maps of John Annerino. Courtesy: USFS Superstition Wilderness.

Page 299: Map 20. Lost Dutchman Trails Map. Courtesy: Lost Dutchman State Park.

Page 299: Superstition Trails Map 20. (Use as a fold-out horizontal trail inside the backcover). Caption: "Superstition Wilderness Trails Map." Courtesy: Tonto National Forest.

About the Author

Author crossing a log jam, West Clear Creek Canyon Wilderness, during a month-long journey run from Mexico to Utah. Remote-triggered self exposure. Copyright © John Annerino Photography

John Annerino is an award winning photographer, author, and journalist of distinguished photography books, illustrated nonfiction books, magazine and news features, and color maps and calendars of the American West and Old Mexico.

John's assignment, consultant, and published work includes ABC News *Primetime* (Sierra Madre, Mexico, and the Devil's Highway, US Mexico Border), *America 24/7: Extraordinary Images of One American Week*, (Blackhawk Helicopter Patrols, US Mexico Border), *Arizona Highways Magazine* ("Between Myth and Mystery: A Cowboy Guide and Navajo Elder,"), *BrownTrout*, Heard American Indian Museum (Native Speaker on Sierra Madre, Tarahumara), *LIFE* Magazine (Pima photography mentor, "Children's Pictures of God" cover story), *National Geographic Adventure* ("National Park War Zone," and "Along the Devil's Highway," both US-Mexico Border), *National Law Journal* (Environmental Law), Native Peoples (Sierra Madre, Mountain Pima), Newsweek (Hopi Tribal Chairman), *New York Times Travel* (Sierra Madre, Tarahumara) *Outdoor Photography* magazine *UK* ("Arizona: A Photographic Tribute"), *People* (Navajo Code Talkers), *Scientific American*, *Time*, *Travel & Leisure*, Sierra Club Books, W.W. Norton, and as a contract photographer for TimePix and Liaison International photo agencies. John received a Book Builder's West Outstanding Photography award for his Sierra Club Book, *Canyons of the Southwest*, Southwest Book of the Year Best Reading awards for *Vanishing Borderlands*, and *The Virgin of Guadalupe*, and a Society of Publication Designers Award for photography in the *National Geographic Adventure* feature, "Along the Devil's Highway."

Explorations:

John spent most of his life exploring the *terra incognita* of the American West and Old Mexico—as an adventurer, conservationist, and scholar of Southwestern history. In his quest to explore its mythic landscapes and secret places, John climbed its hallowed mountains, rowed its wild and scenic rivers, and traced ancient Indian paths on foot through canyons and painted deserts. Among his explorations by foot, raft, rope, camera, and pen, John worked as an outdoor educator, climbing guide, and survival instructor in Arizona and Mexico; helitac wildlands fire crew leader in Alaska's Kenai Peninsula, Washington's North Cascades National Park, Montana's Pasayten Wilderness, and as a forest firefighter on Arizona's White River Apache Reservation; and a white-water boatman-photographer on the Forks of the Kern River, Golden Trout Wilderness, California; Green and Yampa Rivers,

Dinosaur National Monument, Utah; Colorado River, Grand Canyon National Park, and Upper Salt River Canyon Wilderness, Arizona; and *LIFE* magazine-assigned photographer and canoist on the Rio Grande, Big Bend National Park, Texas/Río Bravo del Norte, Maderas del Carmen UNESCO Biosphere Reserve, Chihuahua, Mexico.

John cut his teeth exploring the Superstition Mountains and, later in the Grand Canyon, safely guiding students along rugged trails, and as a veteran Colorado River boatman and paddle captain. Rediscovering routes of Native Peoples and explorers, John made the Grand Canyon's first journey runs: six-day inner-Canyon below the South Rim; seven-day, 210-mile spirit run on the old Hopi/Havasupai trade route from Oraibi to Havasupai; and an eight-and-a-half day adventure run off-the-grid below the North Rim. Tracing Indian paths and historic trails John ran 750 miles of Arizona wilderness from Mexico to Utah, and led the first modern, unsupported crossing of the *El Camino del Diablo*, "The Road of the Devil," on foot, mid-summer. To date, John has explored more than 59,773 recorded miles on-foot of Native American routes and trails in the canyons, deserts, and mountains of the Great Southwest.

MAPS OF THE SUPERSTITIONS

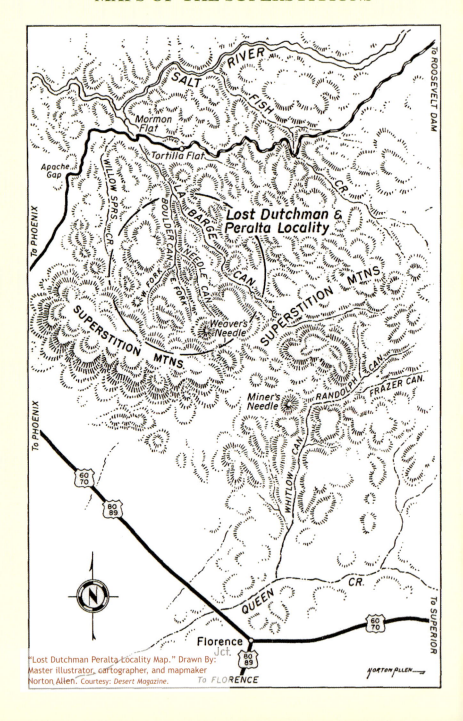

"Lost Dutchman Peralta Locality Map." Drawn By: Master illustrator, cartographer, and mapmaker Norton Allen. Courtesy: *Desert Magazine*.

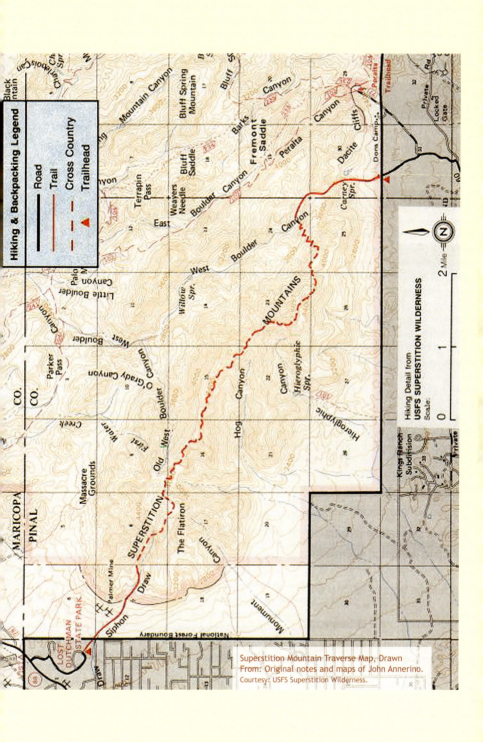
Superstition Mountain Traverse Map, Drawn From: Original notes and maps of John Annerino. Courtesy: USFS Superstition Wilderness.

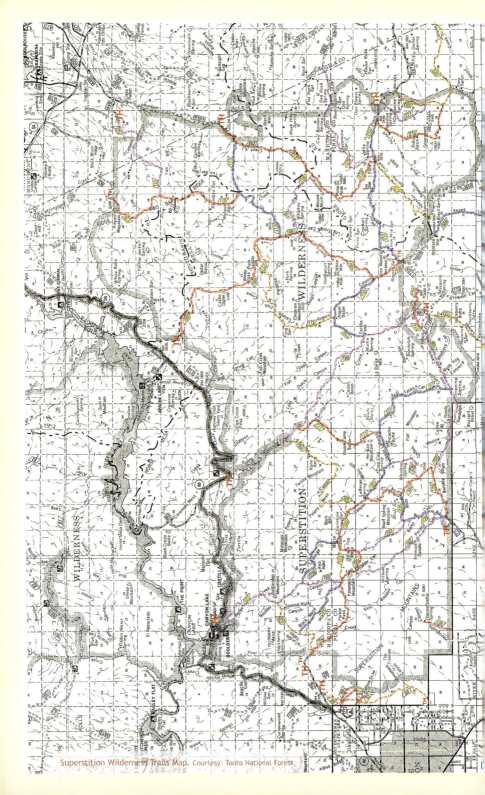

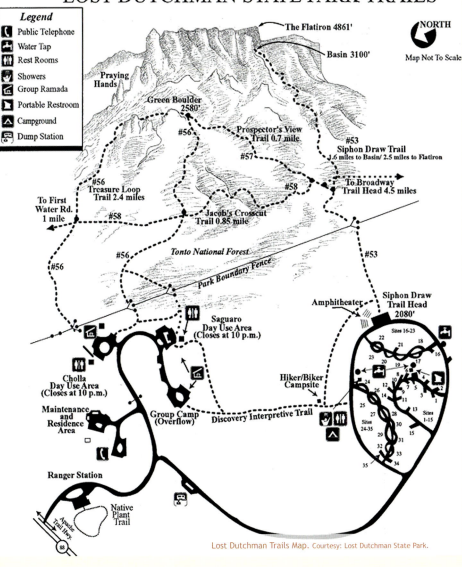
Lost Dutchman Trails Map. Courtesy: Lost Dutchman State Park.